AMCHITKA AND THE BOMB

AMCHITKA AND THE BOMB

Nuclear Testing in Alaska

DEAN W. KOHLHOFF

WITHDRAWN

UNIVERSITY OF WASHINGTON PRESS

Seattle and London

Library of Congress Cataloging-in-Publication Data
Kohlhoff, Dean.
Amchitka and the bomb : nuclear testing in Alaska / Dean W. Kohlhoff.
p. cm.
Includes index.
ISBN 0-295-98255-1 (alk. paper)
1. Nuclear weapons—Testing—Alaska—Amchitka Island.
2. Nuclear weapons—Testing—Environmental aspects—Alaska—Amchitka Island.
3. United States—Politics and government—1945–1989.
4. Amchitka Island (Alaska)—History—20th century.
I. Title.
U264.3 .K64 2002   363.17'99'09798221   2002066513

CONTENTS

Foreword vii

Preface ix

1 / Among the Many Islands 3

2 / On an Anvil of War 13

3 / Before a Mighty Windstorm 26

4 / Nuclear Alaska 40

5 / Under Rufus & Larkspur Scrutiny 48

6 / During a Long Shot 55

7 / Through Milrow Calibration 68

8 / For Safeguard Security 89

9 / Amid More Cannikin Controversy 98

10 / Beyond the Last Bomb 109

Notes 118

Index 157

FOREWORD

Dean Kohlhoff died on June 12, 1997, before he had a chance to complete final revisions on his manuscript for *Amchitka and the Bomb*. Because we knew that Dean's greatest unfulfilled wish was to have his story of the environmental consequences of nuclear testing on Amchitka Island told, Nancy Kohlhoff, Dean's widow, and I decided to take up the work of preparing his early draft for publication. In so doing, we hope that we have been faithful to Dean's goal of representing the struggle between the partisans of national security and the defenders of the Aleutian environment as fairly as possible. Dean's interest in the Aleutians was never simply academic. He always saw himself as advocate and defender of the Aleutians and its Aleut people.

MEREDITH WM. BERG
Valparaiso University
Valparaiso, Indiana

Dean worked on this manuscript until only a few days before he passed away. On one occasion, he said to me, "They won't publish my manuscript posthumously, will they?" From then on, I felt that if I could arrange to have the manuscript published, it would be the last, best thing I could do for Dean. Now, his work is finally complete.

NANCY L. KOHLHOFF
Valparaiso, Indiana

PREFACE

In the 1960s and early 1970s, three underground nuclear tests were carried out on Amchitka Island, a small island in the Aleutian Chain. Each blast had its own name—Long Shot, Milrow, and Cannikin—but the name Amchitka became a code word for all of them. Although these tests were the only ones conducted on Alaska soil, there was a new alchemy at work. The tests linked island to bomb and North Pacific to Central Pacific. Amchitka, like Bikini and Eniwetok, became a byword in a new atomic age.

Much controversy surrounded the tests primarily because the island lay in a national wildlife refuge. But other issues besides the ecological ones emerged. Amchitka's geology is prone to earthquakes and tsunamis. If these natural catastrophes could result from the blasts, people far away would be affected. The tests also were framed in the context of the nuclear arms race. Some officials believed the tests were essential to United States security in the face of the Cold War even though they maintained a measure of sympathy for Amchitka's environment. The debate drew many opinions, including those of politicians, scientists, and policy-makers. In the end, the Supreme Court decided for the largest and last test.

My perspective on Amchitka has been shaped by several experiences. Even before I imagined a study like this, I taught courses on the history of American environmentalism. While traveling in Alaska, I met students whose political consciousness was expressed in protest against the bomb and for the safeguarding of the island. After I picked up this topic in 1992, I listened to interviews in which participants expressed a high level of emotional commitment to Amchitka. Then, in the summer of 1994, I understood why.

On a research visit to Adak Island, I experienced the Aleutians for the first time. Adak Island, which is approximately 200 miles from Amchitka, is teeming with wildlife. Where once a huge military population existed, there now swarm mallards, common teal, loons and ravens, bald eagles, glaucous-winged gulls, parasitic jaegers, and Aleutian terns. Never before had I seen a song sparrow, Lapland longspur, northern phalarope, or gray-crowned rosy finch. In an inlet near Kuluk Bay, harbor seals with doleful-looking faces waited for the tide to deliver their regular supply of food. Fish and wildlife personnel pointed out to me a protective mother sea otter that splashed away with her cub after letting us look on for what felt like an hour. Now, it seemed to me, I understood what Amchitka was really all about!

A study running somewhat parallel to mine has been mounted by my friend and colleague, Dan O'Neill. He, too, has dealt with Alaska's nuclear experience in a pioneering work on Project Chariot called *The Firecracker Boys*. His title refers to nuclear excavation engineers who planned to blast a deepwater port in coastal arctic Alaska. As O'Neill reveals, the project was eventually aborted.

In this book, my objective is to explore why Amchitka Island was used for nuclear blast tests and to report the consequences which followed. I have provided a history of the island and have attempted to reveal the controversies leading to the blasts. Throughout, I have sought impartiality and balance in recording the intense pressures felt by those who believed the tests to be essential and those whose sympathy lay with the preservation of Amchitka's wildlife and environment.

DEAN W. KOHLHOFF
Valparaiso, Indiana
May 12, 1997

AMCHITKA AND THE BOMB

1 / AMONG THE MANY ISLANDS

Islands
between sea and ocean
Aleutian Islands . . .
mountainous bow of storms
belt of emeralds
like the eagle's curved flight above you . . . .

—RAYMOND HUDSON,
"Summer's Bay"

Alaska is an exceptional place by any realistic standards. It is the biggest state in the Union. It holds the most islands, the highest mountains, the largest glaciers, and the greatest number of active volcanoes over any of the other States. Although it was once only a small outpost in the old Russian empire, Alaska is now a giant among its sister states. Aptly, the Russians had called it *Bolshaya Zemlya,* or "Big Land," which is reflected in its modern nickname, the Great Land. Actually, the Russian *Aliaska,* or *Alyaska,* is an adaptation from the Aleut language meaning "the mainland" or "land that is not an island." It covers 586,400 square miles with uncommon natural beauty, extraordinary vistas, and monumental features. The land mass is so dominant that it overshadows the many islands that dot the seas surrounding it on three sides. Bordering the Beaufort, Chukchi, and Bering Seas, Alaska protrudes bulky and peninsula-like into the Arctic and Pacific Oceans. These surrounding seas greatly influenced Alaska's early development, providing resources and accesses for its indiginous people as well as outsiders. Most Alaskans today live in coastal areas with a dizzying cross-hatch of straits, inlets, sounds, channels, passes, narrows, coves, bights, and bays. Alaska's coastline is over twice as long as the combined coasts of the remaining states in the Union.[1]

Two large island groups extend Alaska even farther to the south and west. The Alexander Archipelago lies alongside Canada, running 500 miles south-

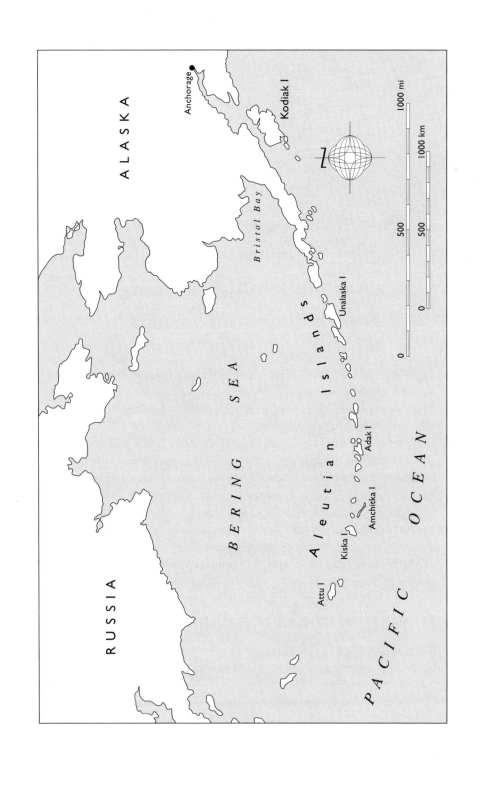

east, while the Aleutian Islands point westerly from the mainland toward Asia, reaching into the eastern hemisphere in a narrow 1,100-mile arc. These islands make Alaska the state of many islands. The Aleutian Chain alone contains over two hundred of them.[2]

Before the Russians explored the region in the eighteenth century, the islands had played an important role in the lives of the Aleuts, Alaska'a indigenous people. A rich Aleutian Island mythology emerged from these ancient, Aleut homelands. Aleut stories traditionally included many heroic characters connected to their beloved island homes. Umnak Island was identified as the exact spot where Aleuts first descended from the skies. Another Aleut tale claimed that human mortality resulted as a punishment when the Deity was criticized for creating the Aleutians. An elaborate narrative was told of the Chuginadak Island Woman, a guardian spirit, whose adventures united island communities in peaceful cooperation. "Land Uncle," an emotive term, supposedly an original Aleut name for the Pribilofs, was also the title of a favorite story celebrating these islands. Tigalda Island boasted of three mighty heroes: Daylight Lifter, Mainland Slayer, and Tusk Breaker—super heroes who conquered their non-Aleut Koniag enemies. In some legends, species such as sea lions, fur seals, and birds were magically changed into human form to benefit Aleutian Island life. In Aleut myths, the islands came first, the people later.[3]

Other Native Alaskan tales also emphasized the primacy of the islands. In the Southeast (as Alaskans call the panhandle), the Tlingit creator, Yeil or Raven, flew to a distant island where he, like Prometheus, appropriated fire for humans. Raven also gave his people the special gift of an island previously reserved only for land and sea animals. According to another legend, the Southeast's many islands were once human ancestors who had been changed into landforms by an eagle. In the north, an Inupiat creation story described the origin of Sevuokuk, now known as St. Lawrence Island. A mythical giant, with one foot planted on Siberia and the other on Alaska, gave Sevuokuk life by squeezing water from sand and stone scooped out of the ocean bed. When dried, the land stuck fast when thrown onto the Bering Sea. Even today, St. Lawrence Island is known as the "island between two continents." Eskimo storytellers proclaimed the deeds of another giant who created Egg and Besboro Islands in Norton Sound. Little and Big Diomede Islands in Bering Strait were affectionately called "island brothers."[4]

(facing page) MAP 1. Alaska and the Aleutian Islands

As interesting as these myths and legends have been, the islands of Alaska also occupy key geographical positions that give them continuing importance. Situated on the northwestern flank of the Pacific Rim, the islands belong to one of the greatest physical features on the globe, the Pacific Ocean. From a global perspective, they are part of an expansive biogeographical area, the Pacific Basin, which contains as many as 25,000 islands, over one-half the world's total. The regional name of the Pacific Islands is appropriate: Oceania, a sea of islands, including those of Alaska and Hawaii. The Pacific Basin is not insignificant or remote. It covers one third of the globe's surface. Its northern boundary is the Aleutian Islands chain. Oceania virtually touches all in the Western hemisphere.[5]

As part of this great global feature, the physical geography of the Aleutian Islands is truly unique. Many earth scientists believe the "Aleutian arc is one of the most striking physiographic features on earth." Its suboceanic trench reaches from Kamchatka to the Gulf of Alaska. The exposed Aleutian ridge joins North America's highest mountains, the Alaska Range. Far from being on a frigid outer rim of the earth, this arc of islands links vital expanses. It is a dividing island chain between the cold Bering Sea, the world's third largest sea, and a warmer north Pacific Ocean. The islands act like baleen filters in an interchange of biota between these two bodies of water. Moreover, a cartographic impression of their detachment is myopic. Actually, the islands are anything but isolated, serving instead as ecological bridges to the Kurile Islands and Siberian maritime regions. Closer in, nearly all the Aleutian Chain islands constitute the western edge of the Gulf of Alaska Basin. In a long semi-circle from Great Sitkin Island in the western Aleutians, the Chain is bounded on the northeast by Cook Inlet, then bends south to include the Alexander Archipelago. Alaska's major population center, Anchorage, and the state capital, Juneau, both lie within this Basin, which is really Alaska's significant underbelly.[6]

The Aleutian region claims many economic as well as aesthetic treasures. Those who know the islands are struck by their natural beauty and the abundance of life found there. For centuries, Aleuts have harvested from the rich intertidal zones and the bordering seas. Russians and Americans have taken from the teeming resources of sea mammals and have converted their pelts into boom-time wealth. To naturalist John Muir, the area seemed rather bleak only in the winter and early spring. Otherwise, he found it "remarkably interesting, its wildlife warm, eager, and swarming." Other naturalists, like Henry W. Elliott, for example, were amazed at the area's rare beauty and "indescribably rich green and golden carpet of circumpolar sphagnum; exquisitely colored lichens." Recently, author John Bockstoce admitted that its vegetation is the "densest, green cover . . . I have ever seen in the North." Similarly, Olaus J. Murie noticed in the wildlife a deep coloration in its birds and foxes. He dubbed the area a "region of giantism" for its jumbo-sized animals. Another researcher, Victor B. Scheffer, was taken by the region's profuse invertebrates and fishes in coastal waters and countless island pools and lakes. On Agattu Island, for instance, Scheffer counted at least two hundred such animals in less than a five-mile radius.[7]

A wholesome and interconnected vitality also made the Aleutians a haven for ancient human communities. Remarkably successful in adaptation, large numbers of Aleuts have enjoyed healthy and extended lives on these islands. Skillful care and maintenance of the environment explain in large part their long, continuous, and rich development. The pre-contact archaeological record is replete with artifacts demonstrating this sustaining relationship between people and the coastal ecosystems.[8]

Europeans first sailing into these waters groped about in frustration and puzzlement. They searched far and wide for the mythical Juan de Gama Land, the Company Land, the *Terra Borealis*, or land in any northerly direction, specifically the North American continent. Vitus Bering is supposed to have called the Aleutians "Obmannui," or "Delusive Islands," probably based on their persistent fog cover which hampered exploration efforts. Because of the climate covering these far-flung islands, studies of the area grew only at a snail's pace, making the Aleutians a special extension of America's "Last Frontier." One island, however, stands out in bold contrast: Amchitka. Because of military development there in World War II and research conducted during the Cold War, Amchitka emerged from the fogs onto the national scene.[9]

Over eons, all islands of the Aleutian Chain were formed by plutonic action spewing forth successive volumes of molten rock from subterranean depths. Born of fire, they are now peaks of a nearly submerged volcanic mountain range. Amchitka is the largest and southernmost island in a group of sixteen islands named *Ostrova Krys'i*, or "Rat Islands," by the Russians. This name seems originally to have come from Aleuts who called these islands *Ayugadak*, or rat, when an accident introduced the species from a shipwreck in the vicinity.[10]

Aleuts called Amchitka *Amtschigda*. The Russians translated that to *Ostrov Amchitka*, Amchitka Island. It has been spelled various ways: *Am-*

attshigda, Amtatka, Amtchitka, and *Amtschitka.* Some believe Bering christened it Saint Makarius or Saint Markiana. Amchitka, the name that stuck, is used also for Amchitka Pass, a fifty-mile-wide stretch of water between the Rat Islands and the Delarof Island group to the east. Geographically, Amchitka is situated north and south between the land masses of Siberia and New Zealand, east and west between Canada and the Kamchatka Peninsula. On the approximate latitude of London, it lies three-fourths of the way out on the Chain, nearly fourteen hundred miles from Anchorage. Amchitka is about forty miles long, nearly five miles at its widest, and looks somewhat like a diminutive Cuba.[11]

Both its geographical position and natural bounty made Amchitka significant for human occupation over many centuries. Based on its crossroads orientation between Siberia and New Zealand, it seems to have played a role in an iron exchange network with Asian peoples during the Iron Age. Rather than being a backwater isolate, Amchitka, it appears, was associated with the northern Japanese islands and northeast Asian maritime provinces. That it supported a relatively large population is indicated by at least seventy-eight archaeological sites which still remain. According to recent radiocarbon dating, it was first occupied between 3,600 and 4,600 years ago. Artifacts demonstrate an elaborate subsistence economy based on abundant island resources.[12]

Russian fur traders coming into the area after 1741 were drawn there to exploit these resources. In the process, ancient Aleutian Island communities were disrupted and their people diverted from traditional ways. However, Aleuts had confronted aggression and intrusions even before Russian contact. Neighboring indigenous people had long been potential enemies, and the ethnocentric Rat Island people had set themselves apart from others by calling themselves *Qagus* or *Qaxus,* an identification that nobody else could possess.

Although little of the earliest history of Amchitka is known, Russian ships, starting with Petr Bashmakov's voyage in the early 1750s, plied its nearby waters to hunt or trade for fur-bearing animals. Skipper Aleksei Vorb'ev established the first Rat Island base in 1761 and remained there until 1763. An impression of Amchitka was recorded in 1761 by seaman Prokopii Lisenkov, who noted, aside from its Native residents, its cormorants, tufted puffins, horned puffins, auks, and geese. While hunting in the area from 1772 to 1776, the Russian Dimitri Bragin observed sea lions, seals, and sea otters lying on its shores, and wrote, too, that "wild geese breed here." A lucrative catch of 91 sea lions, 642 sea otters, 1,106 foxes, and 8,000 fur seals was taken from Amchitka by crewmen of the *Aleksandr Nevskii* during the 1778–1780 season.[13]

Such large catches became scarcer at the end of the eighteenth century, by which time over-hunting had quickly depleted the fur-bearing animals. Russian competitors for these Aleutian resources, furthermore, were challenged by outsiders from Canada and the United States at about the same time that the fur industry reached its peak. Consequently, in 1799, the Russian American Company was handed a monopoly over the area by Czar Paul I. But the Company soon after shifted operations to the east and south for more profitable pelting. Amchitka was left under administrative control of the Company's Okhotsk center until about 1846, when it was placed in the Novo-Arkhangel'sk (Sitka) district for more efficient management.[14]

This Russian intervention brought many changes to Amchitka. As with other islands along the Chain, its population declined from contact diseases brought by outsiders. Its ancient village life suffered from social disintegration. Its resources were reduced to perilous levels. At the beginning of the nineteenth century, Company manager Maksim Lazarev, posted there by the Russians, moved eighty-five Amchitkans off the island to increase the work forces at Adak and Atka. This relocation also was made with the hope of restoring the sea otter populations and the island's subsistence base. Despite the economic justifications for these transfers, many who were moved died of hunger and disease. Nonetheless, when thirty-eight adults were returned to Amchitka in 1812, the island began to recover. Navigator Ivan F. Vasil'ev claimed that "Amchitka is without doubt one of the best islands of the Aleutian Chain. . . . There are many lakes and swamps, where there are many wild geese. The shores slope gently, and on them is plenty of driftwood. . . . Near the shore fishing is good, with pike, perch, cod . . . and others. It is a comforting thought to navigators that here one need not starve."[15]

This alternating pattern of neglect and exploitation in Amchitka's history lasted well into the twentieth century. Sometimes the island was uninhabited; but as in other places in Alaska, occupancy moved in cycles of natural fluctuation, making "uninhabited" merely a temporary description. In the 1840s, the island was emptied of people again; and then sometime in the 1850s, another community was established. A chapel was built which signaled restored Aleut life, but the village lasted hardly two decades. It is uncertain exactly when Amchitka lost this resident community, but it likely happened shortly after 1867, when western Aleut populations declined by nearly two-thirds in the early years of American rule.[16]

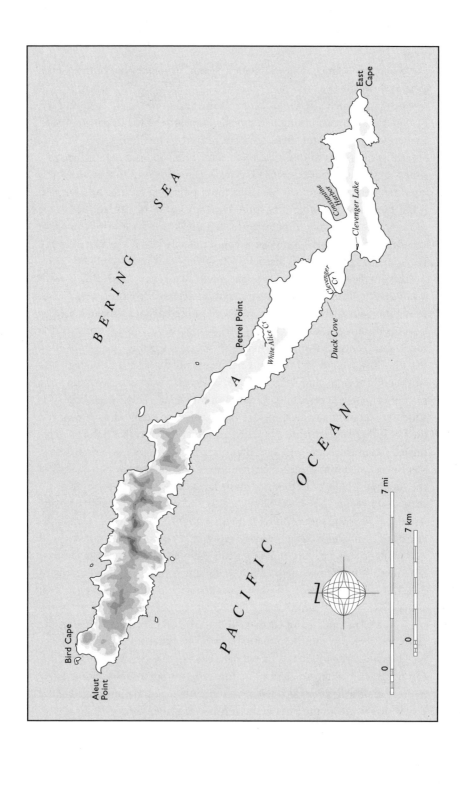

The loss of human occupancy marked a distinct juncture for Amchitka in the late nineteenth century. At that time, it supported no subsistence economy, and the fur industry of old had petered out as well. Hence, its resources could have been rejuvenated, and the island might have become a sanctuary for the animal and plant life which once flourished there. This, indeed, would have been in harmony with the very meaning of *island:* a refuge, a protected place. Thus, to shelter an assemblage of life, Amchitka might well have become itself again.

But Amchitka did not slip back unnoticed into its natural state. By the end of the nineteenth century, the hunting of whales, seals, and sea otters had reduced their stocks to the point of extinction, despite earlier attempts by both the Russians and Americans to arrest the problem. The immanence of the threat to these creatures finally produced important results. In 1911, the United States, Great Britain, Japan, and Russia belatedly signed an agreement to end the pelagic (open sea) hunting of seals. The North Pacific Sealing Convention was the first international conservation measure to touch Alaska.[17]

The salvation of the North Pacific seals encouraged American conservationists to test the limits of their influence. In the enabling legislation passed by Congress in 1912 to make good on the promise of the previous year, protections were expanded to include the endangered sea otter as well as the seal. Unwittingly, the measure helped Amchitka to become a special haven; and true to its role, it emerged as the mother of sea otter restoration in the Aleutians.[18]

The third major victory for conservationists came the next year. On March 3, 1913, President William H. Taft signed Executive Order 1773, which created the "Aleutian Islands Reservation." From Attu in the west to Umnak in the east, islands in the Chain were "reserved and set apart as a preserve and breeding ground for native birds, for the propagation of reindeer and furbearing animals and for the encouragement and development of the fisheries." The Aleutians were now part of a public trust. This was no halfhearted afterthought. The Reservation stretched out over one thousand miles and covered nearly three million acres.[19]

These successes, however, as important as they were in preserving species native to the Aleutian Islands, represented more of an ideal than an actual condition. Many competing economic and ecological interests in this area

(*facing page*) MAP 2. Amchitka Island

ensured mixed usage of the area's resources. Reservation status, for example, was not intended to interfere with the use of the islands for lighthouse, military, or naval purposes.[20] Moreover, species not native to the region, such as reindeer and fox, remained unprotected. Subsequent presidential action further eroded any hope of returning the Aleutians to a pristine state: a whaling station was permitted on Akutan Island, two protected fishery areas were abolished, and limited homesteading was allowed on Amaknak Island.[21]

Nonetheless, the achievement of an approximate stasis between commercial and environmental interests in the Aleutian Chain exerted a healthy effect on Amchitka. The recovery of the sea otter herds began here, although progress was slow. The first sea otter was spotted in 1931; by 1935, their sightings were common. Within two years, the Interior Department's Bureau of Fisheries had erected buildings and had stationed two game wardens on the island to protect this newly discovered treasure. In order to ensure the future of threatened wildlife, including birds, predators, especially the fox, were to be targeted in Amchitka as well as forty-five other islands.[22] Thus, by the eve of World War II, Amchitka had achieved distinction within the Aleutian Islands Reservation. This distinction in turn intensified scientific interest in the area. Agencies such as the Smithsonian Institution, the United States Bureau of Biological Survey, the United States Geological Survey, and the Alaska Game Commission sponsored studies in the Aleutians. From Amchitka alone, one British botanist, Isabel Hutchinson, added over fifty new species to her list of newly discovered flora. Never before had Amchitka and the islands drawn such attention from the outside world. This was the beginning of the region's modern scientific era. Few at the time could have imagined the devastating impact that a looming war would have on this out-of-the-way place.[23]

2 / ON AN ANVIL OF WAR

... barracks blacken in rain, sag
on their foundation. Beyond them
pill boxes and beach, hills
strung with bunkers, the trails
worn into subsoil like contour
lines of a map.

—JERAH CHADWICK,
"Approaching the Improbable"

World War II, which began officially for the United States with the bombing of Pearl Harbor by the Japanese in December 1941, came to the Aleutians in 1942. On June 3 and 4, American military installations at Dutch Harbor on Amaknak Island in Unalaska Bay were bombed by Japanese planes. Soon after, Japanese troops invaded Kiska Island and then took Attu Island in the far western Aleutians close to Japan. This was the onset of what the United States military called the Aleutian Campaign.

Never before had the Aleutians, now a Refuge of the National Wildlife Reservation, been a battle zone of such magnitude or intensity. Yet, for purposes of battle, only the devil himself could have conjured up a more improbable place. Craggy mountains, steep hills, deep valleys, spongy tundra, jagged coasts, shoal-strewn waters, thick fog, mighty winds, and numbing cold, snow, and ice awaited the encroaching warriors. Although the war in the Aleutians ended in the summer of 1943, when Americans in Operation Landcrab retook Attu Island, and, along with Canadians in Operation Cottage, landed on Kiska Island just after it was deserted by the Japanese, over three thousand died in this campaign fought on the islands of the Refuge. Moreover, the conversion of many of the islands into armed camps during the war so damaged the environment as to call into serious question their future fitness as places for animal or human habitation.[1]

Even now, evaluations of the Aleutian Campaign vary greatly. Most agree that its influence was rather ephemeral and failed materially to affect the war's outcome. But the overall balance sheet abounds in ironies. Both sides mistook the intentions of the other, each side thinking the Aleutian Islands could become, if not actual invasion platforms, then at least a pathway to harass the other's mainlands. The occupation of Attu and Kiska as defense posts might have been a morale booster for the Japanese, but it was short-lived. And, when the United States took back the islands, it was done more for political reasons than for military considerations, namely as a response to public outrage over enemy-occupied United States territory. Some said the forces tied up there could have been better used in the central Pacific. The costs of supply were high, weather conditions were horrible, and the lost lives may have been in vain since, as it turned out, the Aleutians were not convenient steppingstones from Japan to the United States. But the persistent fog and low-lying cloud cover in the Aleutians did lead to major improvements in radar technology. When the campaign ended, the United States' dominance of the North Pacific was clinched, which made the later lend-lease shipments to Soviet Siberia safer. In the calculus of war, however, whether the campaign's costs were worth its benefits is still an open question.[2]

Such questioning, nonetheless, cannot discount the sacrifices of the combatants or the experiences of the native Aleuts whose lives were disrupted by this war. All were scarred by the campaign and testify to it still. American soldiers died in the Aleutians, and the native villages in the area were evacuated and/or destroyed by the Japanese and the Americans alike. This campaign was far from trivial. And, the aftermath for Alaska itself was extremely important. The war wrote the Alaska Territory large upon the geopolitical map. Alaska's position became increasingly crucial as the Cold War bore down. Its population was increased by service personnel assigned to bases there or by their choosing the "last frontier" for home after the war. Finally, as a result of huge defense expenditures on infrastructures and military installations, the Territory was propelled toward statehood.[3]

Yet, seldom is there factored into the war's effect the unprecedented amount of damage visited upon this Aleutian Refuge. Military construction, the battles, and the occupation itself took a huge environmental toll throughout the Refuge by dint of the pressures of a large human presence. The United States Army alone sent thousands of construction engineers, not counting thousands more of civilian workers, to build the Aleutian fortress. Reminiscent of ancient Aleut heroes Daylight Lifter, Mainland Slayer, and Tusk Breaker, 34,000 United States troops swelled over the islands and moved relentlessly west. In addition to the United States troops, 10,000 Japanese were garrisoned on Kiska and Attu Islands. By mid-1943, thousands more from the American side followed. At the close of the campaign, six bases in the western Aleutians housed nearly 83,000 Army and Navy personnel. Construction, quartering, maintenance, and supply for these large forces put enormous pressure on an environment which had for so long been only sparsely populated. Historian Brian Garfield called this the "Aleutian population boom."[4]

The Refuge, of course, had not seen such a flurry of alien invasion and subsequent building in all its history. After the Americans took over the most distant island, Attu, it became the largest base after Adak, and it had one of the busiest ports in the Aleutians at Massacre Harbor. In June 1943, it handled "64,000 cubic tons of supplies," rising to "peaks of 102,000 cubic tons in July and 100,000 cubic tons in December." In addition to the military presence on Adak and Attu, military installations were established in the Refuge on Akutan, Aloid, Amchitka, Atka, Buldir, Great Sitkin, Kanaga, Kiska, Little Kiska, Nizki, Ogliuga, Semisopochnoi, Shemya, Tanaga, Umnak, and Unalaska. Brigadier General Benjamin B. Talley, who superintended much of this construction, claimed "we . . . expended nearly 300 million dollars—a hundred and fifty million of it during the spring of 1943, nearly one million dollars a day."[5]

Often working in impossible weather and at breakneck speed, United States military and civilian engineers dramatically changed the landscape of the Refuge. A multitude of new features appeared on the islands' terrains. There were plants for heat, light, water, and sewage disposal; buildings for troop quarters, mess halls, warehouses, garages, workshops, hangars, hospitals, and radio and weather stations. Bridges, docks, roads, airstrips, bomb depots, and fuel tanks dotted the lands. Many gun emplacements ominously silhouetted the skies. Huge sheet metal structures, fifty-five-gallon drums, barbed wire, and machinery cluttered hitherto uncluttered vistas. After the war, much of it lay rusting in dumps of military debris.[6]

From an engineer's point of view, "the battle for the Aleutians was a battle of construction," and bulldozers were its main weapons. Army Engineers Corps and Navy Construction Battalions tore away acre after acre of the soggy "ubiquitous layers of tundra that averaged from three to twenty feet deep." Then, to build roads and airfields, these areas were scoured of ground cover and were filled with countless tons of gravel, rock, and sand, which had been mined from the islands. Known as the "fighting earth movers," these engineers built on a grand scale in "one of the greatest stories of the War, and an epic in construction history." But, of course, this activity was also destructive. Many areas, stripped of protective grass and tundra, became badly eroded. When the winds churned up fiercely, the erosion was further exacerbated. Then, the scarred areas were often sandbagged and covered with steel drums to keep flying bits of sand and gravel out of aircraft engines and away from sensitive instruments. On Unalaska, military roads were built over salmon-spawning streams, which ruined this resource for Aleut harvesting, and the pollution to the surrounding streams and bays harmed the marine birds and mammals.[7]

On Kiska and Attu, two islands the Japanese had taken at the beginning of the war, the Japanese military was unable to marshal such a mechanized campaign. On Kiska, the Japanese did attempt to build tunnels, underground shelters, semi-subterranean dwellings, and an airstrip. But most of this work was done with hand tools. Although that in itself was harmful to the environment, it was the heavy bombardment of the islands by the United States that led to massive habitat destruction. In 3,430 missions, United States planes dropped 624,698 pounds of bombs on Attu, and the Navy weighed in with a heavy shelling of its own before the invasion. Kiska was pounded by 26,910 air strikes and 6,049,522 pounds of explosives. Then, in a softening-up operation before retaking Kiska, Navy men-of-war used so much ammunition—544,000 pounds of it—that they "churned up the muskeg and chipped up the rocks" on nearby Little Kiska Island. Only Rabaul in the South Pacific received more bruising punishment.[8]

Admittedly, protection of the Refuge during the war was impossible, and to assess the total damage is extremely difficult. Statistics of bombing, injury, and death were compiled with regularity, but the trauma to animal and plant life was rarely, if ever, recorded. Harassment of animals was inevitable. One soldier, for instance, described the following scene off Tanaga Island: a plane "buzzed" a dozen sea lions there, "causing great consternation among them." Other service personnel, ignoring the law, took up hunting, mainly as an antidote to boredom. In a flap with the Alaska Game Commission before the war, Major General Simon B. Buckner, Jr., the area defense commander, brought suit in a territorial court to obtain military hunting rights. Although the case ended in a compromise, many servicemen still regarded Alaska as an unrestricted hunting ground. Buckner finally became aware of the extent of this predation and issued a prohibition against it, an act for which he was later praised by Acting Interior Secretary Abe Fortas. General

Buckner applied the order to all of Alaska, stopping "considerable unnecessary destruction of game and fish. . . ." Navy poaching became so problematic that Rear Admiral Frank J. Fletcher, Thirteenth Naval District Commandant, directed that sailors be informed of the 1911 Fur Seal Convention protecting the animals. "Uncured skins" had shown up "as presents," he learned, sent from Alaska to "relatives in Seattle . . . in violation of existing law." Fish and Wildlife Service director Ira N. Gabrielson complained to Interior Secretary Harold L. Ickes at the end of the war that the military was a major factor "in prejudicing the discharge of our responsibilities in the management of the fish and wildlife resources of the territory."[9]

Amchitka's entree into the war was occasioned by American submariners down on their luck. While on a reconnaissance mission soon after the Japanese invaded Kiska and Attu, submarine s-27 was driven out of control by Amchitka's strong currents and stuck fast on a reef five miles off shore. There, the submarine took on water, listed badly, and spewed out chlorine fumes from a damaged battery. Abandoning the ship, the sailors carried food and ammunition ashore in a rubber boat, hunkering down in the Aleut village where the church and other buildings provided havens until they were rescued a week later.[10]

At the beginning of the war, both the Japanese and the American military had been interested in Amchitka. Japan wanted to use the island for protection, and the United States hoped to use it as a launching site for attacking Japan-held Kiska and the Kurile Islands. At a briefing prior to assuming command of the North Pacific Force, Rear Admiral Thomas C. Kinkaid predicted one or the other eventually would build an airbase on Amchitka. But neither side knew for certain if the other had already taken the island or, for that matter, whether it was even worth the effort.

Each side investigated its prospects cautiously. First, a Japanese Army survey party led by Major Kazumi Fujii reported excessively mushy ground dominated by ponds, which would make construction extremely difficult. As a result, the Japanese rejected the island as unfit for military purposes. The Americans, however, came to a different conclusion. Based on a report written by Olaus J. Murie for the United States Army in October 1942, Amchitka was said to have potential for military use. In December, this assessment was reinforced by a complement of Alaska Army Scouts under Colonel Lawrence V. Castner, who concluded that Amchitka indeed had potential for airfield construction. Hence, a plan to use Tanaga Island, some one hundred miles to the east, was shelved in favor of Amchitka.[11]

Before U.S. troops could occupy Amchitka, the island had to be cleared of any enemy who might be lurking there. Consequently, General Buckner ordered "an exploratory air raid" on the island. Colonel William O. Eareckson, a daring pilot of the Aleutian Campaign, was told to "demolish every building of the deserted Aleut village, including the church." Eareckson at first felt rather squeamish about destroying this sacred building, but after having made "several half-hearted passes," he then "bombed the church flat." Air strikes against Kiska and Attu followed on January 5, and the sinking of two Japanese ships with troops and ammunition aboard cleared the way for occupation of the island on January 9, 1943. The invasion of Amchitka had begun.[12]

For two days, the occupation of Amchitka, named Operation Longview, was delayed because of foul weather. However, despite the severity of the Aleutian storms, a small security force put ashore on January 11 from the United States Navy destroyer *Worden*. After unloading, the *Worden* attempted to depart from Constantine Harbor at the east end of the island, but like submarine s-27 earlier, *Worden* was dashed onto the rocks by powerful winds and vicious currents. The ship foundered, then sank. Fourteen sailors drowned in the frigid, turbulent waters, the first of Amchitka's casualties. The following morning, January 12, a detachment of 101 United States Army officers and 1,844 enlisted men under Brigadier General Lloyd E. Jones was offloaded in high winds from the transport *Arthur Middleton*. The howling gale they faced that day destroyed landing boats and swept the *Middleton* onto harbor rocks where it listed for several weeks until repaired. Although not without considerable cost, Amchitka was now occupied by the United States military.[13]

Despite the weather, work by the determined soldiers began immediately. Alaska Scouts, setting out on foot in a blizzard, trudged toward Aleut Point on the island's westernmost tip, laboriously hauling themselves there to establish an observation post. From Aleut Point, on a clear day, one could spot incoming enemy aircraft as far away as the Kiska mountain peaks. It took nearly two weeks for men and supplies to be unloaded at Constantine Harbor in the whipped-up, freezing water and wind. With the stacking of equipment and supplies on the beach, however, the gradual transformation of Amchitka began.[14]

A temporary camp to house occupation forces was built near Constantine Harbor. Most of the troops were unprepared for this environment of muskeg, wind, and cold. For them, tent living on Amchitka meant not digging in but sinking in, as two thousand soldiers churned the soggy tundra into a knee-deep quagmire. The mess grew like some creeping monster when the "warmth within the tents thawed out the tundra, leaving it like jelly." The earth itself seemed to give way. "Gunners set up their batteries and found that the weight of the field pieces forced them deeper into the muskeg, off balance and out of true."[15]

Nevertheless, before January 1943 passed, four thousand more troops settled down on Amchitka in two infantry and four artillery batteries. By February's end, their ranks had swelled to eight thousand. In March, a Navy Construction Battalion arrived following Amchitka's designation as a naval air facility. By the end of October, the island was at full military strength with 14,136 Army and 803 Navy personnel stationed there. Amchitka had become the fourth largest base on the Aleutian Chain after Adak, Attu, and Kiska.[16]

Soon after American occupation in early 1943, the Japanese on Kiska launched floatplane bombers against Amchitka. From January 24 to mid-February, sporadic raids, which the historian Brian Garfield called "the Amchitka Express," slowed down construction, damaged new facilities, and took lives. Three Army engineers were killed in one strike against a partially built airfield runway. In another attack, several soldiers who had dug themselves into foxholes were "smothered when bombs burst near them," and "more men drowned in the muck. . . ." But the persistence and dogged hard work of United States soldiers paid off. Near the end of February, Amchitka-based aircraft flew support and strafing missions against the enemy. Although only two pontoon patrol planes and sixteen fighters were on the island at this time, they helped in the mounting Aleutian Campaign: in February, "156 tons of bombs were spilled out over Kiska."[17]

The aircraft runway from which these planes attacked had been a first construction priority, and its completion in just over a month was an engineering triumph. Engineers had worked round-the-clock using artificial lighting, which also illuminated many overcast daytime hours. The successful construction of the runway, 150 feet wide and 4000 feet long, was based on techniques first used on Adak. The site chosen was at the head of Constantine Harbor, where a flat, narrow valley floor, high on one end, sloped down on the other end to a marsh which flooded at high tide. To solve the marsh problem, engineers built an earthen dam shutting off the marsh area from tidal water. After drainage ditches were dug, the dammed-off area was filled with sand to the higher end's level "without need of an elaborate dewatering pump system." Then, using interlocking pierced-steel planks, called the "Mardsen mat" after its Eskimo inventor, engineers laid down steel sheet segments on both ends of the runway. This created a packed sand midsection "with calcium chloride to make it firm and solid."[18]

Amchitka's landscape was reshaped further in March with the construction of two more runways. The main one, 200 feet wide by 10,000 feet long, was surfaced entirely with steel plank. The secondary one, a cross-runway 5,000 feet long, was made of steel at its ends with a middle section of crushed rock. These two runways, built on a relatively flat, elevated plateau above Constantine Harbor, required stripping the tundra to depths of two to eight feet, filling a large number of small, dispersed lakes, and then covering the area with sand, sometimes to depths of twelve feet. One combat engineer regiment and two regular engineer battalions, consisting of 2,625 men in all, worked on this impressive project.[19]

Although construction on Amchitka was confined mostly to the island's east end near Constantine Harbor, that work required great numbers of bulldozers, dump trucks, and power scoops. Between 20,000 to 30,000 cubic yards of sand and gravel—thousands upon thousands of tons—were hauled daily from two borrow pits several miles away. When construction peaked in October 1943, Amchitka workers had set a record for the use of heavy equipment among all the other westward Aleutian bases. Unfortunately, a record reconfiguration of the terrain also took shape. One soldier noticed that "where a small mountain once stood there is now a yawning man-made valley in which a skyscraper could easily be buried." These indomitable "fighting earth movers," armed with power drag shovels and gigantic scrapers, had cut down one of the most commanding heights of Amchitka, reducing it to a flatness approaching sea level.[20]

In addition to runways, the military also needed unloading docks to move men and supplies from ships onto the island. Without docks, cargo had to be loaded onto barges and grounded straightway into the beaches where it was unloaded by hand. Supplies thus passed hands sometimes up to six times. Often, lumber was merely dumped overboard from the ships and carried in by the tides, where it became entangled in the rocks along the shores. Lumber "cast wildly about by the icy water" threatened injury or death to those attempting to retrieve it. Although docks would eliminate much hand labor and save materials as well as lives, the blustery weather that made them essential also made them dangerous to build.[21]

Without docks, and also without roads, "great mounds of rations, lumber, fuel drums, materials, and equipment sat pyramid-like, piled up ashore." When trucks were used in attempts to move these supplies, the "tractors pulling tread-fitted trailers . . . bogged down hopelessly in the oozing muskeg." Thus, plans called for two docks to be built and linked to the growing military complex by a network of roads. To this end, engineers first built an access road to the harbor and later laid down a forty-mile route nearly the entire length of the island. It was named, appropriately, "Infantry Road." From this main artery, dozens more roads were built around the airfields and other facilities. Some were built by merely dumping sand or gravel over the matted grass. Others required bulldozing and backfilling. Hundreds of acres were marked by these roads and by the scars of extracted materials needed to build them.[22]

But by far the most challenging engineering project at Amchitka was the construction of a breakwater at Constantine Harbor. It was the only one of its kind undertaken in Alaska, and by no means could it be considered routine. To protect the harbor, a breakwater would have to withstand fierce waves and winds off the Bering Sea. And it would be expensive: $1.5 million was allocated for the project. After taking soundings at the bottom of the harbor, engineers planned for a wall 2,300 feet long, which would jut out from the harbor's western shore at Kirilof Point. It was to bend slightly, connecting three small islands and two large submerged rocky areas. Once it was completed, a huge wharf measuring 70 feet wide by 200 feet long, the largest in the Aleutians, would be erected and connected to the breakwater, or jetty, by a large expanse of dumped rocks.[23]

Since United States Army engineers had their hands full preparing bases on the island, noncombatants were brought in to build the breakwater. A contract was given to the West Construction Company. In March 1943, the company arrived with its own drilling equipment, and immediately 103 civilians began working in ten-hour shifts using Army trucks and air compressors. Their first goal was to blast out an access road along the western harbor shore to the breakwater's starting point. The route was rimmed by high rock cliffs which had to be lowered, and quarry rocks needed for the breakwater had to be blasted loose. On April 6, the first explosion jolted Amchitka and dislodged 120,000 cubic yards of rock. Many more blasts followed. Approximately 384,300 yards of rock were eventually quarried, not counting enormous volumes of gravel, small rocks, and "minutely broken fragments of black volcanic glass recemented with silica," which was Amchitka's typical substrata. Then, large chunks weighing twelve tons or more were dragged

across the terrain by heavy tractors. This became the biggest quarry operation undertaken in the Aleutians.[24]

The breakwater was to stand boldly against the water's edge. Its inner
core was to be thirty feet wide and over seventeen feet above sea level. When
topped and held in place by a larger rock layer, its dimensions would reach
thirty-eight feet wide and over twenty-four feet high.[25]

A foreshadowing of things to come was revealed early in the construction of the breakwater. Despite its size and strength, the Bering Sea gave it
scant respect. Some sections were wiped out completely by storms. On two
occasions, waves battered deeply into the core stones and washed them out
to sea. Despite the force of the sea, the project was finally completed in August 1943 and turned over to the Army Engineers for maintenance. Unfortunately, problems that plagued the breakwater's construction continued to
plague its maintenance. Heavy seas continued to wash away areas as long as
three hundred feet. One Army engineer complained that "constant maintenance is required to keep the jetty in usable condition." Repair by drilling
and piling was an ongoing requirement to protect the breakwater from the
relentless breakers.[26]

As military building progressed, the population of Amchitka grew from
a small tent village in January 1943 to a city of 14,939 inhabitants by the end
of the year. This development meant more construction of facilities, more
encroachment upon the wilderness, and more cluttering of vistas. Construction originally had provided housing and utilities for a garrison of only
eight thousand, but capacity was expanded eventually to more than twice
that number. Tents gave way to more permanent dwellings. The Navy preferred steel Quonset huts, while the Army built "Pacific" huts made of wood.
Two airplane hangars, five storage tanks for 1.5 million gallons of aviation
gasoline, two five-hundred-bed hospitals, seven anti-aircraft artillery emplacements, an aircraft warning radar station with a control tower, and over
three hundred other wooden structures joined the growing assemblage.
Solid boardwalks were built to connect these many places and to conduct
personnel safely over the mud. In 1944, the three primitive airfield runways
were paved. By 1945, the base was completed with a capacity of 16,134 personnel, some of whom lived in 1,873 Pacific huts. The base originally had
been budgeted for an estimated $21 million, but the project ended up cost-
ing over $34 million.[27]

Amchitka bore the brunt of the marshaling of resources for the Aleutian
Campaign. The heaviest equipment, the largest wharf, and the only break-

water were foisted upon it by the exigencies of war. Even the campaign's only paratroopers were posted there. Consequently, years after the occupation, signs of the campaign remained. A 1977 survey enumerated 1,489 steel and wooden structures still standing, 143 revetments, 78 reinforced concrete foundation slabs, ordnance depots, open borrow pits and quarries, pickets, patchwork quilts of barbed wire, bulldozers, and dump areas with aircraft parts still in them. Fully over one-third of the island, from East Cape to Petrel Point, held war refuse. A late visitor to Amchitka was shocked by these "signs of man's past presence on the island." To him, the vestiges of war, especially around the harbor area, were "almost overwhelming."[28]

Amchitka's archaeological record, much of which was mismanaged during the occupation, constituted a further assault upon the island's integrity. Many artifacts were unearthed, destroyed, or stolen from Amchitka in violation of the 1906 Antiquities Preservation Act. Historian Brian Garfield called it "the Aleutian bone-hunt."[29]

The pilferage would have been worse had it not been for Captain Paul Guggenheim, an Air Force medical officer with an interest and some training in archaeology. Earlier in 1937, he had accompanied anthropologist Aleš Hrdlička on a Smithsonian Aleutian Expedition. Guggenheim and Amchitka's commanding general had hoped to prevent wanton scavenging, but neither could prevent the amateurish digging and private collecting carried out by occupation troops. "Poachers" began "poking about," Guggenheim complained, and as a result, his "anthropological campaign" on Amchitka became disorganized, fragmented and conducted not "always according to scientific procedure."[30]

Guggenheim, forty-five soldiers, and three West Construction Company employees opened forty archaeological sites on the island. Even so, Guggenheim concluded, these crude efforts did not contribute significantly to Alaska's archaeological record. His most important find was a "very lethal war club." He also purchased artifacts from soldiers who failed to appreciate their real value, but he refused to buy human skeletons. He delivered lectures designed to educate the unprofessional scavengers, but his words fell on deaf ears and were sometimes actually counterproductive. They "seemed only to encourage more vandalism," he rued.[31]

Guggenheim's excavations, as well as the unauthorized treasure hunts of troops, were more often than not macabre. It was disturbing to him when soldiers adorned tent posts with ancient skulls painted red in the eye and nasal sockets. On one occasion, his party, while digging for remains, dutifully snapped to attention while a funeral procession passed by. The party saluted a post inspector, killed in an accident, on his way to burial. Guggenheim confessed to an "embarrassing sense of the bizarre" in this scene—one going to be buried while another was being exhumed. Guggenheim concluded that the digging and scavenging did, in the final analysis, furnish some amusement, thus providing an antidote to the dullness of military service in harsh conditions. He said it was at least "a sanity saver."[32]

Melvin L. Merritt, who worked on Amchitka years after the war ended, said, "I came to think of the island as a beautiful place in a grand, bleak way." But most soldiers, during the occupation, understandably held negative views of it. As Guggenheim observed, military occupation "everywhere raises mud and banishes the life of the earth." One officer stationed on Amchitka compiled a list of the island's plants and wild flowers, which, he thought, was his own "sanity saver." But for the majority of troops, boredom and depression were oppressive. Many undoubtedly would have paraphrased the supplication of the Vikings: "From the fury of the Aleutians, Oh Lord, deliver us."[33]

But, alas, the soldiers were not delivered, and their response to military duty in the Aleutians was mostly negative, albeit infused with a kind of humor. "Repulsive is a GI Word Meaning the Aleutians" is the way *Newsweek* put it. "The chamber pot of the gods" was Gore Vidal's description of it. The "ass-hole of all creations," was one sailor's derogation. Military duty in the Aleutians was likened to a stint in prison—Alaska's own Gulag Archipelago. Umnak Island was called "Alcatraz" and Atka Island "Atkatraz." After the war, one soldier wrote to the president to suggest using the Aleutian Islands "for prisoners."[34]

One service publication, the *Yank*, specialized in Aleutian-bashing humor as a means of providing comic relief. A soldier wrote, for example, that Aleutian scenery "is something I've grown very cold about." The motto on the masthead of the *Attu Sun* newspaper was, "It Seldom Appears." One cartoonist created a mascot, the "Kee Bird." It chirped "Kee-kee Keerist, but it's cold." Worried that the Aleutians would forever ruin the image of Alaska, one captain promoted a kind of debriefing of servicemen by taking them on tours of the real Alaska. This program was written up in a popular magazine, *Alaska Life,* under the title, "Alaska Isn't All Aleutians."[35]

Seldom noted were the softer sides of the Aleutian experience. Courtland W. Matthews and Robert B. Whitebrook, for example, published poetry about their experiences in the Aleutians. Another voice not heard was that of a soldier who wrote, "June and July in the Aleutians is a time of floral extravagance so breathtakingly beautiful that it was difficult to keep the mind on such urgent matters as survival, mobility, and tactics."[36] But these voices were drowned out by the naysayers. *National Geographic* called the Aleutians a "bizarre battleground," a "forbidding no man's land," containing "stretches of barren desolation." *Life* magazine chimed in with the observation that the islands had "few animals." A documentary film released by the War Department spoke of "barren islands." Adak Island, which later became one of Alaska's largest postwar communities and eventually the headquarters of the Aleutian Islands National Wildlife Reservation, in particular was characterized as "next to worthless for human existence." Thus it was that the wartime experience obscured the natural, if raw, beauty of the island chain. The Aleutians actually were rich in all forms of life.[37]

What would become of this Refuge after the war? General Buckner, who took special interest in Alaska and planned to make it his permanent home, had his own ideas. "Many islands in the Aleutians can be developed for sheep raising," he speculated, along with transplanted "mountain sheep, goats and possibly elk." Furthermore, he believed, muskrats should "be planted immediately in the lake region on northern Kiska to determine" whether they could thrive. Perhaps they might become "a good source of revenue," providing fur pelts. In a letter to Frank Dufresne of the Alaska Game Commission, Buckner also suggested introducing rabbits to lure foxes into feasting on them, thus sparing "the ptarmigan and young ducks." The general desired as well "to see the authorization of bird shooting in the Aleutians" for the sake of subsequent military morale.[38]

Dufresne, however, opposed Buckner's suggestions with ideas of his own. Conservation was what he had in mind. He thought the Aleutians should be returned to their status as a Refuge, as originally intended. He cited for Buckner the presidential order of 1913, "wherein no bird nor animal could be taken at any time." The prewar plan of the Fish and Wildlife Service toward conservation of the plant and wildlife on the islands, he said, had been interrupted temporarily by the war, but would be advanced after peace came. Dufresne was optimistic that a brighter future lay in wait for the region. Nonetheless, no one at the time could foretell for certain what might happen to this Refuge after the winds of war would finally subside.[39]

3 / BEFORE A MIGHTY WINDSTORM

When there is going to be a storm,
one has cold feelings inside.

—ancient Aleut presentiment

The war that marked Amchitka so decidedly ended in fiery devastation and ensuing death to thousands of people in enemy territories across the globe. In February 1945, bombs dropped on Dresden by 2,570 Allied planes took at least 35,000 German lives and ignited a conflagration visible for 200 miles. Then, in early March, much of Tokyo was reduced to ashes after two nights of bombing and wind-whipped flames killed 100,000 civilians. More bombs were hurled against targeted sites in Japan until by July eight million were left dead, injured, or homeless. These attacks "killed more Japanese inhabitants than the U.S. military suffered throughout the entirety of World War II."[1]

But that was not the end of the devastation. In August 1945, two atomic bombs, "Little Boy" and "Fat Man," were dropped on the Japanese cities of Hiroshima and Nagasaki by Allied B-29 Superfortresses. This new atomic technology delivered instantaneous death and unprecedented destruction, but it also left the frightening legacy of lingering death by exposure to radiation or "fallout." Five years after the bombs had been dropped, an estimated 274,000 victims had succumbed to radiation-related disease.[2]

The atomic bomb changed the world forever. Its deathly persona in mushroom shape has become a specter looming over all subsequent history. "Hiroshima," "Nagasaki," and "the Bomb," along with other atomic-related idioms like "fallout" and "nuke," are now household words. The "bomb" reshaped foreign relations, spawned another "new" weapons race, and transformed the awful face of war by making plausible the unthinkable—massive radiological warfare which threatens the obliteration of life as we know it.[3]

Not everyone, of course, saw atomic power in such unambiguous ways. Many scientific experts were intrigued by the potential of atomic energy to

26

advance civilization, not just destroy it. Simply stated, atomic energy had the power to divide history. Responding to the atomic bombing of Japan, Connecticut freshman U.S. Senator Brian McMahon foresaw a "new age." He told his Senate colleagues, "Hiroshima was the greatest event in world history since the birth of Jesus Christ." Historians at the time tended to support this interpretation. An official history of the bomb's creation is entitled *The New World*.[4]

Although the initial effects of the bomb's destructive power were available to scientists at Alamogordo, New Mexico, the location of the first test explosion, and later to eyewitnesses at Hiroshima and Nagasaki, systematic studies of both the immediate and long-term effects of the use of atomic weapons were fairly slow in coming. In the summer of 1946, the first round of postwar atomic testing, named Operation Crossroads, took place on Bikini Island in the Pacific. The first of these tests, an airdrop held in June, was followed a month later by an underwater detonation. While the immediate destructive results of these tests on shipping were relatively unimpressive, the environmental impact was nothing less than alarming. In addition to killing countless fish, algae, and coral, the explosions left in their wakes high levels of residual radiation in Bikini's lagoon. This, in effect, rendered the island uninhabitable. Following the second detonation, code-named Baker, water particles containing lethal doses of a unique kind of fallout rained back onto the earth. The test's official historian described the phenomenon as a kind of "kiss of death." "The white billows," he wrote, "carried radioactive fission products equivalent to many tons of radium." Glenn Seaborg, who later became chairman of the Atomic Energy Commission, described the scene as "the world's first nuclear disaster, and one that had been predicted by our own scientists."[5]

The next year, 1947, the Atomic Energy Commission authorized a team from the UCLA Medical School to conduct scientific studies of the original atomic test site in Alamogordo in order to assess the nature of the environmental damage. As one might expect, the scientists and technicians who had conducted the original atomic test in July 1945 had been primarily interested in "getting the job done first." "Safety," according to Barton Hacker, an official historian, "never commanded topmost concern at Los Alamos." Even a high-ranking official of the project's medical office confessed that "the idea was to explode the damned thing. . . . We weren't terribly concerned with radiation." In order to make the most comprehensive assessment possible, the UCLA team included biologists, botanists, entomologists, health physicians, herpetologists, ornithologists, and soil scientists. The potentially controversial nature of this investigation is suggested by the fact that the team's activities were conducted in secret and that its subsequent report remained classified until the 1960s. In any event, the investigators discovered that the land below ground zero had been depressed as much as six feet, "as if a giant sledge hammer had hit it." After two years, the vegetation had just begun to return. Lethal plutonium in the soil and plants was discovered in a radius of "eighty-five miles outside the fenced-in area." Radiation had harmed area birds as well. "Five horned larks had malformations on their feet and claws. One three-year-old jay had a desiccated foot." Rodents suffered eye cataracts and "several ladybird beetles also had abnormal spotting on their backs."[6]

In 1948, three additional test explosions were conducted on Enewetak Atoll, located 200 miles west of Bikini Island. In an ominous change of policy direction, environmental damage assessments seemed to have disappeared as an objective of these tests. Rather, the deepening of the Cold War constituted a mandate for the development of new and more powerful weapons in order to secure the defense of the Western democracies. The first blast of the Enewetak series yielded an explosive force equivalent to 37,000 tons of TNT, the largest single man-made detonation in history. In defense of this program of producing ever more destructive weapons, Test Director Navy Captain James S. Russell argued that "America's preeminence in the field of atomic weapons is not a static thing, it depends upon achievement—day to day, year to year, and test to test achievement." The pride of achievement that occurred at Enewetak is clearly reflected in Atomic Energy Commissioner Lewis F. Strauss's congratulatory letter to Russell: "You are the father of a fine bouncing boy meeting all expectations."[7]

Even as the perceived threat of the Cold War drove the United States to develop more efficient nuclear weapons, so pressures began to build to test these weapons closer to home in order to show that the hazards associated with atomic weapons production had been exaggerated. Rear Admiral William S. Parsons of the Atomic Energy Commission's Military Liaison Committee saw "obvious advantages" in locating a continental test site, one capable of "educating the public [to understand] that the bomb was not such a horrible thing that it required proof-testing 5000 miles from the United States." Subsequent studies suggested that the desert southwest and the coastal southeast, including the North Carolina offshore barrier strands, the Outer Bank islands of Hatteras, Ocracoke, and Portsmouth off the tip of Cape Hatteras, might be well suited for these tests. Although interior Alaska was mentioned in these studies, unfavorable atmospheric conditions there caused concern. Navy Captain Howard B. Hutchinson, the author of the most important of these reports, cautioned that Alaska's weather patterns might trap radioactive waste, causing it "to fall-out on the adjacent country side in the rains or snow associated with minor migrating cyclonic depressions."[8]

Although advocates of further experimentation with atomic energy regarded islands as logical test sites, no one had scrutinized the Aleutian Chain before 1950. Even though World War II in Alaska had been fought in the wildlife Refuge, the islands seemed ready for full recovery after the war ended. Optimistic Fish and Wildlife Service managers revived prewar plans for enhancement of the Refuge's natural resources. As we have already seen, the islands had been surveyed several years before the war with this enhancement in mind. Blue foxes on some of the islands had been slated for extermination in order to promote bird and sea otter preservation. However, the fox had gained a wartime reprieve when the military occupied the islands and subsequently evacuated Aleut trappers. As foxes flourished during the war years, bird populations declined. Soldiers, too, added to the imbalance of natural resources in the Refuge. One of them later reflected on the plight of Adak Island's giant clams: "It was unsettling to learn that we had not been harvesting the clams, we had been mining them." He concluded that "the apparent opulence and vigor of life on these islands is a mirage. It is actually precariously poised, easily obliterated, slow to recover."[9]

As the foregoing suggests, superintending the Refuge had been extremely difficult during the war. Yet, the Fish and Wildlife Service had maintained a presence there, thus indicating a high priority for the area. Refuge manager H. Douglas Gray, proponent of the 1939 plan to convert major islands from fox farming to wildlife preservation, had served in the Navy, but he had been replaced by Frank Beals for the war's duration. Lacking transportation and most other means of support, Beals had hitched rides from the military in his attempts to pursue Refuge work. Ruefully, he noted that service personnel concentrated on post duties and "had no time or interest in wildlife preservation." Hence, Beals had been left "a man alone." Nevertheless, he had managed to conduct an airborne sea otter survey of the Rat Islands region and had compiled field notes, which later served as basic sources for major research on Aleutian birds by Ira N. Gabrielson.[10]

Early in 1946, after the exigencies of the war had subsided, H. Douglas Gray was returned to his managerial position in the Fish and Wildlife Service and immediately toured the Refuge. He noticed military scars on the land, piles of debris, and another recently introduced species, the Norway rat. These conditions alone would have made restoration of natural resources challenging enough, but Fish and Wildlife Service personnel faced an even more daunting problem: the War and Navy Departments were requesting permanent withdrawals from the Refuge of more than seventeen islands for military use. Although islands around Unalaska were on the list, most were located in the western Aleutians, where defense of sea and air approaches to the continent seemed critical. Agattu, Amchitka, and Tanaga—key islands in conservation planning—were included in the proposed withdrawals. Although this was disappointing to conservationists, the determination of the military to withdraw islands for its own purposes was consistent with the legislation which created the Refuge in March of 1913. Reservation status had not been intended to interfere with the use of the islands for military or naval purposes.[11]

But so important was the Refuge to conservationists that Interior Department officials lodged strong protests to the War and Navy Departments against these intended encroachments. In 1948, the contentious parties worked out a compromise. The Fish and Wildlife Service was willing to give up less essential islands if it could be assured control of a right of access to all of them for conservation work, except in "sensitive areas."

In the end, the military withdrew its request for Agattu Island, and the Air Force reduced its request for Amchitka to the east end, where runways and facilities already existed. This accommodation satisfied both sides, thus ending the argument. Prior to the achievement of this compromise, the Interior Department had planned a public hearing at which the protests of the Office of Indian Affairs, the Governor of Alaska, and others would have been voiced. In addition, conflicts over the islands which had existed between the Army and the Navy most likely would have surfaced at some point. The Fish and Wildlife Service was satisfied by the settlement since they likely would have lost all contested issues by the invocation of military necessity or national security. In any case, manager Gray recognized that the match had not been between two equals. "When you have an elephant by the leg," he conceded, "it is better to go along with him."[12]

Although the controversy was settled peaceably, it revealed the Refuge's vulnerability to Cold War pressures. It also highlighted the importance of Amchitka Island as a wildlife sanctuary. Interior Department officials thought the island was a "prize" waterfowl area. "The rare Emperor Goose winters there in about as large numbers as are now found remaining on the North American Continent," one of them pointed out. However, the most important consideration from the conservationist perspective was that military interference would spoil plans for transforming Amchitka into a prime sea otter haven. In 1946, the Fish and Wildlife Service had canceled fox farming permits there in order "to give Amchitka an entirely inviolate status" for the protection of the otters. In two years, it was argued, Amchitka had become home to the "largest herd known and [it] demands complete protection by providing isolation."[13]

Before he resigned in 1947, Refuge manager Gray had recommended assigning patrol boats for sea otter protection around Amchitka. Although no such patrols had been established, his replacement in 1948, Robert D. Jones, Jr., was a committed Refuge guardian who was drawn to sea otter research. He was affectionately nicknamed "Sea Otter Jones." His initial attraction to the Aleutians came as a result of Army service during the war. An electronics specialist, Jones had worked on Amchitka's radar equipment, spending much of his time there on the remote west end at Bird Cape.[14]

As Refuge manager, Jones set himself immediately to sea otter protection in the context of an Amchitka agenda. By 1949, Jones had investigated an unusually high sea otter mortality and had concluded that the culprit disease was not contagious to otters living elsewhere in the Aleutians. However, he felt more laboratory equipment should be purchased for the island and more research conducted. In following Gray's lead, Jones also supported the extermination of fox farming, which would halt the predation of otter pups on the beaches. He hoped to begin this program in July 1949, and he planned to extend his studies by recommending that the Fish and Wildlife Service control the number of outside visitors allowed on the island. In order to facilitate future investigations, he also would tag one hundred animals for identification. Amchitka, therefore, under Jones's leadership, became the headquarters of sea otter studies.[15]

Jones was a physically tough man with "a great heart," as his supervisor described him. Lacking funds and equipment, however, he faced difficult obstacles to his work on Amchitka. Nevertheless, he appreciated the provision of a dory from the United States Air Force transportation unit, which made his job a bit easier when navigating Aleutian waters in search of sea otter colonies. Still, by 1950, Jones looked forward to the military's leaving the island as well as the elimination of the foxes, feral dogs, and rats that endangered infant sea otters. His goal was to restore Amchitka "to its native condition" and to further preserve the Refuge. His determination held promise for conservationists' hopes and expectations.[16]

Despite his plans, Amchitka's immediate future did not lie exclusively in the hands of Robert Jones. Before the end of 1950, the proposal of atomic testing would cast its shadow across the island and would shape its destiny. Ultimately, Amchitka would be chosen for an atomic proving ground because of the relentless push and powerful influence of advocates of further atomic weapons experimentation. Amchitka would become the first North American test site after Trinity in New Mexico in 1945. The island would be used for the military's initial underground and flat-surface atomic explosions to test the bomb's surface-cratering effects. Heretofore, atomic bombs had been detonated on a tower, dropped from an airplane, or exploded under water.

The selection of Amchitka as an atomic test site is in part explained by the vagaries of the Cold War. With the creation of the North American Treaty Organization, or NATO, in April 1949, many believed that Communism had been contained in Europe, and with that accomplishment, the direction of the Cold War had been reversed in favor of the Western democracies. That confidence, however, was soon shaken by a succession of disturbing events. In August 1949, the Soviet Union exploded its first atomic bomb, affectionately named Joe One. Suddenly, the U.S. monopoly on nuclear weapons was shattered. Soon after, in the greatest single setback suffered during the entire history of the Cold War, the pro-American Nationalist regime in China was overthrown by the Communists. In October 1949, revolutionary Chairman Mao Tse-tung proclaimed the existence of the People's Republic of China. Four months later, in February 1950, British atomic scientist Klaus Fuchs was uncovered as a Soviet spy, a demoralizing discovery which caused many to wonder about the security of American nuclear secrets. Finally, in June 1950, the North Koreans suddenly and without warning attacked South Korea, an act of aggression that invited an immediate United States commitment to the defense of that fledgling state. Thus, in the space of less than a year, American security was dramatically threatened by a succession of unforeseen events. Amchitka became one of the casualties of this intensification of the Cold War.

The chain of events that would lead eventually to the selection of Amchitka as an atomic test site was triggered by an action taken by the Defense Department on September 30, 1949. On that date, General Kenneth D. Nichols, chief of Armed Forces Special Weapons Project, circulated a memorandum among key military leaders in which he recommended the holding of underground nuclear tests. Nichols, who had previously served as an assistant to General Leslie R. Groves, commanding general of the Manhattan Project, felt that "Such a test was necessary in order to determine the phenomena associated with such an explosion and to permit a military evaluation of a penetrating (as opposed to an air-dropped or underwater) atomic weapon." The Joint Chiefs of Staff agreed with Nichols's recommendation and approved a five-million-dollar appropriation for preliminary research. The test was judged by the Joint Chiefs as "highly desirable," and they recommended that it be carried out within fifteen months.[17]

But where to test for penetrating, surface, or underground blasts posed a serious problem. In a request to General Nichols on December 14, 1949, the Joint Chiefs of Staff had asked for a specific study of time, location, expenses, goals, and analyses of possible continental test sites. By the spring of 1950, such analyses by several agencies had proved inconclusive. Scientists who were consulted, moreover, advised against an underground test in the continental United States for reasons of safety. Other troubling issues listed by the Defense Department included security, public relations, climate, geology, cost, accessibility, and the size of the test area. One by one, alternative locations fell by the wayside. "Certain remote areas in Canada and other areas within the Commonwealth, such as Australia," were passed up, "even though such areas were made available." Caribbean and Hawaiian islands were rejected because of proximate population centers. Furthermore, central and western Pacific islands failed the size requirement and, additionally, "would entail transplanting a considerable number of people." Test sites in Alaska's interior "were discarded because of unaccessibility, extreme climate, unsatisfactory geology, and the considerable number of trappers and prospectors."[18]

With a sense of urgency and a short timetable, an Armed Forces Special Weapons Project "panel of experts" or "board of competent scientists" was convened in April 1950. It recommended "sites in the Aleutians as suitable from the point of view of safety." At the end of May, General Nichols narrowed the desired location further when he told the Atomic Energy Commission Military Liaison Committee that "the most logical test site appears to be Amchitka . . . which has the advantages of contaminating a small area and has existing docking facilities and an airport." When subsequently informed of this recommendation, President Truman agreed. He fixed his signature to such authorization on October 30, 1950.[19]

The document President Truman signed also approved a surface blast as a companion to the underground test. This above-and-below-the-ground comparative testing reflected an ongoing evolution in military thinking. "There has never been an underground man-made explosion comparable in magnitude to that of an atomic bomb," the document read. Consequently, experts "do not agree as to the size of the crater, earth shock, immediate radiation, or persistence of radiological effects." The goal "is not to prove the functioning of a penetrating atomic bomb but to determine its military effects" for "war planning." An explosion on the flat surface of the earth had never been held, so the tests at Amchitka would demonstrate effects not obtainable from the air, tower, and underwater blasts previously deployed. "It is possible that the USSR may have at this time weapons designed either for surface burst or to penetrate the earth before exploding," Truman was warned. The military felt the Amchitka tests would be vital for the development of a U.S. atomic defense system. Not counting the cost of the bombs and the measurements to be made by the Los Alamos Laboratory, $12.6 million was allocated by the Defense Department, and the Amchitka shots were scheduled to be detonated between September 15 and November 15, 1951.[20]

Rear Admiral Thomas G. W. Settle was nominated to command military Joint Task Force 131 for carrying out this operation, which was assigned the secret code name Operation Windstorm. An estimated time schedule called for exploratory drilling to begin on December 10, 1950, and for refurbishing of the facilities in January 1951. By February, a camp for five hundred personnel was to be completed, and all preparations were to end on August 30, 1951, in time for shot A on September 22 and shot B on October 2. Each of these shots was expected to yield twenty thousand tons of explosive force, about the same as the Trinity, Nagasaki, and Bikini blasts.[21]

The Windstorm test area was situated in the heartland of Amchitka. It commenced six miles northwest of facilities at Constantine Harbor and continued for fifteen miles on both sides of Infantry Road. This large, relatively flat swatch of land nearly touched the coasts on both sides of the island. It comprised about one-third of the island's landmass. Development of the new proving grounds began with a search for geological composition conducive to uniform seismic signals which would come from the shots. Initially, three separate places in the targeted area were selected for surface studies, which were to be followed by placing drill holes in each. The first bulldozed trenches and shallow holes revealed only minimal depths of desired substructure, so only two areas were selected for more extensive exploration. United States Geological Survey geologists kept logs of the drilling, which was done by Navy Mobile Construction Battalion Three and Lynch Brothers, a private contractor with diamond-bit coring equipment. Thirty-four test holes were drilled, ranging in depth from 5 to 428 feet, 6 to nearly 10 inches in diameter, some with casings, some without. No seismic studies were undertaken, but this drilling from February to May 1951, produced important scientific data on Amchitka's geology and hydrology.[22]

Although in 1947, Armed Forces General Kenneth D. Nichols had pressed for sole military control of the bomb, Operation Windstorm inevitably involved other government agencies, especially the Atomic Energy Commission as its civilian caretaker. Atomic Energy Commission Chairman Gordon E. Dean had met with President Truman on October 25, 1950, to push for the Alaska tests, which the president did approve five days later. In November, General Nichols solicited A E C assistance for Windstorm, and a month later Dean pledged Commission "aid and support" for the project "in all possible ways." It was decided that publicity would be handled by a Special Committee of the National Security Council on Atomic Energy, consisting of the A E C chairman plus the secretaries of Defense and State. Military direction with civilian participation thus characterized this effort.[23]

Preparations were to be kept secret, but the Special Committee broke ranks in March 1951 and considered whether to make public the nature of and the need for Windstorm. More and more workers were arriving on the island, and this made secrecy increasingly difficult to maintain. Concern over rumors, possible leaks to the press which the Soviets might use for propaganda, and the necessity to close the area to sea and air traffic were also factors in considering a disclosure. In a proposed draft of a press release from the Joint Chiefs of Staff, however, no mention was made of the bomb or of an underground test. Withholding information drew criticism from A E C Chairman Dean and the secretary of state, who felt a news leak was imminent and that an announcement of details would be better for public relations than not specifying exactly for what purpose Amchitka was being used. The State Department argued that the site of the test was "provocative" to the Soviets unless it were defined as underground, thereby limiting fallout. Dean recommended a delay unless the "true nature" of Windstorm could be stated at that time, admitting that the tests would be "the subject of widespread public discussion" and a "proper . . . fully justified concern on the part of the American people." He suggested a new draft be prepared, "indicating there will be a radiological hazard" on Amchitka and that "after this period the site will revert to something akin to its present status."[24]

The military, recognizing the importance of avoiding bad publicity and its subsequent controversy, agreed to these AEC and State Department objections. A revised draft would be prepared which would announce that tests of fissionable atomic weapons were being planned, that one would be exploded underground, and that after Windstorm had been completed, Amchitka was to be vacated. The Chief of Naval Operations, to whom the commander of Joint Task Force 131 reported, disagreed with the disclosure of the underground nature of the one test, but he thought using the island "can be easily justified" because of its "extended land area" and "remote position."[25]

Just as a press release seemed forthcoming, the secrecy of the operation was, as feared, breached by a leak. On March 28, 1951, the *Anchorage Daily Times* in an Associated Press story printed this headline: "U.S. May Hold Atom Bomb Test on Aleutian Island." The following article, lacking specifics, only speculated about the test's purpose and exact location. Perhaps, the story ran, it would be a deep-penetration, underground weapon chosen for the Aleutians because its climate was similar to conditions in Russia's northern territory. The islands mentioned as possible sites were Shemya, Amchitka, and Umnak. Several other news stories about the tests followed, but they were equally vague. U.S. Senator Warren G. Magnuson of Washington said he thought the United States might be testing an H-bomb there to see what would happen if a saboteur exploded a bomb in a basement or subway of an American city. Closer to the mark, his colleague Senator Henry M. Jackson, member of the Congressional Joint Committee on Atomic Energy, claimed that questions of underground effects, surface damage, and radioactive spread would be answered in due course. In the meantime, he had other questions about the tests: "how deep into the ground would an atomic bomb or guided missile with an atomic warhead have to be sent to bring good results?" and "how will Russia react to an atomic explosion experiment run off so close to her Siberian frontier?" AEC Chairman Gordon Dean remained mum, declining any comment on the testing time or place.[26]

At the same time that these issues emerged, abrupt changes in military plans made all speculation irrelevant. Admiral Settle suggested that Windstorm be rescheduled. He thought the drilling experiments had proved Amchitka's soil to be undesirable and thus might send skewed seismic readings. He also believed that smaller preliminary shots of one thousand tons, for collecting data, could now be safely conducted in California's Camp Irwin or Nevada's Las Vegas area with bombs that had not been available when Windstorm was first planned. He said the bigger blasts could come later. For the Admiral, Amchitka appeared to be the wrong place at the wrong time. Its foul weather was likely to prevent the necessary observations of the air and ground results. Unfavorable weather had already interfered with test schedules, plus the operation had drained personnel and equipment which could better be used elsewhere. He recommended postponement until sometime in May or June 1952.[27]

The AEC, in turn, agreed with this recommendation. Although Commission member Henry D. Smyth saw advantages in saving precious fissionable material which would have been expended in the twenty-thousand-ton Amchitka blasts, other more important considerations prevailed. Uncertainties and the unreliability of estimates presented serious problems. Also, Chairman Dean admitted to Senator McMahon, "the proper selection of instrument ranges and the distance for placement of test structures is proving difficult for the Amchitka tests." Windstorm would be "expensive and logistically burdensome." But the great unknown looming over the proposed tests on Amchitka or at any other site for that matter was "the radioactive particle hazard from a surface or underground burst." Dr. Shields Warren, AEC Division Director of Biology and Medicine, was "gravely concerned about this problem." Other Commission members wondered about testing in "a mine, tunnel, or cave in which the burst could be contained."[28]

The military, too, worried about radiological dangers inherent in surface and underground blasts conducted on Amchitka. The risks were literally incalculable. None of the prior tests in any way replicated the physical conditions found there. As a result, Lieutenant Colonel W. R. Sturges, Jr., of the Defense Department's Division of Military Application, concluded that the tests might yield "startling" results, "comparable to those [yielded by] Trinity." These second thoughts by the military about the viability of Amchitka as a test site caused a reconsideration of plans. These considerations resulted in the emergence of a new goal: how to conduct a presumably safer "Baby Windstorm"—but under AEC auspices. As the U.S. military backed off of any association with atomic tests on Amchitka, large or small, the AEC sensed political danger for itself. Los Alamos Director Norris E. Bradbury, for example, now labeled the Amchitka project a "hot potato."[29]

Even though he was aware of the foregoing debate waged within the ranks of the military and the AEC, Defense Secretary George C. Marshall believed that, all things considered, Amchitka still represented the best site for the proposed atomic tests, and he so indicated that fact when he requested presidential approval for the project. Although temporary postponement was an acceptable option for Marshall, he nonetheless saw no compelling reason why the timetable for the tests should be set back further than the early fall of 1952. This judgment was shared by the Joint Chiefs of Staff. Such endorsement notwithstanding, however, Admiral Settle was determined to scuttle all plans to conduct atomic tests on Amchitka. In an action the admiral described as a "roll-up," he quickly moved to evacuate the island, transferring test personnel, material, programs, and funds to Nevada. In his last command act, the admiral recommended that Joint Task Force 131 be deactivated on July 30, 1951.[30]

No one could have been happier with this sudden abandonment of Operation Windstorm than Aleutian Islands Refuge Manager Robert Jones, who had long since conducted a rearguard action against the operation. He had earlier complained that military personnel had "started drilling without informing us" with the result that the island's fragile terrain had been "scarred." When first informed by a reconnaissance crew on Amchitka in early 1950 of the proposed atomic tests, Jones confessed shock, which soon turned into resolve. He immediately reported the news to Fish and Wildlife Service superiors who, in turn, lodged an official protest over this use of the island. The ensuing controversy led to an October conference in Washington, D.C., between Interior Department and National Security Council officials. Pointing out the progress already made in sea otter restoration, Interior Department Assistant Secretary Dale E. Doty stressed the island's key role in the Refuge. He said test preparations would surely set back the wildlife program. He felt poaching by workers would be problem enough, but his greater fear was the "danger of longlived radioactivity from the fallout being deposited over wide areas of shore line and shallow water and the possibility of its concentration in the invertebrate food of others." Doty's chain of complaints seemed to lead to his inescapable conclusion: "It would hardly have been possible to have chosen a more objectionable area than Amchitka."[31]

Realizing that the odds were stacked heavily against him, Jones began to prepare for the worst. He sought, and received, funds to transfer some of Amchitka's famous sea otters to other sanctuaries.[32] The fact that the first thirty-five of these captured animals had died in captivity prior to their intended transfer only fueled Jones's resentment of all those associated with the U.S. military presence. He described these men as "closed-mouth stranglers" who were totally insensitive to the "necessity to consider humanity." The tests themselves were acts of "malevolence" that threatened the very existence of the Amchitka habitat. If the forces of environmental destruction seemed overwhelming to Jones, he could take small comfort in occasional victories. He was, for example, successful in preventing a group of sailors from killing and stuffing a bald eagle for use as a mascot.[33] One can only imagine the relief felt by this lonely conservationist when he learned that Operation Windstorm had been canceled.

The fate that might have awaited Amchitka had Operation Windstorm been activated as planned is suggested by the results of similar testing that was conducted as part of Nevada's Operation Jangle in November 1951. Even though the Nevada blasts were only one-twentieth of the strength of the proposed Amchitka explosions, the results were impressive. Shot Sugar, the first of these surface detonations, yielded "unbelievably" high radiation in its crater. Its displacement of desert was estimated at fifty thousand cubic feet, leaving behind a hole thirty feet deep and ninety feet wide. Shot Uncle, the second explosion in the series and the first underground explosion, was buried at seventeen feet. It displaced about one million cubic feet of earth and left behind an even larger crater: one hundred feet deep and over three hundred feet wide. Fallout from this explosion was detected as far away as Rapid City, South Dakota.[34]

4 / NUCLEAR ALASKA

I have caught a bear.

'Bring it here.'

It won't let me.

—from Native lore

The predicament of the human and the bear—the trapper and the trapped—is a fitting symbol of the nuclear age. "We" had the bomb, but it just as surely had "us." Which one really dominated, the man or the bomb, was difficult to know. In Native lore, the uneasy relationship between man and bear taught a lesson in humility. But having the ultimate weapon engendered little humility in the man, especially in Alaska.

As previously noted, the Territory was identified for a role in atomic development in the early 1950s when the Aleutian Islands were being investigated for test sites. An *Anchorage Daily Times* editorial, "Atomic Diplomacy in Alaska," hailed this development as an enhancement of national security. Alaska's "atomic playground" was surely selected for its proximity to the Soviet Union. Even if open to observation of atomic tests by Russian submarines, the editor mused, the United States should now be "ready to give the Kremlin some sort of peek into what happens when this nation plays with atoms." He went on to point out that the state of Alaska actually could offer the United States military an even better spot than the western Aleutians for such display of power. Perhaps "Uncle Sam" could have Little Diomede Island in the northwest Bering Strait, "the rock that is separated from Russia by only two miles of water." Possibly, the United States government could even arrange for "some of the debris of the blast to fall on Russian soil" and impress them by shaking "the shingles off their rooftops."[1]

To the extent that this editorial musing was written with "tongue in cheek," the 103 Inupiat (Eskimo) people of Little Diomede village most likely failed to see the humor. In a more serious vein, the editorial went on to argue that picking Alaska for atomic testing demonstrated "realistic thinking" on the part of Washington, D.C., strategists. An atomic presence in Alaska would counter military installations on Russia's Chukchi Peninsula only fifty miles away from Alaska's Seward Peninsula. From Chukchi Peninsula, after all, atomic bombs could be launched against the United States. If further justification were needed, the editor reminded his readers that this type of Alaskan atomic diplomacy would be similar to President Theodore Roosevelt's show of strength by sending battleships around the world in 1907. What the editor failed to mention was that now, in 1951, the implications of power demonstrations were clearly more dangerous.[2]

The editor's boosterism and baiting of the Soviet Bear represented more than just journalistic bluster. It underscored the fact that Alaska occupied a vulnerable position in the weapons race spawned by the Cold War, which in turn precipitated immediate concerns about civilian defense. Reflecting this awareness, Territorial Governor Ernest Gruening and Congressional Delegate Bob Bartlett testified in a 1951 United States Senate armed services subcommittee hearing that Alaska needed underground bomb shelters but could not afford the estimated five million dollars it would cost to build them. The shelters should hold 22,000 people each and would double as hospitals in emergencies. The two pointed out that fully 67 percent of Alaska residents lived in possible target areas. In a further plea for civilian defense planning, a Federal Civil Defense Administration official also testified before Congress that over 90 percent of Alaskans lived in framed housing that would provide no protection from the bomb. This vulnerability, coupled with an attack in winter, would surely create great suffering from exposure to the elements. "Quite possibly," he predicted, "the Territory would be the first to suffer under an enemy attack."[3]

The Defense Department had, in fact, anticipated possible Russian attacks on the interior of Alaska and the Aleutians in order to neutralize United States military bases located there. Given the discouraging course taken by the Cold War in the late 1940s and early 1950s, it is hardly surprising that the Defense Department had made plans during this time to secure the protection of Alaska and the Aleutian Islands. One of the earliest of these defense plans, Operation Dropshot, was premised on the possibility that the Soviets might at some future time decide to bomb Alaska in order to safeguard their Siberian military installations. With this prospect in mind, the Defense Department, beginning in 1949, directed increasingly large appropriations to secure Alaska and the Aleutian Chain against a preemptive strike. For the next five years, these appropriations averaged $250 million a year, incidentally boosting Alaska's economy in unprecedented ways. The central importance of Alaska and the Aleutians in the so-called "Heartland" defense was to provide the earliest possible warning of a full-scale Soviet attack against Canada and the continental United States. This was to be achieved by the construction of a peripheral network of radar stations stretching northeast from Nikolski on Umnak Island (part of the Refuge) to Port Heiden in Bristol Bay on the Alaskan peninsula. Once this radar warning system was in place, its effectiveness was tested by a series of simulated atomic attacks. As sensible a defensive strategy as Heartland might have been for Canada and the United States, the dangers implicit for Alaska and the Aleutians were clear. Essentially, no attempt would be made to defend these outposts themselves in the event of an all-out war. They were seen as expendable pawns in the larger game of protecting Canadians and Americans living in the lower forty-eight states.[4]

The value of having in place an early warning system was underscored by advances made in weapons development during the early 1950s. Between 1949 and 1954, resources diverted to the production of bigger and better bombs burgeoned. Defense Department personnel working on problems relating to the production of improved atomic weapons increased nearly fifty-fold during these five years. At the same time, capital expenditures of the Atomic Energy Commission came to exceed those of General Motors, U.S. Steel, DuPont, Bethlehem Steel, Alcoa, and Goodyear combined. The most important single payoff for this effort was the creation of a new super weapon, the "Hydrogen" bomb.[5]

Despite the proliferation of these bigger and better bombs, throughout the decade of the 1950s and well into the 1960s, advocates of the use of atomic energy for economic development in Alaska pursued the dream relentlessly. Edward Teller, the so-called "father of the hydrogen bomb," titled a *Popular Mechanics* article, "We're Going to Work Miracles." He claimed that "The atom's power is ready to unlock a treasure chest of arctic oil," and he further thought it could be used to "dig open an Alaskan harbor" about one hundred miles above the Arctic Circle on the Chukchi Sea. This area's coal deposits and oil reserves lay untapped, he argued, for lack of a harbor and loading facilities. The use of atomic blasts to open the harbor would be much cheaper than traditional excavations. Finally, he attempted to reassure his readers that fears of radioactive contamination were irrelevant because the site was so remote. All except "10 or 12 percent" of the radioactive byproduct would be trapped beneath the harbor and would "remain practically immobilized in the fused rock."[6]

Project Chariot, the name given to a proposed plan for blasting this harbor, was part of a larger proposal, Project Plowshare, which included numerous plans for the use of atomic explosions for peaceful and economic advances. The story of Project Chariot is recounted in Dan O'Neill's *The Firecracker Boys*. This account demonstrates how government and military officials glossed over hazards to humans and the environment associated with this kind of atomic engineering. Fortunately, the numerous grandiose plans for blasting Alaska into economic prosperity with hydrogen bombs went unfulfilled.[7]

Nevertheless, in the Pacific Islands region, the first test explosion of the hydrogen bomb, Shot Mike of Operation Ivy, which occurred on October 31, 1951, demonstrated the awesome power and dangerous byproducts of this new weapon. The blast released 10.4 million tons of TNT force. It blew Elugelab Island of Enewetak Atoll to smithereens, leaving in its stead an underwater crater 1,500 yards in diameter. Two years later, the Soviets responded with a similar test of their own. Observers of Joe-4, as the test was code named, recorded that "day [was] replaced by night. Thousands of tons of dust were lifted into the air. The huge mass moved slowly over the horizon." The detonation evaporated the shot tower, dug a deep depression, and glazed the nearby earth. Joe-4 left "helpless birds writhing in the grass, well away from ground zero. Wakened by the light from the test, they had taken off, only to have their wings scorched and their eyes burned out."[8]

Perhaps even more devastating than the initial hydrogen blast effects themselves was the residual radioactive fallout left behind. The thirteenth test after Mike, Operation Castle's Shot Bravo on February 18, 1954, for example, produced fallout over seven thousand square miles, a surprisingly wide area. These "ashes of death" caught a hapless Japanese fishing crew aboard the *Lucky Dragon*, which at the time was sailing one hundred miles east of the test site. Unfortunately, its crew was hospitalized, but perhaps more threatening was that the ship's catch of shark and tuna was sold, possibly for human consumption. Bravo continued to deliver extremely high levels of radiation as late as thirty-one hours after the blast, as the crew of an American tanker sailing six hundred miles from the test site unfortunately discovered.[9]

As evidence from various blast sites around the world began to demonstrate the dangers of fallout, military and government officials remained essentially unconvinced. Fallout was an inevitable price to pay for staying ahead in the Cold War and would have to be tolerated by the public. In the words of Atomic Energy Commissioner Willard F. Libby, "People have got to learn to live with the facts of life, and part of the facts of life are fallout."[10]

By 1957, however, concerns about the long-term effects of radioactive fallout had grown to the point where Congress finally conducted formal hearings on the subject. These hearings revealed that Scandinavian and Canadian researchers had found unusually high levels of radioactive strontium 90 and cesium 137 in lichen, caribou, and reindeer in the north temperate zone. American bioenvironmental researchers further discovered that Alaska Natives carried high readings of these and other nuclear blast by-products. These researchers claimed that fallout traveled through a triangular pathway somewhat peculiar to the arctic environment. Because it was present in lichens, a tundra perennial which soaks up wind and rainborne radioactivity like a sponge, particles of fallout were ingested by caribou and reindeer grazing on tundra vegetation. Natives, who depended on these animals for food, in turn unwittingly absorbed this same radiation.[11]

Alaskans, as it turned out, were particularly vulnerable to the hazards of nuclear fallout. Alaska sat astride the central and northern Siberian testing areas in the Soviet Union. Between 1956 and 1962, eighty-two USSR tests were held there, forty-five of which yielded the power of a million or more tons of TNT. One of these tests set an all-time record explosion equivalent to an estimated fifty to sixty million tons of TNT. During this same period, the United States conducted twenty-one tests at the surface, on barges, or in the atmosphere of the central Pacific proving grounds.[12] As a result of this activity, Alaska's Eskimos, reported one prestigious scientific journal, "have four times the strontium 90 content of the average for the world population in the North Temperate Zone." Another study revealed that in four villages above the Arctic Circle, seven hundred Natives were found with abnormally high levels of cesium 137. The isotopes produced by cesium 137 are particularly long-lived and thus create "prolonged internal hazards extremely dangerous to plants, animals and humans." Unlike strontium 90, which is absorbed by bone and marrow, cesium 137 seeks soft tissue.[13]

Although no conclusive evidence existed at the time that such levels of radioactivity were damaging to human health, the unknown conjured up scary images of cell destruction, genetic mutation, birth defects, and cancer. Despite Edward Teller's dismissive claim that fear of fallout was an unwarranted legacy of Hiroshima, Alaskans became increasingly alarmed about it. According to one United States Public Health Service official, "These people in Alaska are quite concerned about fallout."

A year later, in 1962, Alaska's senior United States Senator, Bob Bartlett, took up the cause on behalf of his worried constituents. Bartlett supported passage of the test ban treaty of 1963 which halted aboveground, outer-space, underwater, and underground testing, and later, in 1967, introduced a Radiation Health and Safety Bill.[14] Bartlett's continued concern about the hazards associated with fallout contamination compelled him to insert emphatic warnings into the *Congressional Record*. His philippics included the following: "DANGER IN THE ARCTIC AS RADIOACTIVITY MOUNTS," and "FALLOUT MONITORING: WE MUST DO BETTER: WE COULD HARDLY DO WORSE." Nuclear tests, Bartlett claimed, made Alaska a victim of the "WHIRLWIND OF POISON." The Senator recommended the establishment of a Federal radiological laboratory in Alaska in order to facilitate research into the dangers of fallout.[15]

While Senator Bartlett sounded these alarms in the nation's capital, Alaskans themselves took steps to enhance their own safety. For example, Robert L. Rausch of the Anchorage Public Health Laboratory, together with field researchers from Alaska's Department of Fish and Game and the Department of Health and Welfare, continued collecting wildlife samples for fallout analysis. In addition, the Federal Public Health Service's Arctic Health Research Laboratory received a grant of $100,000 to conduct radioecology studies in Alaska. The Alaska State Senate, for its part, passed a joint resolution in 1965 requesting additional funds for research and urging the Bureau of Indian Affairs to consider "moving the village of Anaktuvuk Pass to a safer location." The legislation incorporating these requests was subsequently passed into law.[16]

The threats posed to Alaska as a nature preserve by all of the foregoing proposals for its use as a defensive outpost and nuclear testing ground had the effect of energizing environmental groups dedicated to the preservation of the habitat. Robert D. Jones, who now took on the duties of both manager of the Aleutian Islands National Wildlife Reservation and the Izembek National Wildlife Refuge, led the counterattack of the environmentalists. Jones's environmentalist credentials were impeccable. During the early to mid-1950s, he had worked tirelessly to restore Amchitka as much as possible to its natural state by eliminating introduced predators. During World War II, military personnel had abandoned hundreds of pet cats and dogs which, upon becoming feral, fed on garbage, birds, carrion, and Jones's prized otter pups. Foxes, which were originally farmed, had also reverted to a wild state. Norway rats, another wartime legacy, were reputed to forage in every niche for bird eggs, chicks, and nesting adults, even on overhanging cliffs.[17]

Thus, Jones's first important project was to rid Amchitka of these intrusive predators. Such was his zeal that he even resorted to the use of the controversial 1080 rodenticide on rats despite the evident risks that its employment posed for other animals and humans. Developed during the war, rodenticide was an extremely toxic natural organic compound of sodium fluoroacetate. In addition, rifle fire, trapping, and more traditional strychnine poison were used to reduce the rat population, even though these means were less effective.[18] By the end of the 1950s, these multiple approaches to reducing the unwanted animal population of Amchitka proved fairly successful. Foxes and feral pets had been totally eliminated, while the rat population had at least been contained.[19]

With the predator population under control, animals native to Amchitka began to flourish. By 1959, Karl W. Kenyon, a sea otter researcher who was drawn to bird studies as well, classified sixty-nine bird species on the island, two of which were new finds in North America. Jones himself identified forty-five species of migrating Asian birds that made a stopover on Amchitka. Samples of birds found on Amchitka were banded to aid future studies of their numbers. Finally, these researchers collected over 240 plant specimens "to determine the part that Amchitka avifauna plays in the world's bird population."[20]

But it was the sea otter for which Amchitka was most famous, and thus it was their fortune which was key to the island's survival as part of the Refuge. At Amchitka, these animals maintained a healthy, nearshore biological community. In a matrix of mutual dependency, sea otters fed on invertebrate sea urchins, keeping their numbers down and, in turn, preventing urchin overgrazing of kelp and sea grass. The healthy presence of otters thus benefited both marine vegetation and sea urchins while continuing their own expansion.[21] Since sea otters are not prone to migrate, the naturally regenerated Amchitka herd was an important source for restoring them in selected former ranges. Undaunted by the failure of an earlier transplanting experiment, Jones and other wildlife personnel launched a new program in the mid-1950s. This effort was, in part, motivated by the fact that the sea otters of Amchitka had prospered to the point that they were in danger of overpopulating their habitat.

Although these transplantation efforts were, in the end, hardly more successful than their predecessors, the results failed to dim the scope of the achievement registered by Jones and his colleagues at Amchitka. Repeated efforts by the Air Force to withdraw Amchitka from the Refuge for its exclusive use, a move that would have constituted a potential death sentence for the sea otters of the island, had been successfully fought off.[22] This, combined with Jones's persistent efforts to control the introduced predator population on Amchitka had, in turn, paved the way for the restoration of other native wildlife species. And, of course, most spectacularly, the sea otter herd had been revived from a threatened condition to a point of near overpopulation. All of these efforts combined to allow Amchitka to reclaim its title as crown jewel of the Refuge.[23]

5 / UNDER RUFUS & LARKSPUR SCRUTINY

Daylight Lifter. . . . got up on top of a high place and,
doing as he did when he formerly fought people,
tucked up his sleeves and lifted up the side of daylight.

—from Aleut mythology

During the 1960s, the unabated arms race with the Soviet Union continued to produce new weapons technologies that required field testing as a preliminary to actual arms production. As the destructive power of these proposed weapons grew, the problem of finding suitable test sites expanded proportionately. Thus, the Atomic Energy Commission and the United States military were increasingly pressed to discover locations where the blast and fallout effects of nuclear explosions would cause acceptable, if not minimal, damage.

Australia attracted attention because of its large landmass and was mentioned as a possibility in a Navy report of 1955. Islands, however, continued to be the most appealing sites. Numerous islands in the South Atlantic, the Antarctic Basin, and the Pacific Basin received careful scrutiny. Most failed to qualify because of weather conditions, topography, foreign government control, or population density. A distinct economic disadvantage to all of these sites was that no facilities were available to house personnel.[1] Although the signing of the Nuclear Test Ban Treaty in 1963 served to rescue for the moment all of the proposed test sites under consideration, Alaska's many islands, small population, and remote location, plus its established military bases, perpetuated the possibility that Alaska would remain a strong candidate for nuclear arms testing. Thus, the reprieve won in 1963 failed to completely assuage the fears of environmentalists about Alaska's future.

The most important single advancement in weapons technology after the mid-1950s was the development of intercontinental ballistic missiles (ICBMs) tipped with nuclear warheads. Between 1955 and 1959, the United States produced 349 ICBMs at a cost of over $1.5 billion.[2] The prospect that

48

the Soviets were developing I C B Ms of their own caused the United States to counter with an improved solid-fuel I C B M called the Minuteman. Test sites were urgently needed to determine the capabilities and effects of this new weapon. In February 1962, the Joint Chiefs of Staff directed the Defense Department to begin a test site search. This request was received by the Atomic Energy Commission's Nevada Operations Office in October of that year. With Minuteman sites scheduled for completion by 1965, it was no doubt inevitable the search would soon yield the name Alaska.[3]

Project Rufus, the nickname given to this search, was officially described as a joint A E C and Defense Department project of "Geological, Geographical, and Meteorological Research." Organizationally, Rufus consisted of a pyramid with A E C and Defense Department officials occupying the top. Three working groups—site criteria, site research, and maximum allowable yield—made up the middle of the structure. Their task was to develop the preliminary research and make initial judgments on suitable locations for testing. Finally, at the bottom of the pyramid, a review panel would scrutinize all recommendations made by the foregoing.[4]

The primary goal of Project Rufus was to identify a site for surface nuclear detonations of one million tons or more of explosive power. These tests would measure the "electromagnetic and seismic effects" of nuclear explosions on the Minuteman missile system. Previous tests conducted at the Nevada test site in July 1962 involved explosions that were too small to have relevance for the Minuteman. According to one researcher, a more powerful bomb in the "10 to 20 megaton range" would be necessary to demonstrate the invulnerability of the Minuteman.[5]

The task of the Rufus organization in recommending a potential test site was constrained by a host of priorities. As one might expect, the safety of the surrounding population was the most important consideration. Because of the size of the blast, no town could be located within forty miles of ground zero. In addition, "downwind" fallout would have to be limited for 150 miles. To make site selection even more difficult, the environment and its habitat would have to be protected. Although the Rufus investigators testified that public pressures "would not directly affect the method of the operation," it was clear that the group was keen to avoid public outcry. Any damage done to natural resources sufficient to cause governmental, public, or conservation group "opposition," the Rufus report concluded, was "undesirable."[6]

The physical requirements stipulated by Rufus were fairly straightforward. A set-aside area measuring from twenty to fifty square miles would be necessary in order to separate the staging areas from the blast site itself. For reasons already mentioned, a detonation yielding the equivalent of ten million tons of TNT would be ideal, although the group admitted that a smaller blast would "satisfy many pragmatic test requirements." With this criteria in mind, Rufus investigators began to search for an actual location for the tests. The larger areas considered included continental United States (including Alaska), the Caribbean, and the Pacific Ocean. Further study narrowed the candidate locations to Nevada, Utah, Montana, and Alaska in the United States, in addition to Pagan Island in Oceana's Marianna group. Of all of these general locations, Alaska (with four) contained the most identified specific sites.[7]

In the end, few areas in Alaska escaped Rufus scrutiny. At one time or another, all of the following regions received some consideration: the Southeast; Kodiak, Chirikof, and St. Lawrence Islands; the Pribilofs; the North Slope; the lower and upper Kuskokwim and Yukon River basins; the Koyukon River area; the Brooks and Alaska Mountain Ranges; the Alaska Peninsula; and the Aleutian Islands. A further refinement of this list led to the selection of Amchitka Island and the Brooks Range North Slope as the "prime sites." This selection seems to have been primarily based upon the recommendations of the Rufus Maximum Allowable Yield Group headed by Dr. Melvin L. Merritt. This task force came to the conclusion that both sites could handle explosions of ten million tons, by far the most of any of the candidate sites.[8] For all of Rufus's original intention to respect the environment in any consideration of site selection, at least to the point of avoiding public controversy, the apparent key factor guiding these deliberations was the physical capacity of the location to absorb maximum destruction. Based on the research of Dr. Allyn H. Seymour, the Rufus review panel concluded that none of the proposed sites should be discounted solely because of estimated damage done to the fisheries or wildlife. Interestingly, the Pribilof Islands were eventually removed from the list of candidate sites, but for commercial rather than environmental reasons. As the report stated, any tests conducted on the Pribilofs would destroy the "breeding grounds for the highly important fur seal industry."[9]

Despite occasional expressions of concern about the impact of atomic tests on Alaskan commercial interests, Rufus was mainly interested in avoiding any site that might threaten human populations. The following three examples show some of the calculations made by Rufus in response to this concern. The Kuskokwim River basin was quickly discarded because of its many Native villages. According to Rufus estimates, as many as twelve villages might suffer "light damage" from a test blast, but twenty-nine were at risk due to the fact that they lay in a path where shocks might bounce back from the ozone layer, especially during winter. Even Anchorage, two hundred miles to the east of the blast site, could expect some "window breaking." The final deterrent to the selection of the Kuskokwim River basin was the location of the Sparrevohn Air Force Station, ninety miles from ground zero. Due to uncertain weather patterns, Sparrevohn might be subjected to nuclear fallout.[10]

Because of its uninhabited status, Chirikof Island for a time drew special attention from Rufus investigators. An additional factor in Chirikof's favor were the prevailing westerly winds which, these investigators believed, might help to carry fallout into the Gulf of Alaska, although weather predicting in Alaska was uncertain at best. But in the end, Chirikof, too, was rejected because of possible damage to adjacent areas. Kodiak, with its five thousand residents, lay within one hundred miles of Chirikof, and thus could not be insured against blast and fallout damage. To make matters worse, sixteen Native villages stood between Chirikof and Kodiak, and thus were even more threatened than were the residents of Kodiak.[11]

The North Slope of the Brooks Range represents yet a third version of this winnowing process. Here, Rufus planners located several possible test sites. Stretching over three hundred miles of pristine settings, the area's eastern edge was marked by Umiat Village, while Cape Beaufort and Cape Thompson on the Arctic Ocean coastal plain indicated its western limit. This potential test area averaged about fifty miles in width and, better still, held no residents. Outside this area, however, there were vulnerable towns and villages with significant populations: Barrow, the largest, with 1600 residents; Wainwright with 253; Point Hope with 325; Kivalina with 142; Noatak with 282; Anaktuvuk Pass with 148; Umiat with 40; and Point Lay with an estimated 104. Moreover, the United States coastal early warning radar stations in the region were likely to suffer some damage. Despite the prospect of physical destruction, fallout here was the greatest cause of concern. Three projections of shot patterns indicated that contamination would fall on the Brooks Range caribou feeding grounds. Aware of the lichen-caribou-Eskimo connection made clear by Project Chariot studies, Rufus investigators calculated that fallout was a particular hazard to the populations of the Brooks Range region. Unlike previous fallout that had been studied, radioactivity in the Brooks Range region would be "fairly concentrated." Nonetheless, Rufus was loath to give up on the Brooks Range sites too quickly. Arguing that the problems associated with fallout might be mitigated by using "very clean devices" producing larger particles which would make contamination "less available biologically" and that winter testing would cause fallout to be diluted by snow, investigators clung to an outside hope that the site might still be usable.[12]

Thus, it was by a process of elimination and diminution that the Aleutian Chain moved upward on the list of sites considered for nuclear weapons testing. Geographically, the islands that comprise the Chain appeared isolated and distant, removed from population and relegated to the kind of obscurity that was so attractive to Rufus planners. At the western end of the Chain, Attu, Agattu, Shemya, Rat, and Amchitka were, for a time, considered prime candidates for testing. On the extreme east edge, Umnak emerged as a possibility. But first appearances aside, both Attu and Shemya housed military installations, while Agattu was much too close to both islands to escape whatever damage might result from a nuclear test. Meanwhile, it was discovered that shots on Umnak would cause "possible moderate damage" to Fort Randall at Cold Bay and produce at Unalaska Island an "oxonosphere blast" during summer months. Even blasts on Amchitka and other Rat Islands were likely to damage windows on Attu, just over two hundred miles to the west, and on Adak, which was nearly the same distance to the east.[13] Other potential sites were gradually eliminated for similar reasons until Amchitka emerged as a top choice as a site for a ten million ton test detonation.[14]

Much of the attractiveness of Amchitka to Rufus planners lay in the fact that projected damage caused by a substantial nuclear blast fell into the classification of "acceptable." "There are many expendable, inflammable structures on the island, most of which would be lost," the planners observed, and its "heavy cover of grass . . . will also be lost temporarily." Likewise, in the vicinity of Adak and Shemya to the west of Amchitka, there were no structures deemed worth saving. At Adak, blast "damage could be repaired or avoided by such measures as opening windows and doors." Moreover, existing regional radar antennae had been built to withstand extremely high winds and would likely be left undamaged. It was further believed that hazards associated with radioactivity would be mitigated by directing fallout toward the open sea to the north and south of the island. The threat of nuclear-blast eye burns could be minimized by firing the surface shots during "periods of greater than average cloud cover" and by restricting ships from entering nearby waters.[15]

In their desire, perhaps desperation, to find a suitable test site, Rufus planners tended to slight the negatives associated with testing on Amchitka. In addition to the imponderables, such as large-scale explosions triggering earthquakes, tsunamis, and volcanic eruptions in an unstable geological area, there was also a calculable list of environmental damages that any test firings would necessarily inflict on the island. Engineers, for example, would leave indelible marks on Amchitka's landscape. Construction sites would require draining ponds and removing "humus and decomposed rock over rather large areas. . . ." Roads would cut deeply into the island's fragile terrain. Birds and wildlife would be at even greater risk. As the Rufus planners themselves reported: "Birds and animals will be vulnerable to the air blast. Birds will most certainly be lost. It remains to be seen if a majority of animals can be trapped and moved." Even seagoing animals, especially sea lions and sea otters, would be affected. In fact, it was estimated that the "lethal radius" for animals in the water might be greater than for land animals, although all life on land could expect to suffer some thermal effects.[16]

Given the central importance of Amchitka to the well-being of the sea otter population of the entire Reserve, the likely effects of nuclear testing on this particular creature received special attention. Sandia Laboratory studies predicted that in a blast of only one million tons, 5 percent of Amchitka's otters would die, a figure that rose to 11 percent in a ten million ton shot. Should the tests be conducted in clear weather, radiation would exact an additional toll. As before, Rufus investigators anticipated that conservationists might make a "fuss" over this projected environmental damage, but this prospect was always seen as a public relations rather than a substantial problem. In any event, no perceived threat to the environment was considered sufficient to suggest postponement, much less cancellation, of nuclear tests on Amchitka.[17]

In the early summer of 1963, Project Rufus moved into a second and more focused phase. Rufus II, or Larkspur, as it was more commonly called, was designed to choose the actual test site and prepare for the implementation of the test firings. Four working units were assigned special missions. The Technical Criteria Group was made up of Lawrence Radiation Laboratory, Los Alamos Scientific Laboratory, and Sandia Corporation personnel chosen for their expertise in nuclear experimentation. The Environmental and External Operational Safety Group, headed by Sandia, was comprised of personnel from the foregoing, supplemented by experts from a variety of institutions, including the United States Weather Bureau, the University of Washington, and the United States Public Health Bureau. A third unit, the Logistical Survey Group, was led by the United States Army Corps of Engineers (North Pacific Division). Its working staff was recruited from the ranks of important defense contractors such as Holmes and Narver and Reynolds Electrical and Engineering. Finally, public relations issues were assigned to a Public Acceptance Group headed by the Public Health Service with the AEC and Department of Defense providing support.[18] By any reasonable standard, Larkspur was an impressive organization, and that fact alone testified to the seriousness with which AEC and the Department of Defense pursued its goal of testing new nuclear weapons in Alaska.

Although Larkspur was commissioned to prepare for actual test firings by 1965, that timetable was demolished by an unforeseen diplomatic event, the successful negotiation of the Nuclear Test Ban Treaty. This treaty, which sought to ease Soviet-American tensions in the wake of the Cuban Missile Crisis, was just partially successful in achieving this goal inasmuch as its strictures covered only underwater, surface, and atmospheric nuclear testing. Thus, expenditures for nuclear-armed bombers, Polaris missiles, and Minutemen actually escalated, while underground testing continued on much as before. Nonetheless, the results of this agreement were sufficiently impressive to cause policymakers to modify the United States nuclear testing program, a decision that made Alaska test sites expendable. As a result, Larkspur was abruptly cancelled. For reasons far beyond their control, conservationists had won an important battle over environmental protection.

Spared the devastating effects of nuclear testing, the Alaskan environment continued to thrive during the 1960s. Most symbolic of this healthy state was the phenomenal recovery of the sea otter herds. By 1962, these herds had become so robust that the Alaska Department of Fish and Game, together with federal wildlife authorities, made the decision to permit the harvesting of sea otter pelts for market. Harvests in subsequent years finally led to the first public auction of these pelts held since 1911.[19]

The victory achieved by environmentalists in Alaska in 1963, however, was far from final. By a lucky coincidence of international politics, threats to the Alaskan environment had won a reprieve, but not victory. For another generation, Alaska would remain hostage to Cold War tensions.

6 / DURING A LONG SHOT

The year 1965 witnessed the corrosive evil of a nuclear bomb explosion
on a National Wildlife Refuge. Life, ecology, evolutionary processes:
all essential features of the worldwide heritage of mankind
to which a . . . Refuge . . . is devoted, were violated.

—ROBERT D. JONES, JR., Manager,
Aleutian Islands National Wildlife Refuge

At first glance, the successful negotiation of the Nuclear Test Ban Treaty of
1963 might appear to have been largely the product of a panic reaction
to the threat posed by the Cuban Missile Crisis. In reality, however, improved means of nuclear test detection, coupled with a genuine desire on
the part of both the United States and Soviet Union to ease Cold War tensions, had paved the way to that achievement. By that time, it had become
possible to measure airborne radioactive contamination by the use of sophisticated air sampling devices. Moreover, methods were also available to
detect acoustic, hydrocoustic, and radio waves, plus electromagnetic flashes
generated by nuclear blasts. Thus, the issue of "cheating" was essentially
confined to underground testing, which left no telltale signs except for those
recorded as seismic signals telegraphed though the earth's crust. These signals were, of course, indistinguishable from those created by natural events
such as earthquakes.[1]

It therefore followed that in the event a reliable method of monitoring
underground tests could be found, and, as a consequence, suspicions about
cheating be eased if not eliminated entirely, a ban on all testing would become feasible. In the absence of such technology, however, the arguments of
preparedness advocates that United States underground tests should be ac-
celerated, if only to counter suspected similar activities by the Soviets, were
difficult to resist. Thus, underground nuclear testing, which increasingly became the focus of all nuclear weapons development by the early 1960s, held
the key to the fate of the arms race during the 1960s. Should the under-

ground testing of nuclear weapons remain undetectable, the United States and the Soviet Union would undoubtedly continue to build new and improved weapons of mass destruction. On the other hand, should such tests for accurate detection prove to be successful, the resulting climate of greater certainty might pave the way to an extension of a test moratorium agreed to by U.S. President Dwight Eisenhower and Soviet Premier Nikita Khrushchev in 1958. Operation Long Shot is the story of the United States' determination to develop a reliable means of detecting such underground explosions and the unfortunate consequences of that determination for the Alaskan environment.[2]

Following the implementation of the Eisenhower/Khrushchev test moratorium, a group of technical experts convened in Geneva to determine the effectiveness of existing mechanisms to detect both underground and atmospheric test blasts that might take place in violation of the ban. By employing scientific instruments located throughout the world on land, ships, and aircraft, the Geneva panel concluded that underground explosions as small as five-thousand-tons yield could be distinguished from earthquakes.[3] Closer analysis, however, suggested that these findings might have been too optimistic. Data derived from a subsequent United States test series, codenamed Operation Hardtack II, revealed that blasts below twenty thousand tons discharged seismic signals that were indistinguishable from those released by earthquakes. Additional discouraging news was received in the spring of 1959 when a scientific panel headed by Robert F. Bacher concluded that even on-site inspectors might not be able to ascertain whether an underground test had taken place.[4]

These scientific setbacks, coupled with the lingering Soviet fear that on-site inspections would lead to spying and the United States' suspicions that the Soviets would undoubtedly cheat in the absence of reliable verification, made the achievement of a permanent test ban difficult. Nonetheless, the obvious importance of the ultimate goal persuaded the United States to continue its efforts to make all forms of nuclear testing verifiable. Code-named Project Vela, this massive scientific project was headed by the Defense Department's Advanced Research Projects Agency.[5] Its aim was three-fold. To improve the monitoring of outer space, the Vela Hotel research program launched orbiting satellites to scan for neutron, gamma ray, and x-ray emissions. Vela Sierra searched for signs of high altitude radiation by using ground-based optical, radio frequency, and geophysical sensing instruments. Vela Uniform was assigned the task of improving seismic detection technology in order to differentiate definitively underground and underwater blasts from earthquakes. Quite clearly, the last of these projects, Vela Uniform, was the most critical for future test ban negotiations.[6]

Given the fact that Project Vela was headed by the Department of Defense, it should come as no surprise that the military would wish to derive additional benefits from whatever testing might be conducted in order to implement the aforementioned programs. Despite President Eisenhower's emphatic public assertion that Project Vela would "not . . . have anything to do . . . with weapon's testing," the Defense Department planned to dig "effects" tunnels near the center of the first test explosion. These tunnels would contain portions of military structures such as missile silos. George Kistiakowsky, the president's science advisor, disclosed that the test would thus "reveal their [the military's structures] resistance to seismic shock, clearly information of some military value." Kistiakowsky's conclusion was that Eisenhower thus risked placing himself in an untenable position should this information become public. As this episode reveals, the difficulties of separating the peaceful and military uses of nuclear testing were inherent in the process itself. The mere possibility that such dual use of testing existed constituted a significant impediment to the construction of any meaningful ban.[7]

Problems arising from dual, and perhaps multiple, uses of underground testing notwithstanding, plans for conducting such tests got underway in late 1959 to determine differences in seismic activity resulting from explosions and earthquakes. The first of these tests conducted by Vela Uniform took place in an active earthquake zone two hundred miles north of the Nevada Test Site, near the city of Fallon. This site was sixty-five miles west of Reno and the state capitol, Carson City. Detonated on October 26, 1963, it consisted of a shaft blast of twelve thousand tons buried at fifteen hundred feet. Despite the possibility of negative public reactions, local authorities were supportive of this test.[8]

A second Vela Uniform test was held in the Tatum Salt Dome, located close to the population centers of Hattiesburg and Jackson, Mississippi, and New Orleans. Here, Vela planners wanted three decoupled blasts. Previously, experts had suggested that decoupling, i.e., detonations occurring in a carved out cavern, would deprive seismic waves a medium in which to travel, thus muffling the blast. This proposal led to internal controversy among Atomic Energy Commission officials. Deputy Director of Operational Safety Gordon Dunning opposed decoupling tests on the grounds that the tests would have no substantive value and were not worth the risks involved. Nevertheless, the first of a proposed three-blast series was detonated on October 22, 1964. It "caused damage much greater than expected," and did not clarify distinctions between readings from blasts and/or earthquakes. The two remaining shots were suspended.[9]

Many other tests followed throughout the remainder of the 1960s. Project Scroll consisted of a shaft test detonated on April 23, 1968. Two tunnel blasts were exploded two years later on May 12, 1970, and July 1, 1970. By 1971, Vela Uniform's test program was considered completed. Although these blast tests, involving both chemical and nuclear explosives, demonstrated no conclusive data with regard to blast/earthquake seismic readings, their destructive impact on the environment at ground zero sites was inescapable.[10]

As has been noted, while other attempts had been made to draw Alaska into nuclear testing, the Vela Uniform project finally accomplished that objective. The most important test in the Vela Uniform series took place on Amchitka Island on October 29, 1965. It was code-named Project Long Shot. This test was the first nuclear explosion ever held in Alaska. It consisted of an eighty-thousand-ton blast detonated at the bottom of a twenty-three-hundred-foot shaft, the largest single explosion of the Vela Uniform series. The Aleutian site was considered sufficiently removed from population centers to warrant Long Shot's size. Alaska's seismically sensitive conditions were viewed as an added attraction. Was it possible to distinguish man-made explosions from earthquakes in such an unstable environment? The two largest underground shots at the Nevada Test Site to date—Aardvark at forty thousand tons and Haymaker at sixty-seven thousand tons—had produced valuable statistics relating to magnitude correlation of "seismic events in the u.s.s.r. and their equivalence in terms of underground nuclear explosions." Even more valuable data could be expected from a larger explosion conducted in the unstable geography next to our most likely foe.[11]

The transformation of Amchitka into a test site began when the first drill rig arrived on May 13, 1964. Two additional rigs were in operation by the end of July. These rigs removed nearly 8,000 cubic yards of material, causing extensive stripping of plants and muskeg.[12] Army engineers, the Interior Department's Bureau of Reclamation, and the Century Geophysical Corporation buried 81 geophone detectors in six holes varying from 16 feet to 50 feet deep. Since drilling was difficult, project personnel buried 2,500 tons of explosive charges in pits dug out by backhoe and power shovel.[13] By the time all exploratory drilling was completed in December, six holes had been sunk in the vicinity of the ground-zero blast point, the deepest of which was 2,883 feet.[14] The shaft for Long Shot itself was formed by drilling a 72-inch diameter hole to the depth of 66 feet. From there, the shaft continued to a depth of 2,346 feet, with the diameter reduced to 54 inches. The shaft was completed and capped on October 2, 1965.[15]

Determining just how much damage to wildlife Long Shot would cause was left to a study of "bioenvironmental safety" to be conducted by the University of Washington Radiation Biology Laboratory, Sandia Corporation, and AEC Operational Safety Division officials. The group pointed out that fallout was a "remote possibility," but if the blast happened to cause underwater land slides, "survival of sea otters, sea lions and other organisms . . . [would be] an unknown factor." The study concluded that "the greatest concern, by far, is with the sea otters." Fisheries, sea lions, and birds were of secondary importance.[16]

Despite the predicted value of Long Shot in determining potential dangers to humans and the surrounding environment, as well as to improving the sophistication of detection technology, they were, in the end, unable to provide conclusive proof of a nuclear explosion as opposed to natural disruptions. It is estimated that between one hundred and two hundred earthquakes with a force of twenty kilotons occur annually in the Soviet Union each year, only half of which can be distinguished from nuclear explosions by seismographs. Moreover, much larger explosions could be disguised by the use of decoupling. Thus, the effort made by the United States to ease the arms race by eliminating the opportunity to cheat in underground testing, in the end, came to very little.[17]

From the outset, Defense Department officials planned to conceal Operation Long Shot in order to gauge whether other countries, especially the Soviet Union, possessed the means to detect an underground explosion of this size. This obsession for secrecy extended to the point where at first the Atomic Energy Commission was excluded from participation in the project. Only later was it discovered that statutory requirements made such exclusion legally impossible. AEC involvement in Long Shot aside, the scope of the preparations for the explosion all but ruled out the possibility that Long Shot could be hidden from the public indefinitely. In fact, rumors reached Alaska as early as March 1964, even before drilling had begun, that a top secret Amchitka project was in the offing. Picking up on these rumors, Refuge manager Robert Jones immediately concluded that a nuclear test was likely. His foreboding deepened when he subsequently learned additional details: a huge supply of military aircraft was headed for Amchitka, and a Canadian drill rig destined for the island had been detained by U.S. Customs in Anchorage. Jones was both saddened and outraged. Once again, the Refuge was threatened by "bomb people" whose goals conflicted with his caretaker responsibilities.[18]

Although not officially announced until the spring of 1965, Long Shot was the subject of a briefing for top Alaska officials a year earlier. U.S. Senators Bob Bartlett and Ernest Gruening, Representative Ralph J. Rivers, and Governor William A. Egan were notified of Long Shot in February 1964, at which time they had raised "no serious objections." However, a month after the disastrous Great Alaska Earthquake on Good Friday, March 27, 1964, Defense Department officials, now worried about perceptions that Long Shot might trigger a similar catastrophe, again consulted Bartlett, Gruening, Rivers, and Egan. Despite the fact that this earthquake was the largest ever recorded in North America, only the governor expressed "reservations" about the "probable psychological effect [of Long Shot] on the populace." Egan's misgivings were eased by assurances that he would be kept fully informed about the progress of Long Shot. He was also brought into line by promises that heavy equipment would not be diverted from the mainland to Amchitka in the event that significant earthquake-related damage occurred as a result of Long Shot.[19]

However, another earthquake erupted in the Rat Islands region on February 3, 1965. Alarmed by its intensity and possible effects on the implementation of Long Shot, Defense Department officials organized an inspection party, which included Congressman Ralph Rivers and the wildlife caretakers Jones and David Spencer, to survey the scene. Although Amchitka had been "well shaken" by the quake, the survey party found little actual environmental damage. To Jones, this foray was a "curious interlude," as the party was offered no information on the upcoming Long Shot blast.[20] In retrospect, Jones felt he and Spencer had been used, as wildlife experts, to validate Long Shot. If they concurred that the powerful earthquake had little effect on the environment, then it would follow that the man-made bomb itself should not be feared. Jones believed the quake had been made into a convenient "heaven sent opportunity for the bomb people."[21]

A public announcement of the pending nuclear test was made on March 18, 1965, some eight months prior to the event itself. The Defense Department's prior policy of secrecy was abandoned largely because the flood of rumors had created so much misinformation that public disclosure was now considered the lesser of two evils. Hence, the public relations arm of the Defense Department joined forces with the AEC's Department of Public Information to keep the record straight, at least to the extent that news about Long Shot would not unnecessarily jeopardize the project.[22] Disclosure thus soon merged with propaganda in order to create as much public sympathy for Long Shot as possible. Governor Egan joined this effort by arguing that Alaskans should be proud of this opportunity to participate "in national security." He further pointed out that over one hundred and forty such tests in Nevada had "proven that there is no danger from radioactivity being released in the test area." "As Governor of Alaska," Egan told his audience on one occasion, "I am pleased that we have been selected as the hosts, so to speak, for this test, and I'm sure I speak for my fellow Alaskans." Either because of misinformation or deliberate neglect, Egan failed to disclose that fifty-six of the Nevada test sites had leaked radioactivity.[23]

When Long Shot finally exploded, what, in fact, did occur? This detonation, like hundreds of previous blasts, evolved in four distinct stages. First, the "explosion energy," created in a millionth part of the first second, produced a pressure elevation of several million atmospheres and a temperature of "about a million degrees." Second, this phenomenon, in turn, set off a huge shock wave that quickly spread out in all directions with a velocity equal to at least the speed of sound in a rock medium, leaving behind a large cavity lined with molten rock. Third, as the cavity cooled, the molten rock at its bottom began to solidify. The final event in this sequence was the collapse of the cavity's roof, which left in the vacated space a "chimney." The speed with which these events occurred, combined with the sheer force of the resulting explosion, was spectacular. Refuge manager Jones described the process as the "hot breath of a nuclear bomb."[24]

Although Long Shot personnel were relieved that the test had run true to form, the excruciating physical effects inevitably caused by a force of such magnitude were clear to all observers. An official follow-up report noted the following conditions:

Surface effects . . . consisted of cracks in uncompacted ground. . . . The cracks were most conspicuous in the roads and occurred as far as 7,400 feet south and 3,700 feet north of Long Shot Ground Zero. Other less common conspicuous effects included slumping of stream banks as far as 3,200 feet from Ground Zero; rockfalls along the Bering seacoast as far as 10,000 feet northeast of Ground Zero; a few mud geysers within 2,400 feet of Ground Zero and principally to the west, south, and east of it; and tilting of ponds.[25]

Additional, more subtle environmental damage was more difficult to calculate. The blast itself had clearly affected communities in the island's ecosystem. Ruptures of muskeg and moss mounds, plus slumping of earthen and coastal banks, were observed within a radius of one mile of ground zero. Water levels in two ponds close to the center of the blast dropped. Ground motion was discovered to have "ruptured banks of settling basins, releasing the contaminants to the drainage" system. Lichens were literally drowned by flooding that occurred in the aftermath of the explosion. These environmental depredations were small but unsettling signals that the long-term ecological costs of Operation Long Shot might be greater than the hopeful test managers had originally calculated.[26]

Further disquieting hints of Amchitka's future were not long in coming. Contrary to scientific predictions, Long Shot had indeed leaked radionuclides into the island's environment. Subsequent on-site drilling and sampling, along with studies conducted by the Lawrence Radiation Laboratory, revealed the presence of explosion-produced "anomalies." Two expeditions to Amchitka in the spring and fall of 1966 discovered four released radioisotopes: tritium (H3) as tritiated water, tritiated methane (CH3 T), iodine (I 131), and krypton (KR 85). Although the levels of these derivatives were found to be "well below" AEC guideline standards of protection in an "uncontrolled area," traces of both tritium and krypton were substantially greater than one might expect to find in a "natural background."[27]

What might happen to this nuclear waste in years to come? Although no one could make a long-term prognosis with any degree of certainty, there was always the possibility that cumulative exposure to radiation would affect Amchitka and its habitat for years to come. Moreover, the migration of these wastes could, in time, adversely affect biota in the nearby Bering Sea and North Pacific Ocean.[28]

Even before post-blast assessments of Long Shot had been made, Alaska environmentalists were suspicious of the easy assurances made by Governor Egan and others connected with the planned explosion. One of the first and most important of these critics was Celia M. Hunter, from the small village of College, located outside Fairbanks. The same day that she first learned of Operation Long Shot from a newscast, Hunter wrote Senator Bartlett a letter expressing her surprise in view of previous Defense Department and

A E C denials that such an event was in the offing. While acknowledging that Long Shot might be perfectly safe, Hunter confessed her skepticism about the capability of existing technology to determine that fact. "The thing that disturbs me [most]," she continued, "is the shroud of supersecrecy which has cloaked this whole program, making it impossible for truly concerned citizens to obtain any indication of what was going on out there." "I fear government decree . . . " Hunter concluded, "for in the past [the Defense Department and the A E C] have shown a willingness to ride roughshod over the wishes of private citizens." Hugh G. Gallagher, Bartlett's legislative assistant, wrote the following response to Hunter: "Senator Bartlett is convinced that the test is necessary in the national interest." He has received "complete assurances that no venting will occur."[29] In taking the "high road" in the public relations battle over nuclear testing, Alaska's public officials were convinced that their own credibility would be sufficient to offset the lack of hard information made available to the public and, thus, stifle any serious open debate on the issue of the merits of such testing.

Her personal misgivings about the credibility of public officials aside, Hunter was also a founder of the Alaska Conservation Society. Established in 1960, this group originally consisted of eighteen persons from Fairbanks, including Ginny Hill Wood, Judy Weeden, and University of Alaska scientists Leslie Viereck, William O. Pruitt, Jr., Robert B. Weeden, and Frederick C. Dean. The Society, Alaska's first in-house environmental organization, had grown from an original spearheading group of eighteen to an influential organization of about four hundred, half of whom continued to live in the state five years later. At first, armed mainly with an ancient mimeograph machine, which produced its quarterly *News Bulletin,* the Society by mid-decade had emerged as an influential education and lobbying resource. Members cared deeply about the environmental consequences of an underground nuclear explosion. The Society's sense of mission to preserve as much of Alaska's wildlife and wilderness as possible was heightened by the belief that statehood, which had been achieved in 1959, would greatly intensify the efforts of investors and entrepreneurs to develop Alaska's natural resources.[30]

Jousting between Alaska's public officials and environmental advocates proved to be an unequal contest. Unable to pry loose important information about the proposed tests, environmentalists were at a loss to mount a serious campaign against Long Shot. In answer to the following question posed by Frederick Dean, president of the Society, to Interior Secretary Steward Udall: "Is it necessary that such activity [i.e., nuclear testing] be permitted on a national wildlife refuge?" he was told, in effect, that the issue was moot inasmuch as such testing would produce no harmful effects to the environment. The insouciance implicit in this response was underscored shortly thereafter when Interior Department officials added that "the d.o.d. has not yet formulated plans for 1965." It is hardly surprising that Dean's written reaction to his dismissive treatment should reek with sarcasm. A month later, after attending an Anchorage press conference which revealed test plan details, he wrote, "The d.o.d. has gained an ability to expedite!"[31]

Following this press conference in March 1965, the Defense Department promised to explain more fully the details concerning Long Shot. However, the most information it was willing to disclose, even at this relatively late date, was that "only one nuclear device would be exploded. . . ." Far more important were the questions left unanswered, questions that were later posed by Dean in the Society's *Newsletter*. Homing in on the choice of Amchitka as the site of the tests, Dean asked: "Was the detailed biological knowledge of the area that is in the hands of the United States Fish and Wildlife Service used in the course of planning? How much danger is there to the ecosystem from blasts, post-blast radiation, impact of the activity on plants, animals, and the environment? Is salvage archaeology needed before another large-scale intrusion is forced on the Island?" Dean's conclusion was evident by the nature of the concerns he raised. An informed citizenry armed with a "full and honest accounting" was vital, he felt, "so the objective evaluation" of Long Shot could be made.[32]

The complaints of Alaskan environmentalists about the shortsightedness of Long Shot planners, however, were never addressed. From first to last, the priority of the Defense Department and the a e c was the efficacy of the explosion itself. Environmental issues were not only of secondary importance, they were considered potentially counterproductive to this primary concern. Moreover, who could reasonably argue that Long Shot was not important to the national defense? Even Dean's anger was deflected by the patriotic implications of this issue. "At the moment," he ruefully informed the Society's members, "we seem to be caught in a dilemma" of clashing values. "No one," he continued, "wants to block an important step toward world peace." In the end, the Society acquiesced in the primacy of national security considerations, refusing officially to oppose Long Shot.[33] Trying to put the best face on a disappointing defeat, Dean concluded that Operation Long Shot might prove to the military and the public at large the need for professional ecological studies as a preliminary to future tests.[34]

The laments of the environmentalists about their failure to save Amchitka from nuclear depredation continued long after the obituaries for Long Shot had been written. Some of this despair was recorded by the national press. *Life Magazine,* for example, wrote, "Naturalists and conservationists bitterly oppose the test on the grounds that it might do irreparable damage to sea otters." There is "considerable resentment . . . over the fact that Amchitka is an official wildlife refuge." A mammalogist at New York's American Museum of Natural History wrote that it would be difficult to persuade young people of the need to conserve wildlife when their own government disregards such advice. Larger conservationist messages, he felt, were similarly compromised. "Now it will be pretty hard to explain to [others], particularly Africans, that they should go home and tell their meat-hungry peoples why they cannot kill native animals for food."[35]

The apparent finality of Long Shot was reflected in an editorial published in *Audubon* magazine by National Audubon Society president Carl W. Buckheister. Commenting a month before Long Shot was to take place, Buckheister mourned that "It is too late to do anything but deplore the act." This piece, entitled "Duplicity and Destruction at Amchitka," represented a blistering indictment of federal policy:

> The reasons for the "top secrecy" was to dupe the Department of Interior—which is supposed to guard over the refuges and which was incredibly naïve—and to get the "official approval" rubber-stamped up and down the line before the public could find out and protest.
>
> The whole point is, there are thousands of square miles of Alaska or offshore islands and Pacific Ocean where Operation Long Shot could have been staged, if it had to be done in that part of the globe. It did not have to be done in a national wildlife refuge.

For Buckheister, the ultimate victim of Long Shot was not Amchitka's environment but the American way of life itself. Our democratic system, based upon representation, information, and honesty, had been undermined by the "arrogant disrespect" of public officials, he charged. What should be done, the Audubon president urged, is to "rock the Defense Department, the Interior Department, and the White House with enough public protest to make them think twice before they engage again in duplicity to invade another wildlife refuge."[36]

Final assessments made by environmentalists about Long Shot showed that there was plenty of blame to go around. While some, like Buckheister, saw the sinister hand of the federal government in Long Shot, others, many of them closer to home, found villains in Alaska. Karl W. Kenyon, mammalogist and supervisor of Alaska refuges, was struck by the insensitivity of bomb workers and their ignorance of refuge principles. Although long-term environmental damage was still a matter of speculation, Kenyon was appalled by the extent to which Amchitka had been despoiled by drilling and construction activities.[37] Robert Jones was angered by the degree to which programs designed to restore the health of threatened ducks and birds, especially the Aleutian Canada goose, had been disrupted. "The fact is," he asserted, "that these people moved onto a National Wildlife Refuge with the most destructive force man has yet harnessed and were not sufficiently concerned to ask what wildlife was there. They were not sufficiently concerned to ask what plans had been made and what projects had been carried to completion and for what purpose!" According to Jones, economics had driven the decision to choose Amchitka rather than some other, less vulnerable location, since usable facilities were already in place on Amchitka.[38]

The battle royal between environmentalists and the proponents of Project Long Shot was set in the corrupted climate of the post-war world and was characterized by bitter frustration and anger on both sides. It is only fair to say that, at the time, neither the Defense Department, the A E C, nor environmental groups enjoyed a clairvoyance about Soviet intentions with regard to the arms race or a ban to reduce or eliminate nuclear weapons production altogether. Further, the ultimate failure of the project could not have been foreseen in 1965, and that failure, in itself, would not have been altered appreciably if public input had been sought.

As for the viability of Amchitka's place in a National Wildlife Refuge, extensive studies of alternate sites in Alaska's ongoing role in nuclear testing had revealed the unacceptable risk of danger to nearby human populations at each site. Then, too, most environmentalists at the time, torn between the ideals of conservation and the nation's security, agreed that the peaceful intentions of Long Shot were notable, perhaps even essential to the survival of the planet. Nevertheless, hindsight, an unattainable luxury in 1965, prompted A E C chairman Glenn Seaborg to state later, "Looking back, I tend to agree with those who feel that our concern about Soviet cheating was exaggerated." He felt that U.S. detection techniques had made considerable advances since 1959. Moreover, he stated, " . . . it is doubtful that the clandestine tests the USSR might have undertaken in violation of a comprehensive treaty would have been militarily significant in the aggregate."[39] Nevertheless, the story of Amchitka Island, caught up in the very unfortunate, but perhaps equally unavoidable, collision of two worthy causes, does not end here. As we shall see, Amchitka will play another vital role in nuclear experiments and experience even greater threats to its environment in only a few years.

7 / THROUGH MILROW CALIBRATION

The AEC and their scientists weren't used to citizen participation.
They were the experts and felt they were right and shouldn't be questioned.
If anyone did, they were suspect. AEC scientists just had no inclination
as experts that they might be wrong or should listen to any questions.

—MARTIN A. FARRELL, JR., Anchorage attorney

Had Operation Long Shot succeeded in discovering a means by which underground nuclear tests could be detected, the history of the postwar arms race might have been written differently. As it was, the hole left by that failure in the Nuclear Test Ban Treaty simply encouraged a new round of weapons development. The most important of these was the creation of the anti-ballistic missile (ABM). The ABM nurtured the belief that the growing arsenal of Soviet ICBMs might be neutralized in mid-air before reaching their intended targets. This goal had such obvious short-term military and political advantages for the United States that the many technical problems associated with ABM deployment were regarded by some as challenges rather than deterrents to its production. The perceived importance of the objective also served to minimize ancillary problems associated with ABM development, such as the environmental impact of any test of the ABM's nuclear warhead. Previous studies that had pinpointed Amchitka Island as suitable for underground nuclear testing now served as an invitation for the use of that site for even larger explosions.

In October 1969, Amchitka was rocked again by a nuclear blast, this time yielding "about" one million tons of explosive force. Originally code-named Shot Ganja in Operation Mandrel, this test was belatedly rechristened Shot Milrow when someone discovered that "Ganja" was the Turkish word for marijuana. Not only was this oversight bad for public relations in and of itself, but it was further feared that the press might add insult to injury by referring to the test as a "pot shot."[1] Thus, Milrow remained a vexing problem for its advocates almost up until the day of its detonation. This chapter recounts the troubled history of the A B M and the role that Amchitka Island played in that history.

The impetus for the development of the A B M can be traced to the immediate post-war period when United States Air Force staff officers proposed that future missiles be tipped with atomic warheads, an achievement that was realized by the end of the decade. Meanwhile, in May 1946, a science panel recommended that the Army build a missile capable of shooting down incoming enemy missiles. The two separate projects were married in 1949 when Defense Secretary Louis A. Johnson appointed a committee to plan such a weapon.[2] Actual development of the "antimissile missile" began in February 1955, when the United States Army Ordnance Corps commissioned a Bell Laboratories study of continental missile defense for the upcoming decade. The equipping of all A B Ms with nuclear warheads was from the very beginning considered absolutely "mandatory" in order to ensure that as few as possible of incoming enemy I C B Ms reached their intended targets. Two years later, in 1957, the Army selected Western Electric and Bell Laboratories as prime contractors for the design and construction of the missile-killing warhead. Soon thereafter, in a parallel move, the Defense Department and the Atomic Energy Commission's Division of Military Application designated Los Alamos Scientific Laboratory to design a nuclear device weighing four hundred pounds for the newly designated Nike-Zeus missile system.[3]

The first tests of the A B M warheads were conducted in the atmosphere in order to simulate deployment. The aim was to intercept incoming missiles as far in space as possible in order to minimize possible ground damage. With this result in mind, two rocket warheads tests, Shots Teak and Orange in Project Hardtack I, were fired near Johnston Island high over the Pacific Proving Grounds. Three more shots were conducted near Gough Island in the South Atlantic, which were followed by an additional four tests held in the Pacific. Then, in August 1963, all atmospheric testing was prohibited by the terms of the Nuclear Test Ban Treaty. Further testing would have to be done underground.

For all of its undeniable attractions, the A B M marshalled a host of detractors who doubted that the weapon would work as advertised. Some Pentagon technicians argued that the Soviets would neutralize the effectiveness of the A B M by swamping United States radar with multiple or decoy warheads. Moreover, metal shreds, balloons, and other objects might be released in order to trick our interceptors. The United States' early warning radar system might also be destroyed by a separate targeted attack. Reflecting the pessimism of these early critics, President Eisenhower's Science Advisory Committee gave a negative recommendation on continued development of the A B M. The President, in turn, ordered the suspension of work on the Nike-Zeus system in May 1959, arguing that its radar and computer components were inadequate to the task of controlling the system.[4]

Eisenhower's dark views about the potential of the A B M percolated down into the thinking of the Kennedy administration. President John F. Kennedy, like Eisenhower before him, took the advice of his science advisors that the A B M was technically too ambitious. In laymen's language, the essential problem was similar to "thousands of bullets hitting thousands of [other] bullets." While not denying the complexity of the technical problems, A B M advocates were so attracted by a weapons system that promised to "shield the country like a great umbrella," to use Edward Teller's romantic imagery, that they continued a persistent rearguard advocacy of A B M development, an advocacy that was not always appreciated by policymakers. Foreign Relations Committee Chairman J. William Fulbright wrote Teller off as an "actor." Kennedy, while not as direct in his criticism, believed that Teller was too stubborn for his own good. There is little question who the president had in mind when he wrote, "There's no doubt that any man with complete conviction, particularly one who's an expert, is bound to shake anybody who's got an open mind. That's the advantage of having a closed mind."[5]

In the face of growing pressures from the Joint Chiefs of Staff and congressional supporters of the A B M, however, Defense Secretary Robert S. McNamara fed anti-missile research some $5 billion a year. In 1966, Congress got into the act by allotting funds for A B M production. This move forced President Lyndon B. Johnson to make a difficult choice. Either he could give his blessing to the A B M with the objective of beating the Soviets to the punch, or he could halt its production altogether, hoping thereby to encourage the Kremlin to accept a total ban on A B M development. At the time, the United States possessed weapons superiority over the Soviets, although the U.S.S.R. had recently expanded its stockpile of ICBMs and had even begun an A B M defense of Moscow. Thus, the time seemed ripe to stop a new wave of weapons competition in its tracks. President Johnson seized the opportunity and ordered the suspension of A B M development pending Soviet-American conversations on the subject.[6]

The resulting discussions held between Johnson and his opposite number, Soviet Premier Aleksei Kosygin, at Glassboro State College on June 23 and 24, 1967, proved disappointing. As the president later wrote, "As soon as I brought up strategic arms talks, he [Kosygin] changed the subject to the Middle East." With no prospect of success on the diplomatic front, and badgered by congressional committees urging the development of costly new strategic bombers, a beleaguered president now ordered McNamara "to yield on the A B M." At a press conference held in San Francisco on September 18, 1967, the secretary delivered a capitulation speech. Having previously opposed a $40 billion A B M defense system aimed against a Soviet attack, McNamara was now forced to justify a $5 billion anti-missile expenditure on the dubious danger represented by Chinese I C B Ms. The explanation was disingenuous. In designating China rather than the U.S.S.R. as the major threat to United States security, President Johnson clearly wished to leave the door to renewed negotiations with the Soviets open at least a crack. As the messenger of the administration's twisted policy rationale, Secretary McNamara was placed in a difficult if not impossible position. McNamara's biographer considered it one of his "bitterest moments," both "eloquent and contradictory." In response to a colleague's later question about the wisdom of basing the need for a sophisticated anti-missile system on the threat posed by China, McNamara ruefully replied, "What else am I going to blame it on?"[7]

The decision to proceed with the development of a less ambitious A B M system was the result of political and military compromise. While the wisdom of that result was questioned and the decision itself was ultimately scrapped in 1967 in favor of another, more ambitious plan called Sentinel, the missile that would constitute the heart of any A B M plan would necessarily carry a nuclear warhead, and that weapon required testing. Thus was created a bizarre Cold War linkage of Amchitka and the defense against Red China.

The search for a suitable site on which to explode what would come to be known as Shot Milrow began broadly. The existing Nevada Test Site was quickly discarded as a possibility because of its proximity to Las Vegas. For various reasons, other sites, located in the United States and abroad, were also eliminated. The finalists included a new location in Nevada, removed from population centers, as well as Amchitka and the Brooks Range in Alaska. President Johnson subsequently approved appropriations of $20 million for the initial development of the Nevada site as well as $5 million for additional survey work in Alaska.[8]

By November 18, 1966, when a formal Site Selection Committee was appointed, the candidate test locations had been further reduced to Amchitka and the Hot Creek Valley area of Nevada. The Brooks Range was relegated to back-up status. Reflecting information previously acquired from Chariot, Rufus, and Larkspur studies, Air Force Brigadier General Delmar L. Crowson, AEC Division of Military Application director, dismissed this western end of the arctic plain because of "problems posed by the game preserve, the Eskimos living in the area, the need for a larger budget, and the length of the site development time." The fact that Amchitka had already been cleared for a test explosion, Long Shot, constituted a substantial argument for its subsequent use. Meanwhile, a weapons-related test slated for December at Nevada's Pahute Mesa would tell the Committee more as the search continued.[9]

The Nevada test revealed unacceptable dangers that ultimately eliminated the state from consideration as a possible site for Shot Milrow. On January 19, 1968, Shot Faultless in Operation Crosstie was detonated 3,100 feet deep with a reported explosive yield of two hundred thousand to a million tons. This blast "opened a 4,000-foot crack across the sage-covered desert floor," a result that proved decisive. A follow-up assessment concluded that "The site is not suitable for shots as large as were required to test the ICBM warhead." By this final process of elimination, Amchitka moved to the top of the list of preferred sites for Milrow.[10]

Meanwhile, military enthusiasm for a test site located on Amchitka began to build. Because of the data accumulated as a result of Long Shot, no "calibration shot" was considered necessary. Rather, investigators were primarily interested in locating alternative test sites on the island. Between November 30 and mid-December, 1966, a sixteen-member geological survey team "made a geological reconnaissance and aeromagnetic survey" of the southeastern end of Amchitka in order to locate sites for the drilling of five deep exploratory holes.[11] General Crowson was so impressed by the potential of Amchitka that he decided to construct a test facility there even before the Site Committee had made its recommendations. His common sense told him that the previous experience of Long Shot indicated that its location would be suitable for future test firings. Surveys of alternate sites would only cause unnecessary delay. Because Milrow's explosive force would far exceed that of Long Shot, however, Crowson was aware that the test hole would have to be very deep in order to avoid the possibility that radioactive material might vent across international borders in violation of the Test Ban Treaty.[12]

The selection of an Alaskan site for Shot Milrow got a surprising and somewhat quirky assist from Howard Hughes. The eccentric billionaire regarded nuclear testing in Nevada as threatening to his Las Vegas properties as well as to his own person. Alerted to the dangers of nuclear testing by radiation sickness suffered by members of his production crew filming the movie *Conqueror* in Nevada, Hughes launched an all-out crusade to stop subsequent tests there. In order to maximize credibility for his cause, Hughes flew Washington University ecologist Barry Commoner, who had previously warned that tests might damage nearby Hoover Dam, out to Las Vegas. Hughes further attempted to enlist the support of high-profile politicians such as Presidents Lyndon Johnson and Richard Nixon, Vice-President Hubert Humphrey, California Governor Ronald Reagan, Senators Robert and Edward Kennedy, and Nevada Governor Paul Laxalt. In the midst of this controversy of his own making, Hughes suddenly discovered Alaska's potential as a nuclear test location. It was not necessary to postpone or cancel planned nuclear tests altogether; they might simply be transferred to a more suitable place such as Alaska. Hughes even offered to pick up the costs of such a move himself. Finally, Hughes persuaded Governor Laxalt to request of the Nevada operation test director that Shot Boxcar, scheduled for April 1968, be switched from Nevada to Alaska. Newly elected Alaska Senator Mike Gravel, for reasons that remain disputed, was added to the Hughes team. Flown to Las Vegas on Hughes's private jet and treated to a fancy hotel suite, Gravel was reportedly promised campaign funding. Appearing on a Hughes-owned television station, Gravel touted Alaska as a test site. Later, the senator reversed his stand and denied having received any money from Hughes.[13]

This strange interlude is more important as an illustration of the depths of feeling provoked by the issue of nuclear testing than it is an explanation for the eventual selection of Amchitka as the site for Shot Milrow. Once the conclusion that the ABM was technically feasible had been reached, continuing controversies about the testing of its warhead mainly involved concerns for national security on the one side and estimates of environmental damage on the other. In this latest round of what was now a familiar battle, anti-ABM physicists Richard L. Garwin and Hans B. Bethe contended in the prestigious *Scientific American* that the Sentinal system would not only be ineffective against China's ICBMs, but would further stimulate a more costly ABM development aimed at the Soviets. This escalation of the arms race, they thought, was a "folly" to build because its contribution to the national defense was illusory.[14] Congressional subscribers to this assessment tried to cut A B M funding in the budget debates of 1968, adding that A B M would hurt arms control negotiations. As cogent as these considerations may have been, uncertainties created by the Chinese Cultural Revolution and the August invasion of Czechoslovakia by the Soviets weighed mightily on behalf of the hawks. After heated debate, Capitol Hill gave the Pentagon more than $1.1 billion for the Sentinal system. This funding was tucked into the largest defense package ever passed up to that time: $71 billion.[15]

Congressional debate on the advisability of continuing work on the A B M resumed the following year. The stakes were now higher. The Nixon administration proposed to spend an additional $759.1 million in order to replace the Sentinal system with the more ambitious Safeguard project, which was geared to protect Minuteman missile sites against Soviet attack. In this initial phase, Operation Safeguard called for research, development, and two installations, one each in Montana and North Dakota. The predictions made earlier by Garwin and Bethe were absolutely on the mark. Sentinel would never serve as an end in itself, but would inevitably lead to the development of a "heavy" A B M system directed primarily at the Soviet Union rather than at China. After a tie vote in the Senate at President Nixon's request, Vice-President Spiro Agnew broke the deadlock and the funding was approved.[16]

The fact that Alaska's two senators split their votes on the A B M funding proposal is reflective of the fracture that existed on the issue in Alaska. As early as 1967, Alaska's newly elected governor, Walter J. Hickel, an ardent partisan of economic development, had come to the conclusion that nuclear testing might prove advantageous to the state. Upon inquiry, Hickel discovered that test officials planned to spend $42 million on exploration during 1967 and 1968. Lesser amounts were to be spent on surveys made of the Brooks Range. One political observer concluded that "apparently Governor Hickel is fishing for justification for extension of the Alaska Railroad and the A E C's potential needs hold out some hope to him."[17]

Additional information concerning its plans for Alaska was soon forthcoming from the A E C. Almost $13 million was designated for drilling alone. Scheduled to begin in May l967, drilling would last for at least two years. Putting together three of the largest rigs ever built, Parker Drilling Company of Tulsa, Oklahoma, was commissioned to drill three emplacement holes, two of which reached down to a depth of 6,200 feet. Other evidence similarly indicated that the A E C's investments might have long-term impact on Alaska. The new test site facility, for example, would be designed to house 350 personnel. "It appears," wrote one observer, "that once in the nuclear era, Alaska is in it to stay."[18]

The prospect that AEC development of nuclear test sites in Alaska might yield significant economic spin-off effects never measured up to Governor Hickel's hopes. While Shot Milrow called for huge financial outlays, most of the money ended up in the pockets of outsiders. The prime contract for the site's "architecture, engineering, and management" was awarded to Holmes and Narver, a long-time AEC Nevada test site favorite. Major subcontracts went to firms based in California, Idaho, Oklahoma, Texas, and Washington State, although eventually small crumbs from this economic table did fall to a handful of Alaskan firms. Reflecting on the reality of Alaska's undeveloped economic status rather than on Governor Hickel's dreams, a temporary 160-man trailer camp deal costing over $900,000 was managed through Penney Trailer Sales of Anchorage, and the Army Corps of Engineers spent $129,900 to hire Walsh and Company of Spenard, Alaska, for dock repairs plus unloading and storage of materials on Amchitka.[19]

With the realization that the federal economic impact of Shot Milrow on Alaska would be minimal, the balance of political support for the project shifted. Most notable was the position taken by newly elected Democratic Senator Mike Gravel. Whatever the nature of his previous relationship with Howard Hughes, Gravel now assumed leadership of the anti-Milrow forces in Washington, D.C., placing Amchitka in the national spotlight and drawing others to the cause. After serving only a few months on Capitol Hill, Gravel introduced Senate Joint Resolution 108 calling for the creation of a "National Commission on Nuclear and Seismic Safety." Gravel was unconvinced that AEC was the best vehicle for determining safety issues connected with its own nuclear testing. Recommending the creation of an independent agency to rule on these concerns, Gravel asserted, "I question the system that permits them [AEC scientists] to be the exclusive judge of their own assessments."[20]

The cue for Gravel's resolution came from former AEC research official and chairman of President Johnson's Science Advisory Committee, Kenneth S. Pitzer, who, at the time, served as Stanford University president. In November of 1968, a national committee of experts chaired by Pitzer claimed that underground tests could create dangerous seismic disturbances. The co-sponsors of Gravel's resolution, Democratic Senators Alan Cranston and Edward Muskie, linked earthquakes to a recent disastrous oil spill from a drilling platform blowout in California's Santa Barbara Channel. For Muskie, the A E C test program unduly discounted such dangers to the region's ecology.[21] In September 1969, Hawaii congresswoman Patsy T. Mink, together with fifteen California co-sponsors, introduced a second resolution calling attention to threats inherent in nuclear testing. House Joint Resolution 899 requested the immediate suspension of the Aleutian tests pending an evaluation of underground nuclear detonations.[22]

Suddenly, nuclear testing had become a hot potato. Encouraged by this groundswell of support, Gravel, together with Hawaii Senator Hiram L. Fong, submitted Senate Joint Resolution 155, which asked for a full investigation into the foreign policy fall-out of nuclear testing. The timing of this resolution was presumably occasioned by reports of Canadian and Japanese complaints about the tests. Foreign Relations Committee Chairman J. William Fulbright, a vigorous foe of the A B M, picked up on this request and scheduled a televised hearing for September 29, 1969. Perhaps public pressure could be brought to bear against President Nixon's decision to proceed with Operation Safeguard.[23]

The Foreign Relations Committee hearings allowed the opponents of underground nuclear testing the opportunity to demonstrate broad grass-roots support for their cause. For example, Senator Daniel K. Inouye, a co-sponsor of Resolution 155, submitted a petition expressing opposition to such testing signed by 325 Hawaiian school children. Similarly, the Hawaiian president of an A F L - C I O affiliate filed a protest signed by 14,000 of his members and their families.[24] Additional congressmen stepped forward to express their reservations. One of these, Wisconsin Senator Gaylord Nelson, found it particularly ironic that the A E C had chosen a wildlife refuge, a place where hunting was prohibited, to test the "biggest firearm of all, nuclear bombs." "Nothing will ever convince me," Nelson testified, "that a wildlife refuge and a nuclear blast go together." It makes "a mockery of the name 'wildlife refuge'." Professional conservationists also had their say at these hearings. National Audubon Society Chairman Elvis J. Stahr, who had previously sent a letter to President Nixon requesting the cancellation of Milrow, now threw the weight of his 80,000-member organization against the tests.[25]

The concerns of Congress about the planned Milrow test failed in the end to dent the administration's determination to proceed with A B M development. As a result, the core of protests about nuclear testing in Alaska shifted to citizens of that state. The first of these came from a variety of sources and focused on safety issues. Columnists writing for the *Anchorage Daily Times*, for example, wondered whether Milrow might affect volcanic

Mount Redoubt, located one hundred miles southwest of the city.[26] As the test date approached, worried constituents registered their fears by writing to their congressional representatives. One of these concerned citizens, after requesting Senator Gravel to halt the test, sarcastically exclaimed, "If the tests are so safe, let them set them off under the Pentagon!" Republican congressman Howard W. Pollock, who had previously announced his support of Long Shot, was confronted by a voter who doubted official assurances that nuclear testing was entirely safe. Recounting the history of quake damage experienced in Alaska, this writer proclaimed, "Alaska is my home and I would prefer to have it solidly under me in one piece." This concern for safety is further reflected in the advice given by an Anchorage couple who urged that possible damage assessments be made by an independent source. Ending on a pleading note, the couple wrote, "If they're really not certain, at least they should have the humanity to listen to our requests."[27]

Other, more organized protests came from environmentalist groups. One of these, the Alaska Conservation Society, evidenced considerable unease about the prospect of another nuclear test on Amchitka, but it had little notion of how to proceed in order to make its reservations effective. Thus, members collectively and singly were reduced to wringing their hands in public. The governing board of the Society, for example, in early 1967, passed a resolution against "atomic experimentation" in refuges and national parks. About the same time, Ginny Hill Wood, a Society founder, alerted fellow members to what she viewed as an insidious, progressive takeover of Alaska as an atomic proving ground.[28] Having preserved its own honor by these exercises, the Society once again backed off from open confrontation for reasons that can only be described as fatalistic. Robert Weeden, the Society's new president, openly admitted that "top-level decisions already have been made that affect Amchitka." Given this state of affairs, the Society's realistic position, Weeden concluded, ought to emphasize the containment of environmental damage caused by the test explosions. Sensing the vulnerability of the Society on nuclear testing per se, and knowing that its members were willing to sacrifice Amchitka if the alternative was the Brooks Range, Senator Bartlett urged that General Crowson contact Weeden in order to reassure him that Milrow was crucial to the national defense and would result in minimal damage to the environment. The strategy worked perfectly. In his reply to Crowson, Weeden admitted that "we cannot realistically hope for anything more from the Commission. It is certainly not our place—or intention—to judge how necessary the project is, or the need to do it on Amchitka." Later, just prior to the Milrow blast, Wee-den suggested that "Alaskan conservation groups . . . not go out of their way to pick a fight with the A E C" because it would only serve to pit conservation interests against national security. Then, too, he lamented, "we don't have the corporate energy to go all out."[29]

In contrast to the demoralized reaction of the Alaska Conservation Soci-ety, the Alaska Sportsmen's Council, an umbrella organization of kindred environmentalist groups, refused to muffle its objections to the Milrow test. Executive Director A. W. "Bud" Boddy wrote to Governor Keith H. Miller requesting information about the expected effects of the explosion to sup-plement the meager disclosures made by the A E C. Had anyone, Boddy won-dered, calculated the risks to commercial fishing should the Amchitka tests produce higher than expected levels of radioactive venting? What would happen if rumors about the existence of "hot salmon" or "hot halibut" began to circulate? "Never under any circumstances," Boddy warned the governor, "allow A E C to substitute its judgment for yours on the question, 'What is an acceptable risk?'"[30]

Governor Miller, who had just been appointed to succeed Walter Hickel when the latter moved off to Washington, D.C., to serve as Nixon's interior secretary, was defensive and unrepentant in his response to Boddy. The gov-ernor chose to depict himself as a victim of circumstance. The initial deci-sion to use Amchitka for nuclear testing, he reminded Boddy, was made while Alaska was still a territory subject to federal jurisdiction. Moreover, Miller pointed out, the acceptance of that decision had been essentially bi-partisan. Governor Egan, a Democrat, was in office when the first explosion took place. In any case, the governor saw no reason at this late date to block Milrow, given A E C data and what he regarded as the federal government's "almost historical right to proceed with the test program." Not wishing to ap-pear totally impotent, however, Miller told Boddy that he would ask A E C and the United States Public Health Service experts to address Alaskans about safety issues and, if necessary, to meet directly with the Sportsmen's Coun-cil. Miller closed his letter to Boddy with the assurance that the exchange of ideas and information that he proposed would "considerably allay your apprehension."[31]

Boddy's challenge to Governor Miller precipitated a public relations blitz to reduce lingering doubts about Shot Milrow to the smallest number possible. In contrast to its decision at the time of Long Shot to withhold as much information as possible from the public, the A E C now took the public relations offensive. From its newly opened Alaska Office of Information, the agency proceeded to spread oil on as many troubled waters as it could find. One dimension of this effort publicized the economic impact of Shot Milrow. The Office of Information pointed out that more than two-thirds of the work force at Amchitka were Alaskans, and that, among these, over ten percent were Natives. Safety fears were addressed by a team of technical experts headed by Sandia Laboratory's Melvin Merritt, who appeared on television to allay the fears of the "misinformed." Finally, California Representative Chet Holifield, chairman of the congressional Joint Congressional Committee on Atomic Energy, sent Alaska's newly appointed Republican Senator Ted Stevens an impressive list of Alaskans who had already been briefed by the AEC. The list included the congressional delegation, state and local officials, representatives of the media, military personnel, scientists, business and labor leaders, churchmen, conservationists, and the heads of Native organizations.[32]

For reasons that are not evident, the initial AEC effort to silence the critics of Shot Milrow did not include the Alaska state legislature, and for that neglect it paid a price. Smarting at having been left out of the information loop, Anchorage Democratic Representative Charles Sassara telegramed AEC Chairman Glenn Seaborg for additional data about the upcoming test, and he further demanded a formal AEC briefing of the legislature. The AEC, belatedly attempting to repair damages caused by its neglect, acquiesced in Sassar's insistence. A public hearing held on September 26, 1969, at the state courthouse in Anchorage was only partly successful in its intended purpose of bringing balky legislators around. Republican Senator Brad Phillips left the hearing still wondering whether Milrow might create another Santa Barbara–like substrata fissure, while the Democratic speaker of the house, Jalmar Kertulla from Palmer, groused that the AEC was "playing Russian roulette."[33]

The last significant remaining pocket of opposition to Shot Milrow was located in Anchorage. In the early summer of 1969, an Anchorage-based group calling itself Democrats for Issues and Action (DIA) entered the fray by sending two resolutions to the governor. The first of these requested a delay of the test until "a national impartial commission" had conducted "a study [of the] possible effects on the fault line and the wildlife of the area." The second resolution opposed ABM funding which, the organization felt, would better be spent on "jobs, Native land claims, clear air, clean water, rural electrification, medical facilities, and Alaska conservation."[34] Despite the fact that the DIA's proposals lay far beyond the jurisdiction of the governor, and thus were stillborn from the moment of their delivery, a nucleus group of the organization reconstituted itself into the Save Our State Committee (SOS) in order to carry on the fight against Milrow. Martin A. Farrell, Jr., a feisty young Anchorage attorney, who had spent ten years in Alaska's rugged backcountry, was elected the committee's chairman. Born of Irish-American stock and reared in New York's East Side, Farrell was not easily intimidated. No novice to the ways of politics, Farrell had previously served on the Washington staff of Senator Ernest Gruening. He and the organization he represented were determined to do everything within their power to make certain that safety issues were resolved before Milrow was detonated.[35]

Using his Washington connections, Farrell managed to raise sufficient funds to launch a last-ditch media campaign against the test. An SOS-sponsored full-page ad taken out in the *Anchorage Daily News* warned readers that Milrow's power was "50 times the amount used to level Hiroshima in 1945." The destructive potential of this bomb in terms of both physical damage and radioactive fall-out could only be imagined. Over thirty SOS marchers carried protest signs outside the state courthouse when the AEC was conducting its hearings before the state legislature. On the very eve of the test blast, SOS organized a youth protest in a downtown Anchorage park. The organization clearly bore the stamp of its leader: it would not go gently into any dark night.[36]

From the perspective of the AEC, which was proud of the strides that it had made in the public relations field since Long Shot in 1965, Farrell was a puzzle. Since the agency could only guess at the reasons for his continued intransigence, it suspected the worst. "It appeared conceivable," the AEC wrote, "that Farrell was working as a paid representative for a client and spoke as directed rather than from personal conviction." Farrell, for his part, was equally certain that the AEC could not be trusted. At one point, he became convinced that his activities were being monitored by AEC and Department of Defense investigators, a conviction that was fueled by the fact that he once caught an Air Force officer taking his picture. The raw state of the relationship between Farrell and the AEC is well illustrated by an event which took place the very day of the Milrow blast. For reasons unknown, Farrell decided to join an AEC-sponsored countdown celebration held in the ballroom of Anchorage's Westward Hotel. Even though he chose to sit in an unobtrusive location by the back door, Farrell was soon spotted by

A E C personnel. He was told in no uncertain terms, "You can't stay here. You'll have to leave or we'll throw you out!" When Farrell made no response to this threat, two men picked him up—chair and all—and unceremoniously deposited him outside the ballroom. Although he laughed off the incident to reporters, Farrell became all the more convinced that A E C officials were intrusive, arrogant, condescending, undemocratic know-it-alls.[37] When it became evident that even bitter-enders like Martin Farrell could not postpone, much less cancel, the Milrow test, the last best resort for conservationists was to try to ensure that environmental damage would be confined and that the federal government would assume full responsibility for dealing with unwanted consequences. This effort was only partly successful. When first informed in December 1966 that Amchitka had been selected for additional nuclear testing, the Fish and Wildlife Service had begun negotiations with officials of the A E C in order to determine the size and scope of the agency's environmental protection program. Ultimately, the two sides agreed that the A E C and the Interior Department would fund the salaries of two part-time Refuge employees who would monitor test preparation effects on the environment as well as two research biologists who would gather data on the impact these preparations would have upon resident wildlife. Finally, the A E C indicated its willingness to clean up any mess left by Milrow and thus restore Amchitka to its 1967 condition.[38]

Consistent with this emerging spirit of good will, the Interior Department hired Battelle Columbus Laboratories to assess Milrow's possible blast and radiation effects on sea otters, terrestrial habitats, and freshwater life. Together with the battalion of scientists sent to Amchitka by Battelle Columbus, five federal agencies, as well as researchers from the Smithsonian Institution and nine universities, eventually became involved with these investigations. Altogether, the A E C spent over $3 million on these combined programs which lasted about two years.[39]

It is not surprising that, given their distinctive place in Amchitka's ecology, the island's sea otter population would receive special attention in these studies. The once fragile sea otter herds had made a spectacular comeback under the watchful care of the Refuge managers, to the point that they now threatened their habitat from overpopulation. Even so, one miscalculated nuclear blast had the potential of wiping out these gains and, perhaps, inflicting even worse damage. Alerted to this possibility by Governor Hickel, A E C Chairman Glenn Seaborg issued a press release assuring the public that both the state of Alaska and A E C officials would do everything within their power to ensure the safety of the sea otters. In order to study the effects that shock waves might have on these creatures, Battelle Columbus sought and received permission from the Fish and Wildlife Service to capture as many as fifteen sea otters for test purposes. Beginning in the summer of 1968, the A EC similarly funded the removal of 364 Amchitka-based sea otters to other, less threatened habitats: forty-nine to Biorka Island in the Aleutian Chain, sixty to the Pribilofs, and the remainder to scattered sites in Alaska's southeast. An additional 118 sea otters were transplanted in a diverse area that included Washington State, British Columbia, and even an aquarium in Tacoma.[40]

In contrast to sea otter and science programs, site preparations generated considerable conflict between Refuge personnel and the A EC. Contractors began arriving in early March 1967 to construct base camps, roads, and communication and supply facilities. By mid-May, Amchitka had been invaded by 260 workers armed with a large supply of earthmoving equipment. The drilling of the first test holes began soon thereafter. All this activity drew the anxious scrutiny of Refuge officials who first noticed environmental damage in the form of oil pollution. Complaints soon followed this discovery. A EC officials, the Refuge officials charged, had been too lax in supervising construction of support facilities. Roads scarred the land while dynamite blasting preparatory to the building of a new dock at Kirilof Point had driven away sea otters.[41]

This initial report was only the prelude to what was to become a litany of complaints. Whether the A EC exercised insufficient supervision over its contractors and subcontractors or whether conservationists had unrealistic attitudes about the amount of environmental damage that could reasonably be avoided is difficult to say. Whatever the cause, an acrimonious breach soon developed between those who were responsible for preparing the test site and the guardians of Amchitka's ecology. Refuge associate supervisor Palmer C. Sekora, now an Amchitka biological monitor, found Holmes and Narver contractors "apathetic" when he met with them in an attempt to reduce construction damage to the habitat. One subcontractor openly confessed that he was "eager to complete the job with as little clean-up as possible." Everywhere the monitors looked, they saw reason for criticism. Veteran Refuge manager Robert Jones suspected that helicopters were a contributing cause to the reduction of bird populations. Another monitor, LeRoy W. Sowl, reported raw sewage draining into Clevenger Lake, thereby contaminating trout and salmon breeding streams. Leakage, which accompanied the off-loading of petroleum products, endangered sea otters and marine birds, while drilling discharges polluted waterways, especially Constantine Harbor. Sowl concluded that the engineers were "not in tune with our wishes." They don't even understand what "is bothering us." Their general attitude seemed to be, "Just what in hell can be hurt in a godforsaken place like Amchitka?"[42]

These dismal reports by environmental monitors on Amchitka were confirmed by outsiders who disparaged the damage being done to the island. George Laycock, in an article entitled, "The Beautiful Sad Face of Amchitka," published in *Audubon,* mourned the ecological depredations inflicted on the island since his previous visit in 1967. Another conservationist charged in a letter to Interior Secretary Steward Udall that the A E C and its contractors "are not paying attention to natural values and are causing serious long range damage both to the land resource and to marine biology." Citing the memorandum of understanding which set forth the ground rules governing Amchitka's use for testing, Udall admitted that competing interests there were difficult to balance. The Department's "competent fieldmen," Udall explained, were working closely with the contractors and A E C to minimize environmental damages to the fullest extent possible. Conservationist Margaret E. Murie doubted the sincerity of these official protests. In a letter of protest written to Senator Bartlett, she complained that the A E C appeared to be using the Battelle bioenvironmental program as a smokescreen designed primarily to make people feel better about conditions on Amchitka. "I very much doubt if much thought is being given to preserving any of the landscape on Amchitka," she told the senator.[43]

Unfortunately, beleaguered environmental monitors in the field received less-than-expected support from their immediate superiors when they complained. Refuge monitor John B. Hakala made the mistake of sending his list of indictments against test employees who failed to follow signed agreements directly to the A E C official in charge. Although Hakala's bill of particulars, which included evidence of oil contamination, terrain disturbance, increasing siltation, drill mud runoff, and garbage buildup, was damning indeed, his bosses in Portland took exception to his procedure. They advised that "a more diplomatic approach in the future may win more cooperation." The same cautious attitude was endorsed by the Bureau of Sport Fisheries and Wildlife, whose director wrote the following advice to fellow Refuge personnel: "I want to caution all of you concerning the need for discretion . . . at Amchitka." We should "realize," he continued, "that we might like it even less if certain other sites were being used." With a timidity borne of a feeling of great vulnerability, the director tried to end on a upbeat note. "We may be able with the help of dedicated, stubborn, field representatives to convince the Atomic Energy Commission . . . that geological explorations can be carried on without excessive damage to the earth's surface."[44]

Caution and denial continued to mark the official policy statements released by the Fish and Wildlife Service in 1968. Commissioner Clarence J. Pautzke, in response to inquiries about environmental depredations at Amchitka put to him by Senator Bartlett, stated unequivocally that such "rumors" were "not true." He personally had attended a conference of Refuge representatives and AEC officials held on Amchitka where he was given promises of new "adequate safeguards" and added cooperation. But, as events were to demonstrate, Pautzke was whistling in the dark. Field reports from Sowl and Hakala repeated the same discouraging story. An exasperated Hakala once exclaimed, "We just cannot continue to operate here under existing conditions." The worst environmental culprit seemed to be drill mud effluent, which leaked from diked areas and spread to tundra, lakes, and streams. In a desperate attempt to change these practices, biological monitors tried to provoke a crisis over ground pollution "through intimidation or the use of scare tactics." After this showdown, Sowl noticed some improvement, but he was sufficiently experienced in the ways of test employees to suspect a "grease job." In the absence of broad-based authentic reform of work practices on Amchitka, Sowl concluded that the Federal Water Pollution Control Administration should be called in to shut down the drilling operation.[45]

No such drastic action was ever taken, and Sowl did notice that the AEC seemed to try harder to discipline contractors to show greater respect for the environment. But drill leakage continued, and a new problem surfaced when it was learned that workers had robbed archaeological middens.[46] As site preparations wound down, instances of environmental damage continued to mount. A spill of caustic soda caused stream pollution. Road construction penetrated into areas that were clearly off limits. Even the pesky black fly was inadvertently introduced to the island for the first time by workers. Associate supervisor David L. Spencer complained of the "frustrating and ineffective atmosphere in which we work." Monitor Sowl characterized the AEC and contractor policy vis-à-vis the disposal of hazardous materials as "dump it." Research biologist Carl E. Abegglen spoke for all the monitors when he concluded that "the attempt to keep the island in its natural condition has been a losing battle."[47]

The final struggle between environmentalists and administration supporters of Milrow occurred over the issue of post-test cleanup. Once the blast itself had become more or less inevitable, arguments continued over the likely extent of the resulting damage. On the one side of the controversy, A E C scientists told A E C Chairman Seaborg that "interested groups may feel reassured that damage to the region . . . will be relatively trivial." Others were less sanguine in their estimates. Interior Department officials foresaw permanent terrestrial damage encircling ground zero. A subsidence crater formed by the explosion would surely be filled with water contaminated by tritium, a claim not disputed by the A E C, although the Commission hastened to add that the levels of radioactivity "will not be hazardous to man." Effects of the explosion on the habitat invited additional speculation. The acting commissioner of the Fish and Wildlife Service continued to withhold endorsement of the test until additional wildlife protection programs were in place. Reflecting a caution keyed to his uncertainty, Interior Secretary Hickel sent his approval of the blast to President Nixon in late August of 1969 with the proviso that any additional tests on Amchitka be contingent on studies of the effects of Milrow.[48]

These differences of opinions were eventually played out in the arena of public relations. While the A E C clung to its original position that Milrow was reasonably safe, scientists outside of government continued to raise troubling questions. A former A E C research official and chairman of President Johnson's Science Advisory Committee, Kenneth S. Pitzer chaired a November 1968 panel of national experts who claimed that underground tests could cause dangerous seismic activity. Then president of Stanford University, Pitzer strongly recommended that an independent panel assess whether nuclear blasts do in fact trigger earthquakes. A scientist at the University of California, Los Angeles, Ronald F. Scott, who was also a member of the Pitzer Ad Hoc Panel on Safety of Underground Testing, wrote, "In Amchitka . . . underwater soil slides may be generated by a nuclear test." Other possibilities included the "development of underwater slides and related tsunamis," a conclusion concurred in by Frank Press of the Massachusetts Institute of Technology. David K. Todd, an engineer at the University of California, Berkeley, and another Pitzer Panel member, pinpointed an additional problem: radioactivity might well empty into the North Pacific and Bering Sea, although he doubted the resulting levels of contamination would be dangerous.[49] While it might not be possible, or advisable, to stifle these contrarious reports by reputable scientists completely, the A E C saw no reason to give them prominence, either. In the end, the Office of Science and Technology recommended against releasing both the Pitzer Panel and AEC reports, arguing that:

> If both are released, the differences between them would be seized upon by the press both to build up the earthquake threat and to underscore differences between the Office and the AEC. Given the present ABM atmosphere, this could produce a further confrontation between the scientific community and the Government and might even get tangled up with the ABM argument since the high-yield tests in question are all for the ABM. This could further complicate the Administration's problem both with the scientific community and with the conduct of high-yield nuclear tests.

Kenneth Pitzer's protests against this one-sided approach were cavalierly brushed aside. He was told that Pitzer Panel members had personal recourse to publish in regular science journals if they so wished.[50]

In the days remaining before the Milrow shot, lingering protests against the test sputtered to an inconsequential conclusion. The most prominent of the naysayers were Senators Warren Magnuson and Mike Gravel. Magnuson took his case to AEC Chairman Seaborg, contending that additional time spent in allaying the "mounting [public] concern" over Milrow would be well worth any inconveniences caused by the delay. The administration, however, was in no mood to placate doubters further. Even Senator Gravel's rather dire warning to the president that "in the event of tragedy, you will be held accountable," had no visible effect.[51]

In a display of its confidence, the administration decided to make Shot Milrow a public show. The event was carefully staged. In phase one, the AEC invited eighty Alaska businessmen, conservationists, legislators, newsmen, and state officials to Amchitka to make their own judgments about the logistical preparations for the test. The island campsite, built to house the workers, had cost an estimated $55 million and included a four-bed hospital, an official United States post office, a barber shop, and even a barroom nicknamed the Rat Island Roost. Workers' leisure time could be spent fishing, watching movies, playing pool, or beachcombing for Japanese glass fishnet floats. A newspaper, the *Am-Chit-Sheet,* helped to break down the worker's sense of isolation. The intended AEC message to these observers seemed clear enough: How dangerous could Milrow be in a physical environment that appeared to be so normal?[52]

As the test date approached, however, the list of guests invited to Amchitka shrank rather dramatically. Phase two of the show was to be much more controlled. The politicians who would actually witness the explosion close up included Governor Miller, congressman Howard Pollock, the Alaska Legislative Council, and California congressman Chet Holifield, chairman of the Joint Congressional Committee on Atomic Energy. Only two newsmen were permitted to witness the blast on the island. Other remaining observers were removed to the aircraft carrier U.S.S. *Princeton*.[53]

Shot Milrow was a thermonuclear or hydrogen bomb "event" designed in part to test the extent to which Amchitka could withstand an explosive force in excess of one million tons of TNT. It was exploded at 12:06 p.m. Bering Daylight Time on October 2, 1969, at the bottom of a shaft 3,992 feet below ground surface zero.[54] According to official AEC reports made after the test, Milrow produced "no significant damage to the ecology of the area and no earthquakes or tsunamis." From the AEC's point of view, Milrow had been a total success.[55]

From other perspectives, however, the AEC's assessment was misleading, possibly deliberately so. The blast effects of Milrow were not inconsequential. Seismic readings indicated that Milrow had caused "hundreds of small, shallow-focus earthquakes" within a three-mile radius of ground zero. These reported aftershocks continued for thirty-seven hours until the blast cavity itself collapsed. Although major damage was avoided, the blast also caused displacement of a fault line running into an intertidal beach on the Pacific Coast at Duck Cove. The uplift on one side of the fault amounted to an estimated five inches. Additional damage to the island included the pulverization (spalling) of rock at depths between one hundred and five hundred feet—and possibly even deeper. The spalling pattern of this debris spread out more than three miles from surface ground zero. Observers noted that the ground heaved upwards some fourteen feet at the point of detonation.[56]

Additional damage occurred at greater distances from the blast. Rockfalls, turf slides, and destruction of sea stack outcroppings used by nesting birds were noted by test personnel. Approximately 2,800 cubic yards of rock and peat fell along coastal areas. Large blocks of inland tundra mantle were torn up and fell into "random orientations." The collapse of the hole chimney later produced fractures in the tundra, leaving behind mounded rows of soil up to five feet. Turbulence caused by the shock wave changed in-stream flow rates, altering some lake levels and increasing water turbidity. Two lakes near the detonation point were tilted and partially drained. The fissures at the bottom of these lakes were still clearly visible six years later, despite encroachment by vegetation.[57]

Wildlife suffered as well at the hands of Milrow. The coastal rock and turf falls buried and obliterated intertidal algae and invertebrates. Duck Cove's fault line shift brought with it recognizable trauma to algae colonies, causing wave action erosion in an area estimated at ten acres. The erosion in turn adversely affected invertebrate species dependent upon this cover. Shock waves cast fish ashore from freshwater ponds in a radius of three thousand feet from surface ground zero and further killed numerous three-spined stickleback fish by rupturing their swim bladders.[58]

These blast effects, combined with the impact of site preparation, camp construction, and drilling operations, produced an ecological chamber of horrors. Siltation and pollution occurred in nine miles of streams covering seven drainages and fifty-five acres of ponds. Mud slides caused "grass morphological changes" in stream beds. In addition, "toxic releases" from drilling in 1968 and 1969 nearly destroyed the Clevenger Creek drainage region. Pink salmon spawning declined, and the overfishing of Dolly Varden by workers caused a notable decline in the species. The aesthetic qualities of the island suffered also from unsightly tundra heaps and piles of quarry spoil left by bulldozers and other earthmoving equipment. Human waste disposal created outbreaks of blue-green algae in streams. Garbage dumps became unnatural havens for bald eagles, gulls, and rats. Amchitka, once part of the protected Refuge, had become an ecological war zone.[59]

In the days immediately preceding the Milrow blast, Alaska Department of Fish and Game Deputy Commissioner Ben Hilliker wrote, "In my opinion, the major problem [of Milrow] is not associated with the calibration test immediately upcoming, but is with widespread public reaction and related concerns about more and higher megaton yield detonations in the future."[60] Hilliker's warning was prophetic. It was much more likely that Milrow was part of a beginning than it was an end. Each nuclear test conducted on Amchitka seemed to provide an argument for the detonation of an ever larger explosion. Where that pattern would culminate was anyone's guess.

8 / FOR SAFEGUARD SECURITY

> The majority of my constituents—virtually 100 percent—
> are against any blast. . . . The Aleut League is unanimously
> against the bombs being set off on Amchitka.
>
> —CARL E. MOSES, Alaska State Representative
> and Aleut League President

By the end of the 1960s, the shape of the argument over nuclear testing in Alaska had begun to take recognizable form. On the one side were the advocates of military preparedness, veteran cold warriors for the most part, who felt that security issues occupied the highest rank among national priorities. Centered in the federal agencies, the most important of which were the presidency, the Defense Department, and the Atomic Energy Commission, these advocates saw themselves as supreme realists and, as such, were little inclined to pay much regard to those whose values differed substantially from their own. On the other side of the debate was a scattered array of dissident groups. While their concerns centered on the issues of human safety and respect for the natural environment, these dissidents also viewed growing international uneasiness about underground nuclear testing as a potential ally. In winning the battle over whether Amchitka might be used for additional nuclear testing, the two sides knew from previous experience the nature of the weapons of victory. For the preparedness advocates, the key issue was to appear publicly as conciliatory as possible while withholding key information that might be used as ammunition against them. Without access to that information, the opposition would remain divided and, thus, largely impotent. The environmentalists and their supporters, on the other hand, needed not only to force out into the public arena meaningful disclosures about the probable consequences of future nuclear tests so that the people themselves might make their own judgments about probable risks, but they also needed to marshal public opinion against what they regarded as wrongheaded public officials.

When Milrow was detonated without apparent incident, AEC officials were not only relieved, they were openly jubilant. The results of the tests, they felt, provided complete vindication of their earlier predictions, and they celebrated their triumph by "[strutting] around [AEC information center in the Anchorage Westward Hotel] like high school football heroes."[1] However, if the immediate battle had been won, at least from a public relations standpoint, the outcome of the war was much less certain. Opponents of the Milrow test were unimpressed by victory statements issued by the AEC or any other federal agency.

The reaction of AEC officials to Milrow notwithstanding, a poll commissioned by Congressman Howard Pollock soon after the Milrow shot clearly revealed that Alaskans themselves had not yet made up their minds on the merits of nuclear testing conducted in their backyards. Of the 1,500 constituents who responded to the congressman's questionnaire, 43 percent approved of the tests in their present form, 24 percent were solidly opposed to all such tests, and the remaining 33 percent desired that "additional safeguards and controls" be put in place prior to the resumption of testing.[2] This division of opinion is further reflected in the rather personal dispute over the issue between Senator Mike Gravel and Governor Keith Miller. Gravel was deeply annoyed when he learned that the governor, a test supporter, had telegrammed three opposing state legislators claiming that their cause was being funded by a "well financed, highly organized, international movement." This attempt to discredit by association struck Gravel as reminiscent of "Joe McCarthy-type tactics." The senator was sufficiently incensed by what he regarded as an underhanded move that he wrote Miller demanding proof or an apology.[3]

When it finally sobered up from its Milrow victory celebration, the AEC realized that the future testing of even larger weapons would require additional groundwork. The centerpiece of the AEC's public relations campaign on behalf of a yet unnamed test blast was the creation of a five-member blue ribbon panel specifically empowered to receive official AEC reports on nuclear test effects. The membership of this panel, which was announced by Governor Miller, was impressive indeed. Included were Alaska Secretary of State Robert Ward, who acted as chair; A. W. Boddy, Executive Director of the Alaska Sportsmen's Council; Democratic state representative Eugene Guess, chairman of the Legislative Council; Robert B. Atwood, editor and publisher of the *Anchorage Daily Times;* and John Asplund, chairman of the Greater Anchorage Borough. This panel would evaluate the AEC reports put to it and make its recommendations directly to Governor Miller.[4] The fact that the AEC's briefings of the panel were scheduled to take place on Amchitka helped to ensure that its work would attract attention.

Having a representative group in place to pass judgments on AEC-generated nuclear test research was one thing; providing that group with sufficient information to justify its existence was quite another. By late November 1969, AEC officials had decided that "the current approach . . . is to take the position in Alaska that Milrow effects studies have not yet been completed," but that since "preliminary studies have not shown any unanticipated problems, . . . we are proceeding with construction leading toward a second Amchitka test." Thus, in one brief policy statement, the AEC rationalized its failure to make full disclosure of Milrow test results as those tests were being completed, thus keeping the panel largely in the dark, while at the same time justified preparations for an upcoming test of unknown size and scope.[5] That maximum secrecy was carefully calculated as a high priority for the AEC rather than as a product of neglect or indifference can hardly be doubted. In a remarkably unguarded moment, AEC information official Dixon Stewart once described the Commission's attitude toward the American public for a Fairbanks radio audience. "Our offerings," Stewart declared, "are designed for the average person, not the nuts and kooks who remember Hiroshima." He concluded by assuring his listeners that "The AEC does not lie. We may dissemble, but we never lie."[6]

In view of the foregoing decision on basic information policy, it is hard to interpret the subsequent AEC determination to send a delegation of experts to Alaska to testify about the safety of nuclear testing as anything other than window dressing. These experts, who represented the Defense Department, Los Alamos, the U.S. Public Health Bureau, the Scripps Institute, and the Sandia and Lawrence laboratories, briefed Governor Miller's staff before holding an open meeting hosted by the governor's blue ribbon panel. It is perhaps sufficient to point out that inasmuch as AEC experts had no more access to Milrow test results than did the blue ribbon panel, they were in no position to shed light on issues specific to Amchitka.[7]

With suspicions growing that the AEC had not changed its stripes on the issue of public disclosure, those opposed to nuclear testing began to mobilize their resources. One of these opponents, state representative Carl E. Moses of Unalaska, attempted to at least contain the threat posed by future nuclear testing. In the spring of 1970, Moses submitted House Joint Resolution 98, which resolved that "further testing of greater magnitude [than Milrow] be discontinued." In a move that carried at least significant symbolic value, Moses made sure that a copy of the resolution was sent to the AEC.[8]

The hearings that followed demonstrated the value of the AEC's policy of information containment. The supporters of Resolution 98, who led off the hearings, were reduced to old and familiar recitations that included constituent misgivings about the unknown, scientific questions about safety, and criticisms about the lack of hard evidence coming from the AEC.[9] The opponents of the resolution, on the other hand, came equipped with expert testimonials as well as visual demonstrations. AEC Nevada Operations Manager Robert Miller, who led off the attack against the resolution, assured the audience that the Commission could "predict . . . with accuracy" the effects of nuclear tests even larger than Milrow. Dr. Harry L. Reynolds, associate director of the Lawrence Radiation Laboratory, added that, since future tests would be buried deeper than Milrow, resulting future blasts would produce even lower levels of ground acceleration and waterborne shock waves, although these reduced shock forces, Reynolds predicted, would probably affect a larger portion of Amchitka than had Milrow. Not content merely to allay the fears of those attending the hearing, the AEC further cited environmental benefits that had resulted from nuclear test planning. An engineer on the AEC team, William D. Smith, Jr., for example, pointed out that AEC-sponsored archaeological research had uncovered finds that might "never have come to light had it not been for the . . . program." While showing a slide of a furry sea otter, Smith boasted that "the AEC is proud that it could—and still can—assist in preserving a part of the lore of your Alaska."[10]

The outcome of the hearings was no contest. Not only was the presentation of evidence one-sided, but the forum itself failed to attract a significant audience. Only about forty people showed up for the daylong event. Moreover, Alaska legislators, reflecting apparent widespread public apathy, seemed to be more concerned about the upcoming elections than they were about the issue of continuing nuclear testing. House chairman Earl D. Hillstrand, who admitted that the main purpose of the hearings was to undercut the position of "last-minute protests," had by the end of the proceeding come to the conclusion that "the AEC critics are simply agitators."[11] Thus, it came as no surprise when the Moses Resolution died in the spring 1970 session of the Alaska legislature. Nuclear test opponents would have to look elsewhere for a vehicle to express their discontent.

Although nuclear tests up to 1970 had provided no nasty surprises, A E C Chairman Glenn Seaborg was not entirely confident that that record could be maintained as the size of the test explosions increased. Prior to the detonation of Shot Handley at the Nevada Test Site in March 1970, for example, the federal government had paid to have the high-rise Bank of Nevada Building in Las Vegas reinforced against possible damage. This one-million ton shot, or "thumper," to use the parlance of the technicians, was a test of a Spartan missile warhead, a type which would be involved in any future Amchitka test.[12] Seaborg was so sufficiently worried about possible thumper effects that as early as February he had proposed to David Packard, deputy secretary of defense, that future A B M warhead tests be scaled down. Despite Packard's initial negative response, Seaborg pressed his case at a later meeting with Packard and the Joint Chiefs of Staff chairman General Earle G. Wheeler. The A E C chairman sensed that congressional opposition to ever increasing nuclear tests was growing. He was especially concerned that Senator Gravel might use his position as chairman of a public works subcommittee to call upon the A E C to provide testimony about the rumored radioactive venting from previous test blasts. Wanting badly to avoid the bright lights of a congressional investigation, Packard, too, agreed that something must be done. He would brief a select group of senators on the status of nuclear testing. Hopefully, that act would buy the A E C additional goodwill and time.[13]

The A E C policy of releasing as little hard information about nuclear testing as possible was further challenged by the recently passed National Environmental Policy Act (N E P A). This act required each federal agency to file "a detailed statement on the environmental impact" of its actions. A watchdog group called the President's Council on Environmental Quality, also created by N E P A, would review these agency reports, which in time became known as environmental impact statements (E I S). The passage of this act in January 1970 provided critics of A E C policies, like Senator Gravel, with a new tool with which to pry loose additional disclosures from the Atomic Energy Commission.[14] As events were to prove, however, the E I S requirement merely challenged rather than changed the A E C's determination to release as little vital information about its testing activities as possible. Over time, and with much practice, A E C officials had become masters of the arts of dissemination and delay. The Commission did not even begin to assemble information for an E I S until the lack of such a statement was called to its attention by Congress during a debate on appropriations. After this late start, an initial draft was put together by the Nevada Operations Office, which was then forwarded to Washington, D.C., for Commission review. After additional review by other federal agencies, the draft was released on June 12, 1970. It was disappointingly weak on specifics. The upcoming test scheduled for Amchitka had not even been named, nor had its size been determined. But the Commission did promise to hold open meetings, issue periodic briefings, conduct site visits to Amchitka, and maintain contacts with concerned Canadian and Japanese officials. In short, the report focused on Commission intentions, dodging the opportunity to describe its primary activities, especially from the perspective of their environmental impact.[15]

For Gravel and his staff, the AEC report was pure whitewash. The senator described it simply as a "P.R. Job." His special consultant on nuclear policy, Egan O'Connor, was more pointed in her criticism. To O'Connor, the silences of the report constituted an actual evasion of the law. Nowhere was there reference to the continuing scientific debate over the possibility that a nuclear test of sufficient size might trigger earthquakes or tsunamis. The Milrow results were at best an uncertain guide to damage estimates caused by larger explosions. Releases of radioactive contamination, O'Connor thought, constituted the worst environmental threat. The AEC's EIS predicted that harmful isotopes would become depleted over time, but it failed to discuss the burden of accumulated pollutants migrating into the region's environment. Long Shot had leaked tritium, and someday Milrow might well release a similar radioactive load. The report further neglected to comment on the danger that such leakage might pose for marine life. In near total frustration and disgust, O'Connor concluded that, based on the report, "no Congressman or citizen could make a judgment about the wisdom of conducting the test."[16]

Perhaps worse than its omissions were the report's evasions and outright deceptions. In March 1970, AEC supported a study, conducted by Teledyne Isotopes Corporation, of Milrow's long-range impact on water resources. Two different models were used. The first suggested that water contaminated by the Milrow blast would not likely reach the ocean for one hundred years. The second, however, indicated a far more serious problem. This study predicted that such contamination might reach the ocean in as few as six years and would continue for an additional sixty-six years to contaminate at levels up to three hundred times permissible concentrations. The fact that this study was completely deleted from the AEC's report struck O'Connor as both deliberate and indefensible.[17]

Armed with information provided by O'Connor, Senator Gravel began a tireless campaign to block congressional funding for Shot Cannikin, as the projected Amchitka test was now called. In a letter to Allen J. Ellender, chairman of the Senate Subcommittee on Public Works, Gravel characterized the AEC's report of its EIS as a "travesty." Widening his attacks to include all ABM development, Gravel, in a speech delivered at the University of Maryland, labeled the ABM program a "grandiose Defense Department Edsel," flawed by such serious risks to the environment that its continued development constituted "sheer folly." As an Alaskan, he especially resented the use of his state as a "happy testing ground." Gravel's open hostility to the ABM and its offshoots invited the standard AEC public relations treatment. He was now invited by Chairman Seaborg to a classified briefing on Cannikin. Gravel, who had become an expert on AEC public relations tactics, refused the offer.[18]

The final skirmish in this round of debates on the wisdom of continuing nuclear testing in Alaska was played out in the halls of the United States Congress. In the fall of 1970, the administration submitted its recommendations in the form of a Defense Procurement Authorization bill for fiscal year 1971, a $19.2 billion package that included President Nixon's Safeguard program. The most that ABM opponents could reasonably offer was the containment of the program to sites already approved, namely Malmstrom Air Force Base in Montana and Grand Forks Air Base in North Dakota. Even this modest resistance to ABM development, however, lost. The president's program would continue on at full speed, and the Cannikin test would receive $118 million of these funds.[19]

Despite the fact that ABM opponents were politely ignored by the AEC and bulldozed when they took their case to Congress, uneasiness about the continuation of nuclear testing refused to disappear. At a December 15, 1970, meeting of the cabinet-level Under Secretaries Committee, this uncertainty surfaced once again. AEC Chairman Seaborg, who testified before this committee on behalf of the Commission, noted that Russell Train, who also served as chairman of the President's Council on Environmental Quality, expressed "continuing concern about these [i.e., nuclear test] hazards and questioned us closely about the possibility of getting by with a smaller warhead or delaying the test." Although Pentagon Director of Defense Research and Engineering John S. Fostor dismissed Train's suggestions as "unaccept-able," Seaborg was disturbed by the lack of consensus that existed among committee members, noting that the atmosphere had changed considerably since the time of the Milrow discussions. Undersecretary of State John Irwin, who chaired this meeting, concluded that "Cannikin presented a very serious problem" which the group "would have to consider again."[20]

The persistent misgivings of ABM opponents about the safety of test shots seemed to be confirmed on December 18, just three days following the meeting of the Under Secretaries Committee. On that day, Shot Baneberry, conducted at the Nevada Test Site, went awry. The blast, totally contrary to expectations, created a surface fissure three hundred feet long and twenty feet wide through which "radioactive debris jetted massively . . . [with] thick black smoke and dust spurting 8,000 feet into the air." It was observed that "vapor drifted from the crack for the next twenty-four hours." Radiation at the test site skyrocketed, requiring the removal and "decontamination" of six hundred workers. A snowstorm carried radioactive fallout in a semicir-cular pattern across Idaho, Wyoming, Montana, North Dakota, Minnesota, Missouri, Arkansas, Texas, and southern California. Seaborg jotted in his diary the following entry: "The event was reported in a sensational manner on the evening national TV news programs. This will clearly be a very trou-blesome matter."[21] Baneberry's surprising results were underscored by the routine nature of the operation. Comparatively speaking, the shot was a mere babe. It had an estimated yield of only 10,000 tons. The implications for a test shot on Amchitka perhaps five hundred times more powerful than Baneberry could only be imagined.[22]

One of the many imponderables that swirled around the proposed Can-nikin test by the end of 1970 was international reaction. The Canadian and Japanese governments had already indicated their displeasure with nuclear testing by sending official protests to Washington, D.C., prior to Milrow. Canada was so upset by the prospect of widespread blast and fallout dam-age that it threatened at that time to bill the United States for Milrow's un-wanted consequences. Hugh Curtis, mayor of Saanich, British Columbia, undoubtedly spoke for many western Canadians when he remarked, "I don't recall in my lifetime any incident which has put such stress on friend-ship which Canadians have held for America." The Japanese newspapers *Asahi Shimbun* and *Yomuri Shimbun* castigated Milrow as "highly de-plorable," especially since the test was conducted in rich international fish-ing grounds. The official Soviet state paper, *Izvestia,* noted that Milrow carried with it the unacceptable risk of triggering earthquakes and tsunamis.[23] Thus, it is perhaps fair to conclude at this point that whereas the opponents of nuclear testing in Alaska had been driven into retreat, they were not altogether bereft of resources. As tested weapons grew ever more powerful, guarantees of safety rang increasingly hollow.

9 / AMID MORE CANNIKIN CONTROVERSY

The game plan was to go out to Amchitka
and stand witness against the bomb.
My stance was political and moral.
The Nazi Holocaust had taught me
to get involved politically.
This is the wellspring of my values.

—RICHARD A. FEINBERG,
crewman on the *Phyllis Cormack*

The controversy that surrounded the final nuclear test held in Alaska, Shot Cannikin, was fueled by a combination of fears of the unknown occasioned by Cannikin's size and an accumulation of frustration and anger suffered by those whose questions about the safety of nuclear explosions had been persistently pushed aside by federal officials. Although in the end apologists for the test would have their way, and Cannikin was detonated by presidential order on November 6, 1971, test opponents managed to mount a challenging and sometimes even inventive resistance that would finally succeed in placing the AEC on the defensive.

Since the unprecedented size of the Cannikin explosion, some five million tons, provided the trigger for the invigorated protests that occurred both in Alaska and elsewhere following the test's announcement, it is perhaps worthwhile to begin this discussion with a description of the scope of the project. W-71, the military designation of the warhead that Cannikin was intended to test, was an integral part of the Safeguard ABM system designed to protect United States Minuteman missile launching sites against an enemy ICBM attack. The W-71 would rest in the nose cone of a three-stage rocket measuring fifty-five feet in length. Using a dummy warhead, this rocket, called Spartan, had already proved its capabilities when, in August 1970, it had intercepted an ICBM in a test conducted above Kwajalein Island in the central Pacific Ocean.[1]

The successful deployment of the ABM vehicle placed added pressure on the AEC and the United States military to complete work on the Spartan's warhead as quickly as possible in order to make operational the weapon as a whole. The test of the nuclear warhead was thus scheduled to take place on Amchitka on November 6, 1971, as part of a larger program called Operation Grommet. The five-million-ton yield of this test would make Shot Cannikin the largest underground nuclear explosion ever undertaken by the United States. By comparison, Shot Boxcar, the greatest nuclear explosion ever conducted at the Nevada Test Site, yielded a force only one-quarter as large.[2]

As one might expect of such an unprecedented undertaking, the preparations for Shot Cannikin were impressive. The warhead itself stretched out the length of a football field and weighed 850,000 pounds. The borehole, drilled down to 6,150 feet, was sufficient to have held four Chicago Sears Towers stacked end-to-end with room to spare. Since the hole was so deep, test engineers had to design a hundred-foot-long horizontal tunnel to drain residual water into a nearby collecting pond. Water that could not be removed by this process was pumped out of the tunnel. The chamber where the detonation would take place, located almost 6,000 feet from the surface, had to be drilled out of rock by hand. Virtually every aspect of the test site preparation involved solving seldom-encountered engineering problems.[3]

The anticipated physical effects of the Cannikin blast were spectacular as well. At surface ground zero, expanding gas and shock waves would leave in their wakes a hot cavity lined with molten rock. Lawrence Radiation Laboratory experts calculated that seven hundred tons of rock would be melted for every one thousand tons of explosive yield. At that rate, Cannikin would probably transform nearly three and one-half million tons of Amchitka rock. After a period of cooling, the blast chamber, a sphere with a twenty-six foot radius, would collapse into itself. Should the so-called chimney above the chamber similarly collapse, the surface ground would sink into the empty space, thus forming a "subsidence crater." This crater would be the most impressive physical signature left by Shot Cannikin. Far more important, however, was the radioactive residue that such a large blast would inevitably create.[4]

In an attempt to neutralize likely protests against Cannikin before they could become effectively organized, AEC officials decided to lobby influential Alaskan public officials. Thus, sixteen members of the state legislature and the governor's staff were invited by the AEC to an all-expenses-paid briefing held in Nevada, where the guests were wined and dined at the posh Las Vegas Stardust Hotel. The obvious intention of the briefings was to re-assure rather than inform. The delegates were told that Cannikin would not create physical trauma such as earthquakes and tsunamis, and further that there would be "no adverse effects to the island from the standpoint of ecol-ogy." Apparently taking their cue from the reactions of the delegates to these disclosures, AEC officials concluded that "rank and file Alaskans do not seem particularly worried about the Cannikin test or its possible effects."[5]

In the meantime, test opponents led by newly re-elected Governor William A. Egan were determined to hold public—and very open—hear-ings on Cannikin, hearings that would reveal all of the accumulated infor-mation relevant to the planned test. Egan's model was the environmental impact hearings that had preceded the construction of the trans-Alaskan oil pipeline. Although neither the Council on Environmental Quality nor the Environmental Protection Agency were required by NEPA to hold such hearings, AEC Chairman Seaborg raised no objections, and the sessions were scheduled to take place in Juneau on May 26 and in Anchorage on May 28, 1971. Eagan hoped that the findings produced by these hearings would be crucial in deciding whether preparations for Cannikin would continue.[6]

Egan's hopes in turn hinged on the role played by the AEC. Would the Commission merely provide expert testimony or would it also act as judge on the merits of opposition arguments made against Cannikin? The gover-nor, fearing the latter, wrote to EPA administrator William D. Ruckelshaus and requested that his agency act as judge at the hearings. As Egan himself said, "I want to make sure the Atomic Energy Commission is being evalu-ated, not evaluating itself."[7] This change in the ground rules that had gov-erned similar past hearings was totally unacceptable to the AEC. The key issue was one of sovereignty, and the AEC would not easily surrender con-trol of any hearing on nuclear testing. Rather, what the Commission had in mind was a replay of the hearings that had preceded legislative action on the Moses Resolution, hopefully with similar results. General Edward Giller of the Division of Military Application believed that "it was extremely im-portant . . . that the AEC seize the initiative [in this matter] so as to have con-trol over the format and aura." In practice, this meant that the Commission would promulgate information and receive feedback. Specifically, the AEC intended that each session of the hearings would begin with the reading of prepared statements by its own experts, after which the official panel would answer written questions that had been provided in advance. The session would then conclude with statements made by "outside speakers who would be permitted to hold the floor for no more than fifteen minutes each." These outside and presumably hostile witnesses could participate in either of the two hearings, but not both.[8] As these ground rules would suggest, the AEC had clearly beaten back Governor Egan's challenge on the important issue of who would control the hearings.

The initial public hearing held at Juneau began as the AEC had expected. The first outside witnesses to take the floor, publicly concerned citizens, were full of righteous anger but little else. Carolyn Burg, a former Save Our State Committee activist, charged that the AEC was guilty of trespassing on Alaskan territory. Bernard Brakel warned that nuclear tests were "playing with my planet at some risk." One Canadian environmentalist chimed in with the suggestion that if nuclear tests were as safe as the AEC claimed, why weren't they held in some place like central Kansas? Since these critics had no hard evidence with which to support their charges, General Giller, speaking for the AEC experts, could afford to be generous in his response. Inasmuch as the world was not a perfect place, the general reminded his audience, nuclear testing was absolutely critical to national defense in the absence of a comprehensive test ban treaty.[9]

Opposition scientists, however, were more successful in denting the AEC armor at the Juneau hearing. Wallace H. Noerenberg, commissioner of Alaska's Department of Fish and Game, admitted that although his agency had initially cooperated with the AEC, it had since become alarmed by the prospect of additional nuclear tests. Turning to the AEC's final draft of its EIS, Noerenberg pointed out that the draft had glossed over estimates of environmental damage caused by nuclear tests. The EIS had understated estimates of damage to seal, sea lion, and sea otter populations, and it had totally neglected to address the issue of residual tritium effects on fish. What bothered Noerenberg the most, however, were the dangers inherent in the unexpected. Hitting an AEC raw nerve, Noerenberg asked the Commission's panel of experts how it could guarantee that an occurrence like the Baneberry "mistake" would not occur at Amchitka?[10]

The public hearings seemed to undergo a shift in atmosphere when the venue moved to Anchorage on May 28, 1971, for their second round. The "aura," to cite General Giller's earlier term, had grown more tense. As one reporter noted, the AEC "phalanx of physicists and other specialists now figited . . . like expectant fathers." Jeremy L. Stone, director of the Federation of American Scientists and an expert on the arms race, was a witness whose authority was not easily dismissed. Stone claimed that not only did nuclear tests represent unproved (and unacceptable) risks that were masked by the AEC's EIS statements, but he also felt that the entire ABM program was unnecessary, "an experiment waiting to be canceled." Quoting another weapons expert, Herbert F. York, Stone concluded that Cannikin constituted "a pointless test of an unnecessary weapon."[11]

Further alarms were sounded when Pentagon officials confirmed that the United States Army had dumped cannisters of lewisite and mustard gas that had been stored as liquids in Aleutian waters several years after World War II. Although this dump site was located 276 miles northwest of Amchitka, some feared that blast waves would rupture the steel burial containers and thus activate these highly toxic chemicals. The critics finally had something tangible into which to sink their teeth. Senator Gravel, seizing the initiative, fired off a telegram to Army Secretary Stanley R. Resor demanding "full disclosure immediately and an explanation of what happened to these blister warfare agents." Making sure that the sense of urgency that he attached to this issue would not be lost upon Resor, Gravel concluded, "The state [of Alaska] should be informed as soon as possible!" By the conclusion of the Anchorage hearing, which was extended by a day to accommodate the thirty-two hostile witnesses, the two sides found themselves increasingly at odds. Over and over again, questions about the safety of nuclear testing were met by bland assurances of panel experts that there was no known cause for concern. As Melvin L. Merritt of Sandia Laboratory testified, "Milrow was what is popularly called a dirty bomb, . . . but what is being tested here is a clean, thermonuclear bomb." Such facile explanations only served to further exasperate the critics of government policy.[12]

The AEC's definitive answer to these and other criticisms came in the form of its final EIS on Amchitka tests. This document, entitled *Final Environment Statement—Cannikin,* represented a complete vindication of its previous decisions and planning. Issued on June 21, 1971, the EIS reported that the Cannikin test represented a "vital part of the U.S. weapons development program." In addition, potential environmental threats were characterized as small and inconsequential. Radioactivity, the AEC predicted, would solidify in an underground rock-glass formation from where it would never escape. Eventually, decay would render it entirely harmless. Physical damage to the environment was expected to be minimal. A small number of seals, somewhere between twenty and one hundred, "could suffer adverse effects." The Commission foresaw no important seismic activity, and thus fears of test-triggered earthquakes or tsunamis, it pointed out, should be discounted. This test was expected to be so safe that the nearest military personnel posted at Adak and the Shemya Islands two hundred miles from ground zero would "barely feel the motion." Finally, the A E C assured its audience that earlier environmental damages caused by the preparations for Cannikin would eventually be repaired.[13] The Juneau and Anchorage hearings had altered the A E C's thinking not a measurable whit.

Just as A E C Chairman Seaborg had earlier feared, congressional opposition against continued nuclear testing was beginning to build despite the Commission's assurances that such testing was necessary and entirely safe. When the A E C released its final E I S on Cannikin, Senator Gravel reacted by announcing that he would repeatedly use the Senate floor as a forum in which to voice his opposition to nuclear testing in Alaska. On July 15, 1971, Gravel was joined by Representative Patsy T. Mink, a long-time fellow A E C critic, who moved to ammend House Resolution 9388, a bill to authorize fiscal year 1972 A E C expenditures, by striking $19.7 million for the Cannikin blast. Although the proposal was eventually defeated in the House by a lopsided vote, Senators Gravel and Daniel Inouye hoped to keep Mink's strategy alive when the budget debate moved to the Senate.[14]

In the end, Gravel's own initiative to curtail, or perhaps even cancel entirely, funding for Cannikin attracted the support of nearly forty senators, a surprisingly large number, although not sufficient to secure passage of the implementing amendment. A compromise submitted by Rhode Island Democrat John O. Pastore to delay the test "unless the President gives his direct approval" was also defeated. The opponents of Cannikin were loath to surrender, however, and the action returned to the House, where Representative Mink attempted to amend another funding bill by eliminating expenditures for nuclear testing in the vicinity of Amchitka. In the final vote, this proposal was defeated 275 to 108. Thus, all efforts to block congressional funding for Cannikin ultimately failed. But the minority that opposed such funding had grown in size and had become more vocal as well. In these crucial debates, Alaska's governor, two senators, and one representative had lined up solidly against the Cannikin test.[15]

Within the A E C, Chairman Seaborg alone was moved by these public and political demonstrations of opposition to nuclear testing. He now saw the need for "candor" in the administration's revelations about Cannikin's purpose and expected yield. His, however, was a solitary voice, completely overwhelmed by his own colleagues as well as Defense Department officials who were convinced secrecy was the most productive policy to use vis-à-vis the Soviets. When Senator Hubert Humphrey came out against the Cannikin test in April, an ambivalent Seaborg confessed that, whereas his official persona was fully committed to Cannikin, his private persona sympathized with Humphrey. But, in the end, he blamed the environmental movement for stirring up public hostility toward the AEC.[16] Seaborg's misgivings aside, the Nixon administration was fully committed to carrying through with the Cannikin test. To this end, the AEC planned a "D minus 180" (i.e., six months in advance) public relations effort on behalf of the controversial test. Fairly modest in scope, "D minus 180" was intended to allay fears while not offering test opponents a tangible target.[17]

As the test date approached, continued opposition to Cannikin mainly took the form of various public protests. President Nixon's arrival in Anchorage in late September 1971 to meet with Emperor Hirohito provided an occasion for anti-test demonstrations. These were mainly the work of an ad hoc group calling itself the Alaska Coalition Against Cannikin. When city officials had at first denied the Coalition a parade rally permit, it had appealed the decision to the Alaska Superior Court and won. Announcing its existence and advertising its purpose, the Coalition took out a full-page in the *Anchorage Daily News* just prior to the presidential arrival. As a result of this publicity, the presidential motorcade was confronted on parade day by several hundred protesters, some of whom carried anti-test posters. A few of the heartier protesters even chased after the motorcade.[18]

The Alaska Mothers' Campaign Against Cannikin represented a variation of the protest of the Alaska Coalition Against Cannikin. Chaired by Lillie H. McGarvey, Aleut League secretary, the Alaska Mothers consisted of a core group of fifty women who were determined to solicit and forward as many letters and telegrams of protest to President Nixon as possible. More interested in numbers than gender exclusiveness, the Alaska Mothers soon widened its membership to include all manner of human beings, including fathers, children, and grandparents. To encourage the flow of protest to the White House, the Alaska Mothers handed out brochures, sold "stop Cannikin" bumper stickers, and passed out "I'm against Cannikin" buttons at the agricultural fair at Palmer, Alaska. In less than a month, members had succeeded in gathering one thousand signatures on petitions and had garnered eight hundred letters.[19]

Increasingly, both formal and informal protest seemed to be the order of the day. An ad hoc group calling itself Concerned Citizens Against Cannikin emerged at Ketchikan under the leadership of a local high school teacher, James R. Musson.[20] Fifteen University of Alaska, Fairbanks, students organized themselves into the Alaskans Against Amchitka. After an unsuccessful effort to meet with Interior Secretary Walter Hickel in order to persuade him to use his influence with the president to cancel Cannikin, these students collected 1,200 signatures on a protest petition, which they forwarded to the White House.[21] Established organizations got into the act as well. Both the Alaska Nurses Association and the Alaska Medical Association, worried about health hazards, passed strongly worded resolutions against the proposed blast. The Kodiak-Aleutian chapter of the Alaska Conservation Society asked Nixon to cancel or delay the test until additional research could more accurately ascertain expected results. Individual public officials joined the parade of protesters. One of these, Mayor Swen Haakanson of Old Harbor on Kodiak Island, became downright threatening. If a blast-caused "earthquake and tidal wave destroys our villages," the feisty mayor warned, "we will file a suit against the government that will make the Native land claims look like pocket money."[22]

By far the most bizarre and enduring of all the protests precipitated by nuclear testing in Alaska was that organized by Greenpeace. A product of the rising social consciousness of the 1960s, Greenpeace was a mixture of high, if sometimes uncertain, purpose and theater. For all of their curious antics, however, Greenpeace members were convinced that history had placed the organization at a very important crossroads—and its name was Cannikin. To Greenpeace, Cannikin represented nothing less than "Armageddon," a clear threat to "generations unborn." Reluctant to define its program in clear, straightforward language, Greenpeace often resorted to vague and frightening imagery in order to scare the pants off of its audiences. Thus, it warned the world that "Angels and bat-beings were locked in a deadly, groaning embrace." The current crisis, it suggested, was not much different from the "famous battles [of] the Second World War."[23]

The history of Greenpeace traces back to the Milrow shot of 1969. Shortly after that test, a Vancouver-based protest group, Don't Make a Wave, staged a benefit rock concert at which it raised a total of $17,000, which was intended to fund its opposition to future nuclear tests. With additional funding provided by the Friends Service Committee, the Sierra Club, and other kindred organizations, the Don't Make a Wave group decided to make a novel and dramatic statement against nuclear testing: it would acquire a boat and sail defiantly into the waters surrounding Amchitka on the eve of the explosion.[24] To this end, a "weatherbeaten, wooden-hulled halibut packer" by the name of the *Phyllis Cormack* was purchased. Rechristened *Greenpeace* in order to reflect the group's pro-environment and anti-war orientation, the ship carried a crew of twelve—eleven Canadians and a lone American, Richard Feinberg.[25]

On September 15, 1971, this strange venture departed from Vancouver, hoping to reach its objective in two or three weeks. As the *Greenpeace* neared its destination on September 23, its crew learned that Cannikin had been rescheduled. Uncertain as to its next move, and wary about an extended stay aboard a leaky and potentially dangerous vessel, the *Greenpeace* crew decided to anchor off Akutan Island in the eastern Aleutians. In the process of seeking a safe harbor, however, the crew unwittingly broke United States regulations on formal entry and was thus subject to arrest. After being escorted by the Coast Guard cutter *Confidence* to Sand Point, Unga Island, on October 3, the intended Amchitka protest was abandoned entirely. *Greenpeace* headed back to Vancouver. Feinberg's confession that "We had botched the whole thing" was hardly an exaggeration.[26]

Despite its troubled beginning, it is important to note that Greenpeace, as an organization, survived and prospered. Somehow, the boldness of the intended demonstration managed to capture the public's imagination regardless of the outcome. Crew members became heroes. At a Kodiak stopover, they were greeted by "Thank You" signs. A banquet in their honor followed, attended by the mayor, the police chief, and several city councilmen. The local newspaper published an editorial in which the "nine strange men" who visited "in the name of Peace and Sanity" were praised. Celebrities in their own right, the crew members were courted by state legislators and were the centers of attention at public gatherings. Similar receptions awaited the crew at Juneau and Ketchikan, *Greenpeace*'s last port of call in Alaska.[27]

The final efforts to short-circuit the Cannikin test through official channels took the form of litigation. At the second AEC-sponsored open hearing held at Anchorage on May 28 and 29, 1971, Aleut League president Iliodor Philemonof from St. George in the Pribilof Islands had indicated that his people were so "upset" by the possibility of radioactivity fouling the ocean that he might well ask League attorney Les Miller to seek an injunction in federal court to stop the test.[28] This threat was made good on September 2, when Hugh W. Fleischer of the Alaska Legal Services Corporation, an advocacy agency involved in civil rights and Native causes, filed a motion for a preliminary injunction in Anchorage. Eleven days later, U.S. Attorney G. Kent Edwards countered this move on behalf of the federal government by filing a motion for dismissal. In the two days of testimony that followed, Fleischer tried to demonstrate Aleut fears that Cannikin constituted a real threat to their livelihoods by presenting direct testimony by Aleut leaders such as Philemonof, as well as submitting affidavits from a variety of concerned Natives living near Amchitka. The government, for its part, tried to neutralize the value of this testimony by presenting A E C-generated evidence demonstrating that these fears, though perhaps real enough, were in fact groundless.[29] Since both sides had agreed to forego a jury trial, the ruling by presiding Judge Raymond E. Plummer was final. He thus decided that the A E C had violated no procedures, nor had its reports indicated the existence of any conditions resulting from Cannikin that constituted a true physical or economic threat to nearby Aleuts. In short, the problem was essentially psychological rather than substantial. As a remedy, the A E C was therefore directed to station test monitors on several islands close to Amchitka, as well as hold briefings in nineteen Native villages prior to the test.[30]

Meanwhile, a similar legal test was undertaken in Washington, D.C., by eight separate organizations. The lead group in this action, the Committee for Nuclear Responsibility, had been founded in January 1971 for the express purpose of blocking the Cannikin test. It was joined in this effort by the Sierra Club, Friends of the Earth, the Wilderness Society, the National Parks and Conservation Association, the Association on American Indian Affairs, Amchitka Two, and Sane, Inc. The motion to stop the Cannikin test was filed in the United States District Court for the District of Columbia on July 9, 1971. The centerpiece of the legal debate that followed was the adequacy of the A E C's Cannikin E I S. Presiding Judge George L. Hart, Jr., denied the motion only to be reversed by the three-judge United States Court of Appeals, which sent the case back to the lower court. Once again, Judge Hart denied the motion, whereupon an appeal was made to the Supreme Court.[31]

In an unusual Saturday morning session on November 6, 1971, the Supreme Court sat in judgment of the only nuclear test litigation ever to reach the highest court in the land. After reviewing the key question of the adequacy of the A E C's Cannikin E I S, the Court, in a four to three split decision, ruled in favor of the A E C. Justices Warren Burger, Potter Stewart, Byron R. White, and Harry A. Blackmun voted with the majority, with Justices William O. Douglas, William J. Brennan, Jr., and Thurgood Marshall dissenting. The closeness of the vote, however, was misleading inasmuch as all of the dissenters based their decision on the need for additional time in which to review the evidence.[32]

With the last obstacle to the Cannikin test now swept aside, all was made ready on Amchitka for the blast. Once notified of the Court's decision, new AEC Chairman James R. Schlesinger authorized the final countdown. The explosion itself occurred milliseconds after noon, Alaska Standard Time, on November 6, 1971. The resulting force, just under five million tons of power, registered magnitude 7.0 on the Richter seismic scale. Twelve minutes after detonation, Schlesinger announced from the control room located twenty-three miles from surface ground zero, "All preliminary indications suggest that the Cannikin test has been conducted both successfully and safely." Everyone was relieved. AEC public affairs official Henry G. Vermillion spoke for many when he later summed up his feelings about the Amchitka nuclear test program: "It was a very interesting five years, but I don't think I would want to go through it again."[33]

The legacy of distrust left behind in the test program's wake, however, could not be disposed of so easily. One of the conspicuous casualties of the United States' decision to use Alaska as a test site was Canadian-American goodwill. Canadians from all walks of life openly demonstrated their displeasure with this decision. The Canadian Coalition to Stop the Amchitka Nuclear Blast, for example, included environmentalists, labor, social workers, women, and religious denominations ranging from Anglican to Zoroastrian. Elementary and high school students marched in protest. Some college classes were cancelled in order to allow concerned faculty and students the opportunity to demonstrate. In Ontario, a United Auto Workers union official proposed a one-day embargo on goods coming from the United States. In Winnipeg, hostility was so great that the United States Counsul-General was placed under round-the-clock police protection.[34] At the official level, the Canadian Parliament in October passed a resolution condemning Cannikin, while Mitchell W. Sharp, Canada's External Affairs Secretary, not only registered his government's "deep sense of regret" with Secretary of State William P. Rogers, but indicated as well that Canada now intended to support a total nuclear test ban treaty, even without on-site inspection, a position that the United States had consistently opposed.[35] While the AEC, not surprisingly, took pride in the fact that the nuclear tests conducted in Alaska under its auspices had resulted in no catastrophes or even major incidents, the cost-benefit discussion of those tests would continue for a long time.

10 / BEYOND THE LAST BOMB

To President Richard M. Nixon . . .
When you press the button to detonate the bomb known as Cannikin,
please remember . . . that there was . . . spirit in men, vegetation,
marine life, and clean atmosphere . . . in the Aleutians.

—Tlingit Auke Tribe Council

On the evening before the Cannikin blast, members of the Auke Tribe, headquartered in Juneau, raised the stakes one notch higher in another last-minute attempt to stop the test. They called the president's attention to the Tlingit traditional belief that all of the islands in the Aleutians were imbued with spirit. This belief, passed down from generations of ancient, indigenous peoples, emphasized that their beloved islands, alive with spirit, were not mere rocks to be blasted and despoiled in dangerous experiments. From this Native perspective, Amchitka represented a vital component of the core of an ancient religion. It was not to be regarded as worthless, a kind of throwaway place.

In a highly competitive world, driven by scientific technology, it may well be asked: What, exactly, is the value of a sea otter spirit, a moss spirit, or an algal spirit? How does one evaluate eagle and falcon spirits? The meaning of spirit may defy definition in scientific terms, but to those who attempted to spare Amchitka by invoking sacred imagery, nothing less than the desecration of the island was at stake. This concept, however, apparently made no impression on pro-defense planners. It was marginalized, despite its uniqueness, along with all of the other protests. Cannikin, the last nuclear test to be conducted in Alaska, went off as planned.

More than a quarter-century has now passed since that milestone, and the passions that infused both sides of the test debates at the time have cooled to the point where, perhaps, a more objective assessment can be made. The basic problem of whether Amchitka, a jewel in the Alaska Refuge crown, might also be a suitable place in which to conduct tests of the most potent and dangerous explosives known to man goes back to the year 1913, when the United States Congress authorized military use of the Aleutian Refuge. From its turn-of-the-century perspective, Congress had no way of even imagining how intrusive a subsequent, undefined military presence might become. Just how compatible were the environmental, economic, and spiritual needs of resident Natives and conservationists with a five-million-ton explosive force, however confined?

For all of the Atomic Energy Commission's repeated and calming assurances to the contrary, considerable damage did occur to Amchitka's environment as a result of the three nuclear tests held on the island. The A E C had predicted that Cannikin would cause small rock falls and turf slides along only two miles of coastline, dislodging 7,000 cubic yards of material. Post-test assessments revealed, however, that the coastal area affected was more than twice that size and that dislodgement totaled nearly 46,000 cubic yards. Intertidal marine life had, consequently, been smothered. Pre-test estimates held that only between 20 and 240 sea otters were endangered; post-test assessments made by the Alaska Department of Fish and Game concluded that between 700 and 2,000 of these animals were destroyed by the Cannikin blast.[1]

Sea otter fatalities, however, failed to tell the whole story of habitat damage. Nearly three hundred deceased rock greenling fish were found offshore, and rock sole catches in the Bering Sea declined substantially, signaling a similarly large kill-off. Assessors further discovered the remains of ten thousand three-spined stickleback fish and seven hundred Dolly Varden in Amchitka's lakes, streams, and ponds. Four harbor seals were known to have died as a result of pressure damage attributed to Cannikin. Fifteen perching aquatic birds, with legs jammed into their bodies by violent, upward ground motion, were autopsied.[2]

For over one mile along the intertidal Bering Sea coast, the blast uplifted a fault line as high as forty-two inches, killing algae and invertebrate life. About fourteen acres were adversely affected, and the area's natural erosion patterns were changed. Six lakes close to surface ground zero were drained as a result of earth-tilting, in the process of which the lake bottoms, lined by fissures, were revealed. Everywhere streams were filled with particulates discharged by fierce ground motion. Drainage configurations were wrenched askew, and a thirty-acre lake was created in the thirty-one-foot deep subsidence crater left by the blast. Lake Cannikin, as this technological anomaly was named, became Amchitka's largest and deepest body of water. Thirty-six acres around the test site were completely denuded. Immediately following the explosion, a drill fluid dike, holding bentonite mud, leaked pollution a quarter of a mile out to sea. In addition to this blast-related damage, about one thousand acres of island habitat was "destroyed or severely disturbed" during construction of the test site.[3]

Although some blast consequences could be reversed, irretrievable loss occurred at an ancient Aleut site nearly two miles from Cannikin on the island's Pacific side. A University of Alaska archaeological team had partially excavated the site the previous summer. Hoping to contain anticipated explosion damage to the remainder of the site, the archaeologists had shored up the exposed area in October. Despite these precautions, the site's walls were caved in by ground motion, and approximately fifty-four square yards of the site disappeared forever with a cliff fall into the ocean.[4]

Unfortunately, the damage to Amchitka did not end with Cannikin's detonation. Additional drilling was required in order to obtain core samples of shot debris relevant to the performance of the Spartan warhead. This post-shot, drill-back procedure was fraught with risk of contamination, especially since similar tests had not accompanied either Long Shot or Milrow. Thus, officials were deprived of prior experience on which to fall back. To guard against possible radioactive spills, the drill rig was erected on a metal, drip-pan base with two attached sump pumps. The hole itself was drilled directly into the blast-melt area and reached a total depth of 7,200 feet. Drilling began on November 17, 1971, and ended on February 18, 1972. Twenty-five core samples were subsequently shipped to Lawrence Livermore Laboratory for analysis.[5]

During this drilling process, equipment was subject to varying degrees of radioactive contamination. On February 13, 1972, the first contact with radioactive blast material was made at the 6,919-foot level. Affected tools were carefully decontaminated or wrapped in plastic for future use. For all of these precautions, however, the operation still produced "low level, unavoidable contamination" on tools, pipes, and small parts of the drilling platform, according to test officials. Radioactive liquids were flushed back into the hole, and when the work had been completed, drilling tools were similarly dispatched to the bottom of the test cavity. Contaminated solids, along with other affected equipment, were sealed, packaged and sent off to the Nevada Test Site. This radioactive waste totaled over twenty-two thousand tons and included four special containers of extremely dangerous cesium 137, cobalt 60, and several plutonium isotopes.[6]

After core samples had been taken, the drill-back hole was used to monitor down-hole water flow into the cavity and chimney areas. Measurements were taken twice daily, beginning on May 21. Four days later these procedures had to be halted when gas started to seep upward. This gas, it was discovered, was laced with above-normal levels of krypton 85 and carbon 14. A build-up of these dangerous gases inside the drill-back building threatened an explosion as well as contamination. Officials were then faced with two options: either the noxious gases could be bled off into holding tanks, or they could be released directly into the atmosphere. They chose the easiest and most dangerous of the alternatives. Gases were slowly allowed to enter the atmosphere, after which water monitoring resumed.[7]

Long-term radiation was undoubtedly the most feared of all of the threats represented by Cannikin. Several months before the Cannikin shot, epidemiologist Carolyn V. Brown of the Alaska Area Native Health Service questioned whether this risk carried unique implications for Aleuts and southwestern Eskimo people. Although data on radionuclide body burdens were available for Interior and North Slope Natives, none existed for residents closest to the test. Thus, she recommended that baseline investigations be undertaken. As a result of Brown's concern, a program was initiated in September 1971, whereby blood and urine samples were taken from fifty-three Aleuts on Atka Island, which is located about three hundred miles east of Amchitka. These samples were then sent to Las Vegas for cesium 137, tritium, and iron 55 analysis. Meanwhile, a few extracted teeth were saved for strontium 90 studies. A year later, comparative testing was repeated on thirty-seven of the Atka village group, and the study base was extended by gathering additional data from Natives at Akhoik Village on Kodiak Island and from Anchorage. These studies found no evidence of unusually high levels of radioactive contamination.[8]

Workers at the test site may not have been so lucky. "Downwinders," as mammal biologist Carl M. Hild called people who stayed on Amchitka for extended periods of time, seem to have suffered unusually high levels of diseases linked to radiation exposure. Nick Aleck, who was likely subjected to tritiated water plus an assortment of other radioactive isotopes while working at the test site, later died from radiation-related cancer. Aleck's wife, Beverly, is pressing for epidemiological studies of all Amchitka workers. She claims that "they are now suffering high rates of radiation-associated pathologies."[9]

Greenpeace has touched off yet another controversy over the possibility that residual radioactivity might still plague Amchitka's environment, including adjacent coastal waters. Greenpeace members, whose initial protest demonstrations in 1971 failed to reach Amchitka, returned in the summer of 1996 in order to conduct their own investigation of radioactive contamination. For six days, Greenpeace scientists collected and packaged plant, soil, and water samples for later laboratory analysis. Contrary to the AEC's earlier pronouncements, the revelations made by Greenpeace were considerably less cheerful. Its findings revealed traces of plutonium 239, plutonium 240, and a plutonium by-product, americium 241, in moss and algae specimens. Long-lived and highly toxic, these residue isotopes pose a continuing danger to food chains. Greenpeace researchers were especially alarmed by the presence of americium 241 in White Alice Creek, a fast-flowing stream that exits into the Bering Sea. The culprit, these scientists believe, is the blast chamber, which continues to leak contaminants.[10]

The Greenpeace report was sufficiently alarming to catch the attention of federal agencies. Since that time, officials of both the Department of Energy and the Environmental Protection Agency have met with Greenpeace representatives to discuss the organization's findings. Energy Undersecretary Thomas P. Grumbly has admitted that should the Greenpeace research prove correct, "It would have implications for [monitoring and sampling] at other test sites." Starting in the summer of 1997, a survey team headed by Douglas H. Dasher of the Alaska Department of Environmental Conservation attempted to corroborate Greenpeace discoveries. Simultaneously, this federally financed investigation hoped to expand the existing toxic monitoring of Amchitka. Thus, the possibility that Cannikin might wreak its havoc on Amchitka for years to come continues to haunt Alaskans and federal officials alike down to the present day.[11]

Despite these known and suspected ravages, was it possible for Amchitka to reclaim its status as a nature preserve? Fortunately, the will of those committed to this objective seems commensurate to the demands of the task. The process of returning Amchitka to its rightful place within the Refuge began with an Interior Department needs assessment. The inventory of nuclear test-related damage made by the Interior Department at that time was impressive, if not entirely discouraging. It found numerous terrain scars, deep ruts created by tracked and off-road vehicles; areas of liquefied soil slides; spoil, borrow, gravel, and rock quarry pits; drilling fluids in dike ponds; and sewage lagoons filled with effluent. Even before Cannikin, Refuge workers had catalogued over five hundred acres that needed contouring and seeding. The landscape was also marred by clutters of instrumentation cables on the ground and tangles of wires strung overhead, temporary camp structures, assorted debris, piles of trash, construction pads, and petroleum farms containing both exposed and buried tanks. Metal scrap was scattered far and wide. Five ugly antenna clusters littered the horizon. During the summer of 1971, AEC officials, working with the Institute of Agricultural Sciences of the University of Alaska, Fairbanks, plotted their counterattack against this array of man-made intrusions. Cleanup operations were to begin in early July 1972. They would last eighteen months, employ 225 workers, and cost $13 million.[12]

The AEC contributed to the restoration of Amchitka in other ways as well. In its process of "demobilization," the AEC not only removed agency personnel, but it also dismantled the testing infrastructure, sealing drill holes, disposing of contaminated materials, and monitoring the environment for possible hazards associated with the three nuclear tests. Usable equipment was transferred to the Air Force for deployment elsewhere. As a sign of its concern for the long-term health of Amchitka, the AEC sponsored a Sea Otter Studies Advisory Panel and agreed to fund the cost of maintaining one Interior Department official on the island to ensure that its withdrawal procedures were environmentally responsible.[13]

The process of rolling up and clearing out began in late February 1972, when post-shot radiochemical drilling had been completed. During the following summer, seismic stations were removed from the island, all thirty-four drill holes were sealed, and shipments of disassembled facilities were begun. About four hundred structures left over from World War II were eventually burned. The following summer, recontouring, reseeding, camp demobilization, and cleanup took place. Having completed its "evacuation" of Amchitka, the AEC officially "relinquished" the island to the Interior Department on September 8, 1973, with the proviso that future "excavation, drilling . . . or removal of materials" from areas adjacent to the three test sites be prohibited. In addition to unofficial reminders of Amchitka's military history, such as a dump of rusting metal, the AEC left behind three brass plaques set in concrete to mark the locations of the Long Shot, Milrow, and Cannikin tests, to describe the island's nuclear test history, and to warn auditors of dangers associated with disturbing the sites.[14]

Amchitka's emergence as a fully restored part of the Refuge dates from 1974, when Christian A. Herter, Jr., United States State Department special assistant for environmental affairs, announced that the island had been designated a "biosphere reserve." As such, Amchitka became part of UNESCO's "man and the biosphere" program designed to encourage international research into and preservation of plants and animals deemed to have unique importance. Another sign of Amchitka's rehabilitated status came in 1976 when it, along with the other parts of the Refuge—a combined total of 1,000,940 acres—was placed in the Alaska Maritime National Wildlife Refuge system.[15]

Amchitka's recent history demonstrates the delicate balances that are inherent in any mixed-use facility. The Fish and Wildlife Service continues to experiment with methods of enhancing the stocks of endangered species, such as a program designed to increase the population of migratory geese.[16] In the meantime, the Defense Department environmental restoration program continues to clean up World War II debris, including unexploded ordnance. This phase of the cleanup program began in 1986 and cost an estimated $6,726,000. As late as 1991, the Navy was still burning napalm bombs that had been stored on Amchitka in addition to numerous explosive boosters, fuses, blasting caps, and detonators. Even so, the work remains uncompleted. The Navy still considers Amchitka's east end to be very dangerous.[17]

Amchitka's restoration as a wilderness preserve notwithstanding, the Defense Department still regards the island as militarily useful. In May 1987, Navy Seabees, along with civilian workers, landed on Amchitka to begin construction on support facilities associated with a Relocatable-Over-the-Horizon Radar system (ROTHR). Built by the Raytheon Corporation, ROTHR was designed to snoop on Soviet bomber and surface ship movements in the North Pacific, thereby reducing the need for marine patrols. The facility consisted of two control camps located at either end of the island, a one-hundred-foot high transmitter complex situated to the northwest, and 372 pairs of 19-foot-high receiver antennae that stretched out for two miles midway up the island on the Bering Sea side. For the first time since Project Windstorm in 1951, over 250 Navy personnel and civilians, who were needed to operate this radar system, encamped on Amchitka.[18]

Although habitat requirements and military necessity were never a good fit, previous experience helped to soften the disagreements that incompatible usages often occasioned in the past. The new Navy radar facility did, in fact, negatively affect Amchitka's environment. Two hundred acres of migratory bird habitat, in the form of wet tundra and ponds, were lost. Electromagnetic pulses at the ROTHR transmitter endangered eagles and seagulls that liked to perch on tall structures. And, there was pollution. A discharge of 20,000 gallons of partially treated sewage, and an accidental spill of toxic polychlorinated biphenyl, contaminated the soil.[19]

At the same time, however, military personnel assisted Fish and Wildlife workers in carrying out Refuge goals. The Navy was often generous in sharing its supplies, facilities, transport, and other equipment with Refuge officials. Refuge headquarters were, in fact, moved from Cold Bay on the Alaska Peninsula to a more centralized position on Adak Island because the military made available its facilities there. Thus, although the managers of the Refuge on Amchitka occasionally feel "stepped on" by military operations on the island, Amchitka continues to serve as an important wildlife preserve. Considering birds alone, it is home to sizeable populations of Eurasian green-winged teal, peregrine falcons, and rock ptarmigan, as well as the largest dabbling duck and tern flocks in the Aleutians.[20] In the postwar period, Amchitka has come to represent what is still possible in the real world where ideals are constantly challenged by presumptions of necessity.

For more than a generation following World War II, Amchitka became a pawn in the chess game of Cold War politics. In addition to demonstrating the feasibility of a new generation of weapons, the nuclear tests held on Amchitka provided United States presidents, and especially Richard Nixon, with negotiating cannon to force the Soviets into an acceptance of a satisfactory arms limitation agreement. Nixon's strategy was to trump Soviet ABM development with an equivalent United States program, thereby paving the way to what he hoped would be a satisfactory arms reduction treaty. Like his predecessor, Lyndon Johnson, Nixon was fond of comparing diplomacy to poker. The number and power of one's chips was the key to success. "I need," he once said, "to have the most bargaining chips from the outset . . . to get the best deal." Thus, he insisted that "Congress must not send me to the negotiating table as the head of the second strongest nation in the world." After three hard years of difficult negotiation, Nixon realized this ambition: he and First Secretary of the Soviet Communist Party Leonid I. Brezhnev signed the Strategic Arms Limitation Treaty (SALT I) in Moscow on May 26, 1972. This interim agreement set limits on future missile deployment and restricted each side to the operation of only two ABM sites. A subsequent accord negotiated two years later reduced this number to one each.[21]

The relative value of the SALT agreements has been endlessly debated. The ultimate goal of these agreements, to maintain the peace by assuring that in any future conflict the United States and the U.S.S.R. possessed the unquestioned ability to destroy each other, provided cold comfort for the American public. The process by which these agreements were brought into being is equally controversial. Some, like A E C Chairman Glenn Seaborg, believed that the United States had conceded too much based upon faulty estimates of Soviet A B M development. Retrospective judgments contend that the A B M was never as crucial to national defense as its proponents had hoped. After constructing one A B M site near Grand Forks, North Dakota, in 1974, at an estimated cost in excess of $7 billion, the site was abandoned only two years later "largely because it was considered ineffective." Spartan missiles, the designated vehicle of the A B M, were subsequently stored in Army depots and later dismantled. Production of the W-71 warhead, which was tested in the Cannikin blast, suffered a similar fate. A total of about thirty W-71 warheads had been assembled by mid-1975, when production was halted. These warheads were deactivated soon thereafter and placed in storage where, to all accounts, they remain. Chairman Seaborg is perhaps as entitled as anyone to deliver the A B M's obituary. "The huge effort that went into their development and testing," he later observed, "can stand as a monument to the futility and wastefulness of the nuclear arms race."[22]

When the last chapter of the Cold War is finally written, the history of Amchitka Island during that time might provide an interesting and illuminating footnote. As is so often the case during times of stress, treasured national values become the victims of unpleasant necessity. Given the level of insecurity that existed in America following World War II, it is hard to imagine that the struggle between environmentalists and national security advocates over the use of Amchitka might have had a different outcome. Yet, the lessons of Amchitka are not confined either to regret or wishful thinking. The current status of the island testifies to the importance of learning from experience. Amchitka can continue to exist both as a military outpost and a nature preserve, as difficult as that combination of purposes might be, if all interested parties bring to the recurring conflicts that must arise a combination of patience, good will, and above all, a desire to accommodate. But, for now, Amchitka Island, not ecologically remote and never a wasteland in an interconnected Earth, holds the sad and unfortunate distinction of being the only nuclear graveyard in a national wildlife refuge.

NOTES

Epigraph from *Alaska Geographic* 7, No. 3 (1980): 223. Hudson, an author and poet, was a long-time resident in the Aleutians.

1. Knut Bergsland and Moses L. Dirks, eds., *Unangam Uniikangis ama Tunuzangis: Aleut Tales and Narratives* (Fairbanks: University of Alaska Native Language Center, 1990), 2; *Academic American Encyclopedia*, 1991 ed., s.v. "Alaska," by Donald F. Lynch; *World Book Encyclopedia*, 1989 ed., s.v. "Alaska," by F. Patrick Fitzgerald and Claus-M. Naske.

2. The Aleutians were once called Katerina Archipelago after Catherine the Great and have appeared on maps as the *Aleoutiennes, Aleotskia,* Fox Islands, and Billy Mitchell Islands. *Alaska Geographic* 7 (1980): 206, 210, 213–14, 216–18, 220–21.

3. Lydia T. Black, "Eskimo Motifs in Aleut Art and Folklore," *Etudes/Inuit/Studies* 7 (1983): 12, 13; "The Chuginadak Woman," Waldemar Jochelson, comp., Knut Bergsland, ed., *Unangam Ungiikangin: Aleut Traditions* (Fairbanks: University of Alaska Native Language Center, 1977), 17–50; Bergsland and Dirks, *Aleut Tales,* 107 n.a. 115, 165, 167, 191, 193, 221, 229, 231.

4. Anatolii Kamenski, *Tlingit Indians of Alaska,* trans. Sergei Kan (Fairbanks: University of Alaska Press, 1985), 62, 64–65; "Story of the Eagle," printed on a banner in possession of author; Margaret Murie, *Island Between* (Fairbanks: University of Alaska Press, 1977), 1; Emily Ivanoff Brown, *Tales of Ticasuk: Eskimo Legends & Stories* (Fairbanks: University of Alaska Press, 1987), 49–50, 111.

5. Felix Riesenberg, *The Pacific Ocean* (New York: McGraw-Hill, 1940), 3; Frederica M. Bunge and Melinda W. Cooke, eds., *Oceania, a Regional Study,* 2d ed. (U.S. Army, 1984), 3.

6. Department of the Interior, *Tectonic Setting of Amchitka Island, Alaska,* R. Ernest Anderson, preliminary draft, U.S. Geological Survey, 474–75 (Denver: U.S.

Geological Survey), 1970, 8–9; Carl H. Lindroth, "The Aleutian Islands As a Route for Dispersal across the North Pacific," J. Linsley Gressitt, ed., *Pacific Basin Biogeography* (Honolulu: Bishop Museum Press, 1963), 121–31; Donald W. Hood and Steven T. Zimmerman, eds., *The Gulf of Alaska: Physical Environment and Biological Resources* (Washington, D.C.: U.S. Department of Commerce, 1986), 8–9.

7. William S. Laughlin, *Aleuts: Survivors of the Bering Land Bridge* (New York: Holt, Rinehart and Winston, 1980), 20–21; John Muir, *The Cruise of the Corwin: Journal of the Arctic Expedition of 1881 in Search of DeLong and the Jeannette,* ed. William Frederic Bade (Boston: Houghton Mifflin Company, 1917), 8–9; Henry W. Elliott, *Our Arctic Province: Alaska and the Seal Islands* (New York: Charles Scribner's Sons, 1887); John Bockstoce, *Arctic Passages: A Unique Small Boat Journey through the Great Northern Waterway* (New York: Hearst Marine Books, 1991), 173; Olaus J. Murie, *Fauna of the Aleutian Islands and Alaska Peninsula* (Washington, D.C.: U.S. Fish and Wildlife Service, 1959), 17, 365, 387.

8. William S. Laughlin, "The Earliest Aleuts," *Anthropological Papers of the University of Alaska* 10 (April 1963): 73, 76–77; Allen P. McCartney, "Prehistory of the Aleutian Region," David Damas, ed., *Arctic,* vol. 5, *Handbook of North American Indians* (Washington, D.C.: Smithsonian Institution Press, 1984), 119–35.

9. Marvin W. Falk, "Images of Pre-Discovery Alaska in the Work of European Cartographers," *Arctic* (December 1984): 562–73; Hubert H. Bancroft, *History of Alaska, 1730–1885,* The Works of Hubert Howe Bancroft, vol. 33 (San Francisco: A. L. Bancroft & Company, Publishers, 1886), 102; Don E. Dumond, *The Eskimos and Aleuts,* rev. ed. (London: Thames and Hudson Ltd., 1987), 70. For studies sponsored by the United States Atomic Energy Commission, see Melvin L. Merritt and R. Glen Fuller, eds., *The Environment of Amchitka Island, Alaska* (Oak Ridge, Tennessee: Energy Research and Development Administration, 1977).

10. *Alaska Geographic* 7 (1980): 18; Bancroft calls the Aleutians "quaking islands," Bancroft, *History of Alaska,* 3; Raymond A. Brechbill, "Status of the Norway Rat," Merritt and Fuller, *Environment of Amchitka,* 261.

11. James R. Masterson and Helen Brower, *Bering's Successor, 1745–1780* (Seattle: University of Washington Press, 1948), 18, 35; Donald J. Orth, *Dictionary of Alaska Place Names,* Geological Survey Professional Paper no. 567 (Washington, D.C.: U.S. Department of the Interior, 1967; rev., repr., 1971), 70; *Alaska Geographic* 7 (1980): 210. Amchitka's recorded size varies. These are my estimates based on U.S. Geological Survey maps. Amchitka lies between 51 degrees 22' and 51 degrees 44' north latitude; 178 degrees 45' and 179 degrees 30' east longitude. Its highest point is 1,008 feet in elevation, and the island covers 113,790 acres. These statistics are in National Archives, Washington, D.C., Record Group 22, Fish and Wildlife Service, Wildlife

Refuges, General Information, file Aleutian Islands 1920–37, box 1, (hereinafter cited as RG 22 FWS).

12. McCartney, "Prehistory," 132, and "Prehistoric Human Occupation of the Rat Islands," Merritt and Fuller, *Environment of Amchitka,* 75; Ron Kent, comp., *Synopsis of 1985 BIA ANCSA 14(H)(1) Field Investigations on Amchitka Island,* 1 (Anchorage: Bureau of Indian Affairs, 1986), ii; Roger J. Desautels et al., *Archaeological Report: Amchitka Island, Alaska, 1969–1970* (Archaeological Research, Inc., 1970), 1, 351; Lydia T. Black, *Atka: An Ethnohistory of the Western Aleutians,* ed. R. A. Pierce (Kingston, Ontario: The Limestone Press, 1984), 27–40. For recent essays on the anthropology of the area, see William W. Fitzhugh and Valerie Chaussonnett, eds., *Anthropology of the North Pacific Rim* (Washington, D.C.: Smithsonian Institution Press, 1994).

13. Black, *Atka,* 52, 53, 83; Masterson and Brower, *Successors,* 75; Raisa V. Makarova, *Russians on the Pacific, 1743–1799,* trans. and ed. Richard A. Pierce and Alton S. Donnelly (Kingston, Ontario: The Limestone Press, 1975), 61, 72–73.

14. Makarova, *Russians on the Pacific,* 77–78, 117; Black, *Atka,* 82, 103–04.

15. Margaret Lantis, "The Aleut Social System, 1750 to 1810, from Early Historical Sources," Margaret Lantis, ed., *Ethnohistory in Southwestern Alaska and the Southern Yukon: Method and Context* (Lexington: University Press of Kentucky, 1970); Kiril T. Khlebnikov, *Notes on Russian America: Parts II–V: Kad'iak, Unalashka, Atkha, The Pribylovs,* comp. R. G. Liapunova and S. G. Federova, trans. Marina Ramsay, ed. Richard Pierce (Kingston, Ontario and Fairbanks, Alaska: Limestone Press, 1944), 212; Black, *Atka,* 96, 104, 158–59.

16. Khlebnikov, *Notes on Russian America,* 250–52; William H. Dall, "On Succession in the Shell-Heaps of the Aleutian Islands," *Contributions to North American Ethnology* 1 (1877): 44; Black, *Atka,* 105, 192.

17. Henry W. Elliott, "The Loot and the Ruin of the Fur-Seal Herd of Alaska", *North American Review* 185 (June 7, 1907): 426–36; Nigel Bonner, *Seals and Sea Lions of the World* (New York: Facts on File, Inc., 1994), 183–84; Trefethen, *An American Crusade for Wildlife* (New York: Winchester Press and The Boone and Crockett Club, 1975), 326–37; "Convention between the United States and other Powers Providing for the Preservation and Protection of Fur Seals," *Statutes At Large* 37, pt. 2, 1542 (1911); *Pacific Historical Review* 4 (1935): 1–14.

18. "An Act to Give Effect to the Convention between the Governments of the United States, Great Britain, Japan, and Russia for the Preservation and Protection of the Fur Seals and Sea Otter Which Frequent the Waters of the North Pacific Ocean, Concluded at Washington July Seventh, Nineteen Hundred and Eleven," *Statutes at Large* 37, pt. 1, 373 (1912); Kurt Dorsey, "Putting a Ceiling on Sealing: Con-

servation and Cooperation in the International Arena, 1909–1911," *Environmental History Review* 15 (Fall 1991): 27–30, 43–44; Trefethen, *Crusade,* 334–35; Karl W. Kenyon, "The Sea Otter," *Smithsonian Institution Annual Report 1958:* 399–407; Calvin J. Lensick, "The History and Status of Sea Otters in Alaska" (Ph.D. diss., Purdue University, 1962), 55–67. See also Ted C. Hinckley, "Alaska and the Emergence of America's Conservation Consciousness," *Prairie Scout* 2 (1974): 79–111.

19. Besides Executive Order no. 1733 creating the Aleutian Island Reservation, others were established as follows: Bering Sea Reservation (1037), Bogoslof Reservation (1049), Chamisso Island Reservation (1658), Fire Island Reservation (1038), Forrester Island Reservation (1458), Hazy Island Reservation (1459), Pribilof Reservation (1044), St. Lazaria Reservation (1040), Tuxedni Reservation (1039), and Yukon Delta Reservation (1041). See Clifford L. Lord, ed., *Presidential Executive Orders, Numbered 1–8030, 1862–1938,* vol. 1, *The List;* and vol. 2, *The Index* (New York: Hastings House, Publishers, 1944), 6. See Trefethen, *Crusade,* 129–378; Oliver H. Orr, Jr., *Saving America's Birds* (Gainesville: University of Florida Press, 1992), 190–91; and Robert P. Allen, "The Wild-Life Sanctuary Movement in the United States," *Bird Lore* 36 (February, 1934): 80–84.

20. Executive Order 1669, December 19, 1912. See Lord, *The List,* 144.

21. Executive Orders 2242, 4020, 4021, 5243, 5318. See Lord, *The List,* and Presidential Proclamation 2416.

22. Corey Ford, *Where the Sea Breaks Its Back: The Epic Story of a Pioneer Naturalist and the Discovery of Alaska* (Boston: Little, Brown and Company, 1966), 198–99; Frank Dufresne, *Alaska's Animals & Fishes* (New York: A. S. Barnes and Company, 1946) xv–xvi, and *My Way Was North* (New York: Holt, Rinehart and Winston, 1966), 247–49. Also, Olaus J. Murie, "Aleutian Report, 1937," 45, Alaska and Polar Regions Archives, Rasmusen Library, University of Alaska Fairbanks, Olaus J. Murie Papers, file 68, box 3 (hereinafter cited as UA Fairbanks); Karl W. Kenyon, *The Sea Otter in the Eastern Pacific Ocean,* North American Fauna, no. 68 (Washington, D.C.: Bureau of Sport Fisheries and Wildlife, 1969), 1; Spencer, "Refuge," 49; Carnahan, "Fox Farming," 88.

23. There had been, of course, previous scientific exploration in the area. See Kurt Dunbar and Chris Friday, "Salmon, Seals, and Science: The *Albatross* and Conservation in Alaska, 1888–1914," *Journal of the West* 33 (October 1994): 6–13; "Report of Examination," June 15, 1936 to Nov. 5, 1936, Wildlife Refuges, RG 22 FWS; Spencer, "Refuge," 68–69; Olaus Murie, *Fauna;* Eric Hulten, *Flora of the Aleutian Islands and Westernmost Alaska Peninsula with Notes on the Flora of Commander Islands* (Stockholm: Bokforlags Aktibalaget Thule, 1937); Isabel Wylie Hutchinson, "Riddle of the Aleutians," *National Geographic* 82 (December 1941): 769, 783.

Epigraph from Jerah Chadwick, *Absence Wild: Aleutian Poems* (Seattle: Jugum, 1984), 3. Chadwick is a teacher and poet who lives at Unalaska.

1. H. P. Willmott, *The Barrier and the Javelin: Japanese and Allied Pacific Strategies, February to June 1942* (Annapolis: Naval Institute Press, 1983), 319. Standard accounts of the Aleutian Campaign are found in official histories. See Stetson Conn, Rose C. Engelman, and Byron Fairchild, *Guarding the United States and Its Outposts,* United States Army in World War II: The Western Hemisphere (Washington, D.C.: Department of the Army, 1964); Wesley F. Craven and James L. Cate, eds., *The Pacific: Guadalcanal to Saipan, August 1942 to July 1944,* The Army Air Forces in World War II, vol. 4 (Chicago: University of Chicago Press, 1950); Samuel Eliot Morison, *Aleutians, Gilberts and Marshalls, June 1942–April 1944,* History of United States Naval Operations In World War II, vol. 7 (Boston: Little, Brown and Company, 1961). For a popular history, see Brian Garfield, *The Thousand-Mile War: World War II in Alaska and the Aleutians* (New York: Doubleday, 1969).

2. Elmer B. Potter and Chester W. Nimitz, eds., *Sea Power: a Naval History* (Englewood Cliffs, N.J.: Prentice-Hall, 1960), 731; Morison, *Aleutians, Gilberts and Marshalls,* 3; Garfield, *Thousand-Mile War,* 200–201, 266–67; United States Strategic Bombing Survey (Pacific), *The Campaigns of the Pacific War* (New York: Greenwood Press, 1946), 83–86.

3. An excellent summary of this dimension is in Fern Channdonnet, ed., *Alaska at War, 1941–1945: The Forgotten War Remembered* (Anchorage: Alaska at War Committee, 1995). The Aleut experience is recorded in Dean Kohlhoff, *When the Wind Was a River: Aleut Evacuation in World War II* (Seattle and London: University of Washington Press, 1995). For an account of the war's effect on Alaska, see Naske and Slotnik, *History of the 49th State,* 131–33, 140, 279–80, and Jonathan M. Nielson, *Armed Forces on a Northern Frontier: The Military in Alaska's History, 1867–1987* (New York: Greenwood Press, 1988), 179–81.

4. Garfield, *Thousand-Mile War,* 195; Colonel James D. Bush, Jr., audiotape of interview by John Haile Cloe, 4 May, 1982 (University of Alaska Fairbanks, Oral History Program), tape H84. Estimates of troop strength are found in Conn, Engelman, and Fairchild, *Guarding Outposts,* 282, 295–96. Figures of base occupation are derived from "Approximate Army and Navy Personnel in Alaska-October 1, 1943," *U.S. Navy Command History* (excerpts), Alaska and Polar Regions Archives, Rasmusen Library, University of Alaska Fairbanks (hereinafter cited as UAF Archives), microfilm 32.

5. "History of Camp Earle, Attu, January 1943 thru June 1944," p. 41, National

Archives Modern Military Branch, Suitland, Maryland, Record Group 338, Records of the Alaska Defense Command (hereinafter cited as RG 338 AK Command), Alaskan Department Historical Reports 1941–47, box E-G. For Aleutian Island military construction, see U.S. Army Corps of Engineers, *Aleutian Islands and Lower Alaska Peninsula Debris Removal and Cleanup: Draft Environmental Impact Statement* (Anchorage: U.S. Army Corps of Engineers, Alaska District, 1979), ii. Benjamin B. Talley, *Building Alaska's Defenses of World War II* (Anchorage: Cook Inlet Historical Society, 1969), 12.

6. For Army construction projects, see James D. Bush, Jr., *Narrative Report of Alaska Construction, 1941–1944* (Anchorage: U.S. Army Corps of Engineers, Alaska District, 1944); *Draft Environmental Statement*, 64–65, 125. Dump sites are vividly pictured in the film *Alaska At War,* produced and directed by Lawrence Goldin, 55 min., Alaska Historical Commission, 1987, videocassette.

7. Allan Merritt, "Aleutian Engineers," *Alaska Life*, December 1943, 17; LeRoy W. Page, "The Navy's Victory Builders," *Alaska Life*, June 1944, 6; L. D. Kitchener, "The Fighting 'Earth Movers'," *Alaska Life*, July 1944, 5, 8; Joseph D. Bodman, "Peculiarities of Aleutian Military Design," *Civil Engineering* 15 (September 1945): 403–04; Testimony, Philemon Tutiakoff, Sept. 17, 1981, Unalaska, Hearings of the Commission on Wartime Relocation and Internment of Civilians, National Archives Microfilm Publication, M 1293, vol. 6, frame 626.

8. Film, *Alaska At War;* U.S. Army, *Official History of the Alaskan Department, June 1940–June 1944* (Washington, D.C.: Office of the Chief of Military History, n.d.), n.p; Morison, *Aleutians, Gilberts and Marshalls,* 46, 55–56, 61.

9. Gaston Shumate, "On Tanaga Volcano," *Alaska Sportsman,* July 1946, 17; Morgan Sherwood, *Big Game in Alaska: A History of Wildlife and People* (New Haven: Yale University Press, 1981), 1–3, 126–37; Major General S. B. Buckner, Jr., to Frank Dufresne, Nov. 21, 1941, and Acting Secretary Abe Fortas to Henry L. Stimson, Oct. 15, 1943; RG 22 FWS, Bureau of Biological Survey, General Correspondence 1890–1956, file Ag-L legislation, box 1, and file Alaska Game Law Regulations, box 3; Commandant 13th Naval District to Commander, Alaska Sector, Dec. 14, 1942, National Archives, Northwest Branch, Seattle, Record Group 181, Records of Naval Districts and Shore Establishments, Regular Navy Files, file EG-3/As-F, box 145. (These records have been transferred to the National Archives—Alaska Region, Anchorage). Memorandum, Governor Ernest Gruening for the Secretary, Dec. 6, 1943, Bartlett Papers, Personal File General 1943, box 12, UA Fairbanks.

10. Captain Ralph C. Parker to Commanding General, Feb. 20, 1942, Official Correspondence of Maj. Gen. Simon B. Buckner, Jr., 1941–44, RG 338 AK Command, box 3; Samuel Eliot Morison, *Coral Sea, Midway and Submarine Actions, May 1942–Au-*

gust 1942, History of the United States Naval Operations In World War II, vol. 4 (Boston: Little, Brown and Company, 1961), 215.

11. Olaus J. Murie, "Report on the Aleutians for the Army, October 1942," file 62, box 9, UAF Archives; Walter Karig and Eric Purdon, *Battle Report: Pacific War: Middle Phase* (New York: Rinehart and Company, Inc., 1947), 297–98; Conn, Engelman, and Fairchild, *Guarding Outposts,* 275.

12. Garfield, *Thousand-Mile War,* 158; Forrest C. Pogue, *George C. Marshall: Organizer of Victory, 1943–1945* (New York: The Viking Press, 1973), 154–55; Morison, *Aleutians, Gilberts and Marshalls,* 17–18.

13. U.S. Army Corps of Engineers, Alaska District, *World War II in Alaska: A History and Resources Management Plan, Final Report,* 1 (Anchorage: Envirosphere Company, 1987), sec. 5–24; Morison, *Aleutians, Gilberts and Marshalls,* 18; Garfield, *Thousand-Mile War,* 171; United States Army, Alaska, "Building Alaska with the U.S. Army, 1867–1962" (pamphlet), Aug. 10, 1962, p. 90; Conn, Engelman, and Fairchild, *Guarding Outposts,* 276.

14. Garfield, *Aleutians, Gilberts and Marshalls,* 171–72; Karig and Purdon, *Battle Report,* 299.

15. Karig and Purdon, *Battle Report.*

16. Ibid., 300; *U.S. Navy Command History,* "Approximate Army and Navy Personnel in Alaska," Appendix A, microfilm 32, UA Fairbanks.

17. Garfield, *Thousand-Mile War,* 172; Murray Morgan, *Bridge to Russia: Those Amazing Aleutians* (New York: E. P. Dutton, 1947), 157; Karig and Purdon, *Battle Report.*

18. Karl C. Dod, *The Corps of Engineers: The War Against Japan,* United States Army in World War II: The Technical Services (Washington, D.C.: Department of the Army, 1966), 289; James D. Bush, Jr., *Narrative Report,* 193, 195; Harold W. Richardson, "Alaska and the Aleutians," in Waldo G. Bowman et al., *Bulldozers Come First: The Story of U.S. War Construction in Foreign Lands* (New York: McGraw Hill, 1944), 96.

19. Richardson, "Alaska and the Aleutians"; Bush, *Narrative Report,* 194. For engineering unit personnel numbers, see Dod, Corps of Engineers, Appendix B., 685–86.

20. Bush, *Narrative Report,* 194–95; Merritt, "Aleutian Engineers," 19.

21. Bush, *Narrative Report,* 193; Merritt, "Aleutian Engineers."

22. Merritt, "Aleutian Engineers." My estimate of road mileage is based on the end-pocket map found in Merritt and Fuller, *Environment of Amchitka;* Richardson, "Alaska and the Aleutians," 99–100.

23. Bush, *Narrative Report,* 195–96, 252–53.

24. Ibid., 196, 253, 383.

25. Ibid., 254.

26. Ibid., 196, 254.

27. Ibid., 194, 196; U.S. Army Corps of Engineers, "Resources Management Plan," sec. 5–24, 25; U.S. Navy Command History, "Approximate Personnel in Alaska," UA Fairbanks; Richardson, "Alaska and the Aleutians," 103; "Historical Reports 1941–47," RG 338 AK Command, Suitland, box Fort Randall; Merritt and Fuller, *Environment of Amchitka*, 128–29.

28. "Resources Management Plan," sec. 5–25, 26; *Debris Removal and Cleanup Study, Aleutian Islands and Lower Alaska Peninsula, Alaska* (Anchorage: Alaska District, Corps of Engineers, 1976), 116, map; Merritt and Fuller, *Environment of Amchitka*, 128.

29. *Act for the Preservation of American Antiquities, Statutes at Large*, 34, pt. 1, 3060 (1906); Shumate, "Tanaga Volcano," 17–18; Garfield, *Thousand-Mile War*, 196; Paul Guggenheim, "An Anthropological Campaign on Amchitka," *Scientific Monthly* 61 (July 1945): 21–32; Kohlhoff, *When the Wind Was a River*, 148–49, 157–64.

30. Bush, audiotape interview; Merritt and Fuller, *Environment of Amchitka*, 128; Guggenheim, "Anthropological Campaign," 21, 27, 32.

31. Guggenheim, "Anthropological Campaign," 24, 27–28, 32.

32. Ibid., 27–28; Merritt and Fuller, *Environment of Amchitka*, 128.

33. Guggenheim, "Anthropological Campaign," 21; Garfield, *Thousand-Mile War*, 196; Merritt and Fuller, *Environment of Amchitka*, v.

34. Amchitka had its share of ills, such as gambling, accidents, murder, and suicide. See Donald M. Goldstein and Katherine V. Dillon, *The Williwaw War: The Arkansas National Guard in the Aleutians in World War II* (Fayetteville: University of Arkansas Press, 1992), 259–60; *Newsweek* 26, Nov. 1945, 63; Gore Vidal, *Williwaw* (New York: E. P. Dutton, 1946), 77; Charles A. Spears, U.S. Navy Memoirs, WWII Miscellaneous Collection, War College, Carlisle Barracks, Pennsylvania; Garfield, *Thousand-Mile War*, 138, 194; Richard Rhodes, *The Making of the Atomic Bomb* (New York: Simon and Schuster, 1986), 586; Osowski interview, transcript of interviews for "Alaska At War" film, p. 5, University of Alaska Anchorage Archives (hereinafter cited as UA Anchorage).

35. *Yank*, 3 Dec. 1943, 11; and 30 Mar. 1945, 11; *Alaska Life*, Dec. 1945, 37.

36. For Aleutian wartime poems, see Courtland W. Matthews, *Aleutian Interval* (Seattle: F. McCaffrey, 1949), and Robert B. Whitebrook, *Aleutian Years* (Palo Alto, California: Pacific Books, 1959); Charles C. Bradley, *Aleutian Echoes* (Fairbanks: University of Alaska Press, 1994), 74.

37. Lonnelle Davison, "Bizarre Battleground—the Lonely Aleutians," *National*

Geographic 82 (September 1942): 316; *Life,* 13 Mar. 1945, 71; Darryl F. Zanuck and John Houston, *Report from the Aleutians,* film produced in Washington, D.C. for the War Department, 1943; U.S. Navy Command History, "Approximate Personnel in Alaska," UA Fairbanks.

38. Buckner to Gruening, Sept. 24, 1943, Alaska State Archives, Juneau, Record Group 01, Papers of the Territorial Governors (hereinafter cited as RG 01 Juneau), series 130, box 573; Buckner to Dufresne, Apr. 1, 1944, RG 22 FWS, Bureau of Biological Survey, General Correspondence 1890–1956, file Alaska Game Law Regulations, box 3.

39. Dufresne to Buckner, Apr. 11, 1944, RG 22 FWS, Bureau of Biological Survey, General Correspondence 1890–1956, file Alaska Game Law Regulations, box 3.

3 / BEFORE A MIGHTY WINDSTORM

Epigraph from "Presentiments" in Bergsland and Dirks, *Aleut Tales,* 209.

1. Mark Selden, "Introduction: The United States, Japan, and the Atomic Bomb," in Kyoko Selden and Mark Selden, eds., *The Atomic Bomb: Voices from Hiroshima and Nagasaki* (Armonk, New York: M. E. Sharpe, 1989), xii–xvi; John W. Huston, "The Impact of Strategic Bombing in the Pacific," *Journal of American-East Asian Relations* 4 (Summer 1995): 171.

2. See The Committee For the Compilation of Materials on Damage Caused by the Atomic Bombs in Hiroshima and Nagasaki, *Hiroshima and Nagasaki: The Physical, Medical, and Social Effects of the Atomic Bombings* (New York: Basic Books, 1981). The detonation over Hiroshima "had an energy yield equivalent to that of 15,000 tons of TNT," while the one over Nagasaki yielded 21,000 tons. Department of Energy, *United States Nuclear Tests, July 1945 through September 1992,* "United States Nuclear Tests—by Date," DOE/NV-209 (Rev. 14), December 1994 (Washington, D.C.: U.S. Government Printing Office, 1995), 1; Selden, "Introduction," xviii, xxii.

3. Truman wrote: "It is a harnessing of the basic power of the universe. The force from which the sun draws its power has been loosed against those who brought war to the Far East." See U.S. President, *Public Papers of the Presidents of the United States* (Washington, D.C.: Office of the Federal Register, National Archives and Records Service, 1961), Harry S. Truman, 1945, 197. Association of the bomb with the actual Holocaust is discussed in John Whittier Treat, *Writing Ground Zero: Japanese Literature and the Atomic Bomb* (Chicago & London: University of Chicago Press, 1995). For a popular view of the ultimate nuclear weapons threat see Jonathan Schell, *The Fate of the Earth* (New York: Alfred A. Knopf, 1982).

4. Richard G. Hewlett and Oscar E. Anderson, Jr., *The New World, 1939/1946,* A

History of the United States Atomic Energy Commission, vol. 1 (University Park: Pennsylvania State University Press, 1962), 436.

5. Jonathan M. Weisgall, *Operation Crossroads: The Atomic Tests at Bikini Atoll* (Annapolis, Maryland: Naval Institute Press, 1994), x–xi, 32, 328; see also *U.S. Nuclear Tests,* i and viii; William A. Shurcliff, *Bombs at Bikini: The Official Report of Operation Crossroads* (New York: Wm. H. Wise & Co., Inc., 1947), 159; Weisgall, *Operation Crossroads,* ix, 3, 227.

6. Ferenc Morton Szasz, *The Day the Sun Rose Twice: The Story of the Trinity Site Nuclear Explosion, July 16, 1945* (Albuquerque: University of New Mexico Press, 1984), 28, 29, 83, 136–137, 140; Barton C. Hacker, *The Dragon's Tail: Radiation Safety in the Manhattan Project, 1941–1946* (Berkeley: University of California Press, 1987) 5, 104–05. Soviet attitudes about safety ran parallel to ours. See for example David Holloway, *Stalin and the Bomb: The Soviet Union and Atomic Energy, 1939–1956* (New Haven: Yale University Press, 1994), 194–95, 365.

7. Richard G. Hewlett and Francis Duncan, *Atomic Shield, 1947/1952,* A History of the United States Atomic Energy Commission, vol. II (University Park and London: Pennsylvania State University Press, 1969), 140, 164, 175–76; *U.S. Nuclear Tests,* i and viii; "Statement of Captain James S. Russell, USN, Test Director, Task Force Seven, at Press Conference, Headquarters, USARPAC, Fort Shafter, T. H., May 18, 1948," p. 3, National Archives, Washington, D.C., Record Group 326, Records of the United States Atomic Energy Commission, Office files of David E. Lilienthal, Subject Files 1946–1950, box 5 (hereinafter cited as RG 326 Lilienthal); Commander F. L. Ashworth to Lewis L. Strauss, Apr. 14, 1948, Herbert Hoover Presidential Library, Lewis L. Strauss Papers, Atomic Energy Commission Series, file Memoranda for the Record 1948, box 66 (hereinafter cited as Strauss Papers).

8. Paul T. Preuss to James S. Russell, Feb. 10, 1949, Department of Energy, Las Vegas, Nevada, Coordination and Information Center, document Accession number 0028600 (this collection hereinafter cited as CIC); Barton C. Hacker, *Elements of Controversy: The Atomic Energy Commission and Radiation Safety in Nuclear Weapons Testing, 1946–1974* (Berkeley: University of California Press, 1994), 40–42; PROJECT "NUTMEG," 51–54, RG 326 Lilienthal, box 9.

9. Frank Dufresne to S. B. Buckner, Jr., Apr. 11, 1944, RG 22 FWS, Bureau of Biological Survey, General Correspondence, 1890–1956, file Aslaka Game Law Regulations, box 3; Bradley, *Aleutian Echoes,* 138–39.

10. David L. Spencer, Claus-M. Naske, and John Carnahan, *National Wildlife Refuges of Alaska* (Anchorage: Arctic Environmental Information and Data Center, 1979), 59–60, 88.

11. Ibid., 60.

12. Minutes of Meeting on Proposed National Defense Land Withdrawals in and Near the Aleutian Islands, May 4, 1948; H. Douglas Gray to Chief, Division of Wildlife Refuges, Jan. 27, 1947, U.S. Department of the Interior, Fish and Wildlife Service, Aleutian Islands, microfilm, roll 2, UA Anchorage; Spencer, Naske, and Carnahan, *Wildlife Refuges of Alaska,* 89.

13. Albert M. Day to Fred W. Johnson, Oct. 17, 1946; H. Douglas Gray to The Director, Sept. 30, 1946, Aleutian Islands, microfilm, roll 2, UA Anchorage.

14. H. Douglas Gray, "Special Report on the Aleutian Islands National Wildlife Refuge to the Director Fish and Wildlife Service, Jan. 15, 1956 to Nov. 22, 1946," Aleutian Islands, microfilm, roll 2, UA Anchorage, 16; Spencer, Naske, and Carnahan, *Wildlife Refuges of Alaska,* 60, 90.

15. Robert D. Jones, Jr., "Quarterly Refuge Narrative Report, Cold Bay Game Management, 1 Jan. 1949-30 Apr. 1949," 12–13, 19, 23, 25, 30, U.S. Fish and Wildlife Service Headquarters, Anchorage, Alaska (hereinafter cited as Anchorage FWS). For his early research, see Robert D. Jones, Jr., "Present Status of the Sea Otter in Alaska," *Transactions of the Sixteenth North American Wildlife Conference, March 5, 6, and 7, 1951* (Washington, D.C.: Wildlife Management Institute, *1951*).

16. *Transactions,* 381; Jones, "Quarterly Narrative Report," *Transactions,* 23, 31; Spencer, Naske, and Carnahan, *Wildlife Refuges of Alaska,* 61; Robert D. Jones, Jr., to Frank L. Beals, May 20, 1949, and Jones to Regional Director, May 22, 1950, Records of the Aleutian Islands Refuge, Adak Island Headquarters, file Jones (hereinafter cited as FWS Adak).

17. A. Costandina Titus, *Bombs in the Backyard: Atomic Testing and American Politics* (Reno and Las Vegas: University of Nevada Press, 1986), 46; Windstorm Handbook, CIC 0128172; Hewlitt and Duncan, Atomic Shield, 28, 166.

18. CIC 0128172; James S. Lay, Jr., to the President, Oct. 27, 1950, Harry S. Truman Library, Papers of Harry S. Truman, President's Secretary's File, subject file NSC-Atomic-Atomic Test, box 20 (hereinafter cited as Truman Papers). Lay was the executive Secretary of the National Security Council.

19. CIC 0128172, and Lay to the President, Oct. 27, 1950, Truman Papers, box 20; Military Liaison Committee, Minutes of Forty-Fifth Conference, May 31, 1950; Hacker, *Elements of Controversy,* 42. National Archives, Washington, D.C., Record Group 326, Records of the United States Atomic Energy Commission, General Advisory Committee, Minutes and Reports of meetings, file AEC-MLC minutes, box 9 (hereinafter cited as RG 326 AEC).

20. Lay to the President, Oct. 27, 1950, Truman Papers, box 20.

21. Draft Minutes, Fifth Meeting of the General Advisory Committee, July 28–29, 1947, box 1, RG 326 AEC; Joint Chiefs of Staff to Chief of Naval Operations, Nov. 18,

1950, and Chief of Naval Operations to Joint Chiefs of Staff, Nov. 29, 1950, National Archives, Washington, D.C., Record Group 218, Records of the United States Joint Chiefs of Staff, Central Decimal File 1951–1953, file CCS 471.6 (9-30-49), sec. 1, box 161 (hereinafter cited as RG 218 Joint Chiefs); CIC 128172; Hacker, *Elements of Controversy*, 60–61.

22. CIC 128172; Arthur M. Piper, *Operations Windstorm and Jangle: Geologic Hydrologic, and Thermal Features of the Sites* (Portland, Oregon: United States Geological Survey, 1952), 5, 33–44.

23. Roger M. Anders, ed., *Forging the Atomic Shield: Excerpts from the Office Diary of Gordon E. Dean* (Chapel Hill: University of North Carolina Press, 1987), 85; Gordon Dean to Robert LeBaron, Dec. 21, 1950, CIC 0030391; Lay to the President, Oct. 27, 1950, Truman Papers, box 20; S. Everett Gleason to Secretary of State, Secretary of Defense, Chairman, Atomic Energy Commission, Mar. 2, 1951, CIC 0030384.

24. Draft, Executive Secretary to the President, Mar. 2, 1951, and Dean to S. Everett Gleason, Mar. 8, 1951, CIC 0030384; James S. Lay, Jr., to Secretary of State, Secretary of Defense, Chairman, Atomic Energy Commission, Mar. 3, 1951, CIC 0030383; L. W. Rogers to Colonel Carter, Mar. 28, 1951, and attached statement, National Archives, Record Group 330, Papers of the Department of Defense Secretary, Combined Policy Committee Files, 1947–1954, file Past Tests, box 8 (hereinafter cited as RG 330).

25. Chief of Naval Operations to Joint Chiefs of Staff, Mar. 20, 1951, RG 218 Joint Chiefs, sec. 2, box 161.

26. *Anchorage Daily Times*, Mar. 28, 1951, 1, 3; May 5, 1951, 1; May 23, 1951, 1; July 30, 1951, 1; *New York Times*, May 5, 1951, 2; July 31, 1951, 5.

27. Excerpts from CJTF Serial RD0010, Mar. 21, 1951, and T. G. W. Settle, Notes for AEC/Defense Department Meeting, Mar. 28, 1951, CIC 0030377.

28. Atomic Energy Commission, Minutes of Meeting 543, Mar. 29, 1951, RG 326 AEC file 1/2/51–2/23/52; Gordon Dean to Senator McMahon, Mar. 9, 1951, CIC 0130189, and Dean to Robert LeBaron, Mar. 30, 1951, CIC 0030377.

29. W. R. Sturges, Jr., Memorandum for Record, May 2, 1951, CIC 0103845; N. E. Bradbury to A. C. Graves, May 27, 1951, CIC 0126065.

30. George C. Marshall to Executive Secretary, National Security Council, May 21, 1951, Truman Papers, President's Secretary's File, file Atomic Test, Windstorm, box 202; T. G. W. Settle to Chief of Naval Operations, July 30, 1951, RG 218 Joint Chiefs, Central Decimal Files 1951–1953, file CCS 471.6 (9-30-49), sec. 3, box 161.

31. Robert D. Jones, Jr., telephone interview with author, Anchorage, Alaska, 14 June 1994; Spencer, Naske, and Carnahan, *Wildlife Refuges of Alaska*, 61; Dale E. Doty to Lay, Oct. 13, 1950, Truman Papers, President's Secretary's File, file Atomic Test, box 201.

32. Doty to Lay, Oct. 13, 1950, Truman Papers, box 201. Lay to The President, Oct. 27, 1950, Truman Papers, box 20; Spencer, Naske, and Carnahan, *Wildlife Refuges of Alaska,* 61; Department of the Interior, Bureau of Sport Fisheries and Wildlife, *The Sea Otter in the Eastern Pacific Ocean,* Karl W. Kenyon, North American Fauna no. 68 (Washington, D.C.: U.S. Department of the Interior, 1969), 288, 320.

33. Robert D. Jones, Jr., "Refuge Narrative Report, April thru August, 1960," 9, FWS Adak. In this report, Jones recounted his reaction to test activities of 1950 and 1951. Doyle C. Akers, "A Seaman's Personal History of Mobile Battalion Three, Book II: The Island . . . Amchitka," Unpublished manuscript (UA Fairbanks, 1982), 557–66.

34. Windstorm Handbook, CIC 0128172; Richard L. Miller, *Under the Cloud: The Decades of Nuclear Testing* (New York: The Free Press, 1986), 130–33; "Summary of Preliminary Jangle Results," RG 330, file Past Tests, box 8.

4 / NUCLEAR ALASKA

Epigraph Anonymous

1. *Anchorage Daily News,* March 29, 1951, 2.

2. Ibid. For Little Diomede's population figures see U.S. Census, 1950, vol. 1, *Population,* "Number of Inhabitants", table 5, pt. 50–7; Stalin had stationed troops on the peninsula should invasion of Alaska be necessary. See Holloway, *Stalin and the Bomb,* 242.

3. *Anchorage Daily News,* April 27, 1951, 1, 8. Statement of Samuel H. Sabin, General Counsel, Federal Civil Defense Administration, on S. 1244, 82nd Congress, Bartlett Papers, Federal Departments and Agencies, file Civil Defense 1945–1951, box 1.

4. Anthony Cave Brown, ed., *Dropshot: The United States Plan for War with the Soviet Union in 1957* (New York: Dial Press/James Wade, 1978), 132; Naske and Skolnick, *History of the 49th State,* 136–38; Nielson, *Armed Forces on a Northern Frontier,* 184–89. Photographs of readiness maneuvers are found in the National Archives Still Pictures Branch, Washington, D.C., U.S. Army Signal Corps photos, number 545957 "Caribou Creek", 580629 "Willow Freeze", and 610954 "Polar Siege."

5. Thomas B. Nolan to Leo H. Saarela, Jun. 20, 1950, Record Group 57, National Archives, records of the Geological Survey, Trace Elements Planning and Coordinating Office, file AEC Chronological 1947–1962, box 2; Ralph J. Rivers to William A. Egan, Apr. 25, 1963, RG 01 Juneau, file 390.l, 1961–63, box 4838; National Archives—Alaska Region, Anchorage, Record Group 77, Corps of Engineers, Alaska District History Files, circa 1971, box 2. Alaska Governor William A. Egan felt that many nuclear power plants would be built in Alaska in the coming years. He suggested that

measures be taken to assure that "design, location, and operation" of such plants would not endanger fish and wildlife. Egan to Walter Kirkness, Jan. 10, 1962, State of Alaska Archives, Juneau, Record Group 11, Department of Fish and Game, series 537, file U.S. Department of Fish and Wildlife Services 1969–1970, box 6863 (hereinafter cited as RG 11 AK Fish and Game); Dan O'Neill, *The Firecracker Boys* (New York: St. Martin's Press, 1994), 285. See also William Johnson, "Testing Nuclear Power in Alaska: The Reactor at Fort Greely" (M.A. thesis, University of Alaska Fairbanks, 1993). AEC news release, May 25, 1964, UA Fairbanks, Ralph J. Rivers Papers, Department File 1965–1966, Independent Offices: Atomic Energy Commission, box 43.

6. Edward Teller, "We're Going to Work Miracles," *Popular Mechanics,* March 1960, 97–100.

7. O'Neill, *The Firecracker Boys,* 285; "Project Chariot: How Alaska Escaped Nuclear Excavation," *Bulletin of the Atomic Scientists* (December 1989); Peter Coates, "Project Chariot: Alaskan Roots of Environmentalism," *Alaska History* 4 (fall 1989). The abandonment of Project Chariot also "stemmed from the prohibitions imposed by the 1963 partial Test Ban Treaty, which banned detonations that produce debris or fallout that could not be contained within the borders of the nations exploding the mechanism." See Richard T. Sylves, *The Nuclear Oracles: A Political History of the General Advisory Committee of the Atomic Energy Commission, 1947–1977* (Ames: Iowa State University Press, 1987), 203.

8. Holloway, *Stalin and the Bomb,* 306–7, 322–23; *United States Nuclear Tests,* 1–4; Robert LeBaron to Lewis L. Strauss, Jun. 26, 1953, Strauss papers, file LeBaron, Robert 1949–68, box 59; Anders, *Forging the Atomic Shield,* 4–5, 28–30, 286; Richard G. Hewlett and Jack M. Hall, *Atoms for Peace and War, 1953–1961: Eisenhower and the Atomic Energy Commission* (Berkeley: University of California Press, 1989), 3.

9. Samuel Glasstone and Philip J. Dolan, comp. and eds., *The Effects of Nuclear Weapons,* 3d ed. (U.S. Department of Defense and U.S. Department of Energy, 1977), 37; Hacker, *Elements of Controversy,* 148–51; Sylves, *Nuclear Oracles,* 172, 182; Anders, *Forging the Atomic Shield,* 24–25; AEC Minutes of Meeting 1062, Feb. 23, 1955, RG 326 AEC; Hewlett and Hall, *Atoms for Peace and War,* 264–69; Robert Gilpin, *American Scientists and Nuclear Weapons Policy* (Princeton, New Jersey: Princeton University Press, 1962), 140–43. For a discussion of the fear of fallout, see Allan M. Winkler, *Life under a Cloud: American Anxiety about the Atom* (New York and Oxford: Oxford University Press, 1993), 84–108.

10. AEC Minutes of Meeting 1062.

11. Congress, Joint Committee on Atomic Energy, *The Nature of Radioactive Fallout and Its Effects on Man: Hearings before the Special Subcommittee on Radiation,* 85th Cong., 1st sess., May 27, 28, 29, and June 3, 1957; Alaska Department of Fish and

Game, *Radioactivity Report,* by Leslie A. Viereck, vol. 4, Annual Project Segment Report, 405 (Juneau, 1963); Norman J. Wilinovsky and John N. Wolfe, eds., *Environment of the Cape Thompson Region, Alaska* (Washington, D.C.,: United States Atomic Energy Commission, 1966), 1151–62.

12. Test statistics are derived from C. Wilson, *Radioactive Fallout in Northern Regions* (Hanover, New Hampshire: U.S. Army Materiel Command, Cold Regions Research and Engineering Laboratory, 1967), 23–26, and *United States Nuclear Tests,* 3–17. For an account of the Zemlya Island blast, see Victory Adamsky and Uyri Smirnov, "Moscow's Biggest Bomb: The 50-Megaton Test of October 1961," *Cold War International History Project Bulletin* 4 (fall 1994): 3, 19–21.

13. Arthur R. Schulert, "Strontium-90 in Alaska," *Science* 136 (April 13, 1962): 146–48; Harvey E. Palmer, et al., "Cesium in Alaskan Eskimos," *Science* 142 (October 4, 1963): 66–67; *Science* 174 (February 5, 1964): 620; and 152 (May 20, 1966): 1062–63. The best collection of scientific analysis on Alaska fallout is found in the "Radioactivity" section of Wilimovsky and Wolfe, *Environment of Cape Thompson,* 1115–1200. For descriptions of fallout, strontium 90, and cesium 137, see Glasstone and Dolan, *Effects of Nuclear Weapons,* 36–38, 442–43, 604–08.

14. Edward Teller, *The Legacy of Hiroshima* (Garden City, New York: Doubleday & Co., Inc., 1962), 167; Jay S. Stefanek to E. C. Anderson, Nov. 16, 1961, CIC 0010800; Claus-M. Naske, *Bob Bartlett of Alaska—A Life in Politics* (Fairbanks: University of Alaska Press, 1979), 181–85. Senator Gruening and Governor Egan were also concerned about nuclear contamination. Gruening wrote that "while the concentrations in Alaska are the highest in the nation they are still far short of what is considered the danger level." Gruening to Egan, Aug. 28, 1963, RG 01 Juneau, file 390.l, 1961–63, box 4838.

15. Congress, Senate *Congressional Record:* (April 4, 1963), vol. 109, pt. 5, 5745–52; (May 14, 1963), vol. 109, pt. 7, 8423–28; (September 12, 1963), vol. 109, pt. 23, 16901–04; (August 31, 1964), vol. 110, pt. 16, 21071–73; Donald R. Chadwick to E. L. Bartlett, Jan. 28, 1965, and Sidney D. Heidersdorf to Hugh G. Gallagher, Apr. 20, 1965, Bob Bartlett papers, Independent Agencies, file AEC Fallout 1965, box 3.

16. Viereck, *Radioactivity Report,* 5; Senate Joint Resolution no. 59, Mar. 30, 1965, in Bartlett Papers, Independent Agencies, file AEC Fallout 1965, box 3.

17. For Amchitka's problem with rats, see Raymond A. Brechbill, "Norway Rat," in Merritt and Fuller, *Environment of Amchitka,* 261–63; Robert D. Jones, Jr., to Frank L. Beals, May 20, 1949, and Jones to Regional Director, May 22, 1950, FWS Adak, file Jones; "Quarterly Refuge Narrative Report, 1 Jan., 1949–30 Apr., 1951," 3–5, Anchorage FWS.

18. *Van Nostrand's Scientific Encyclopedia,* 1958 ed., s.v. "Rodenticides"; Clarence Cottam to Olaus J. Murie, Jul. 21, 1950, and Murie to Cottam, Jul. 27, 1950, FWS Adak; "Refuge Narrative Report, April thru August, 1960," 13, Anchorage FWS.

19. "Refuge Narrative Report," 13–14, 18–19, Anchorage FWS; Spencer, Naske, and Carnahan, *Wildlife Refuges of Alaska,* 62; Clifford C. Presnall to Director, Bureau of Sport Fisheries and Wildlife, Mar. 12, 1959, RG 22 FWS, General Correspondence 1890–1972, file Alaska General 1949–65, box 3.

20. Spencer, Naske, and Carnahan, *Wildlife Refuges of Alaska,* 61–62; Karl W. Kenyon, "Birds of Amchitka Island, Alaska," *The Auk* 78 (July 1961): 307–09; "Refuge Narrative Report," 18–20, Anchorage FWS.

21. James A. Estes and John F. Palmisano, "Sea Otters: Their Role in Structuring Nearshore Communities," *Science* 185 (Sept. 20, 1974): 1058–60; Charles A. Sinenstad, James A. Estes, and Karl W. Kenyon, "Aleuts, Sea Otters, and Alternate Stable-State Communities," *Science* 200 (April 28, 1978): 403–10.

22. J. Clark Salyer II to Regional Director, Jun. 13, 1951, and Clarence Cottam to Director, Bureau of Land Management, Jun. 15, 1951, U.S. Department of the Interior, Fish and Wildlife Service, Aleutian Islands, microfilm, roll 22, UA Anchorage. Another story of Defense Department defeat in the early 1960s is told by Kennedy press secretary Pierre Salinger. Upon hearing of plans for nuclear test sites in Alaska, the president, alarmed by its proximity to the Soviet Union, phoned Defense Secretary McNamara, who had not been informed. He "brought the whole idea to a shuddering stop." See Pierre Salinger, *With Kennedy* (Garden City, NY: Doubleday and Co., Inc., 1966), 137.

23. Robert D. Jones, Jr., "Present Status of the Sea Otter in Alaska," 38; Calvin J. Lensink, "The History and Status of Sea Otters in Alaska" (Ph.D. diss., Purdue University, 1962), 2; Karl W. Kenyon, *The Sea Otter in the Eastern Pacific Ocean,* 288, 320–32; Spenser, Naske, and Carnahan, *Wildlife Refuges of Alaska,* 64; Kenyon, *Otter in the Eastern Pacific,* 153, 288–90, 320–31; Murray L. Johnson, "The Sea Otter in Captivity," *Sea Otter in Eastern North Pacific Waters,* comp. Alice Sneed (Seattle: Pacific Search, 1972), 18–19; Karl W. Kenyon to Daniel L. Leedy, Mar. 10, 1958, RG 22 FWS, Records of the Commercial Fisheries and Seal Management 1892–1968, entry 285, file Sea Otters 1897–1958, box 14; Robert D. Jones, Jr., "Refuge Narrative Report, April thru August, 1960," 10, Anchorage FWS.

5 / UNDER RUFUS & LARKSPUR SCRUTINY

Epigraph from Bergsland and Dirks, *Aleut Tales,* 165. The Daylight Lifter tale is chapter 17.

1. C. B. Momsen to Chairman, U.S. Atomic Energy Commission, May 3, 1955, CIC 0128168. Glenn T. Seaborg to Stu [Udall], Jun. 30, 1964, CIC 0073398.

2. Jacob Neufeld, *The Development of Ballistic Missles in the United States Air Force, 1945–1960* (Washington, D.C.: U.S. Office of Air Force History, 1990), 119, 131,

212–15; Gilpin, *Scientists and Nuclear Weapons,* 146–47; Richard Reeves, *President Kennedy: Profile of Power* (New York: Simon & Schuster, 1993), 228–29.

3. *Anchorage Daily Times,* April 11, 1962, 1; Neufeld, *Development of Ballistic Missiles,* 186–87, 237; Robert E. Miller to Rufus Group, Jan. 18, 1963, CIC 0133727; "Project Rufus Site Selection Summary Report," May 4, 1963, CIC 0123373; "Preliminary Criteria For Selection of a Site For a Large Yield Land Surface Explosion," prepared for Chief, Defence Atomic Support Agency by Roland F. Beers, Inc., Alaska Department of Environmental Conservation files (hereinafter cited as ADEC), file 4, box 1. This collection of documents pertinent to Alaska is from the Las Vegas Department of Energy archives.

4. L. F. Wouters, "Thoughts on Criteria for a High Yield EMP Test," Aug. 17, 1962, ADEC, file 4, box 1; Robert E. Miller to Rufus Group, Nov. 13, 1962, CIC 0133726; "Project Rufus," May 4, 1963, CIC 0123373, 4–5, 7.

5. "Project Rufus," May 4, 1963, CIC 0123373, 4–5, 7.

6. Ibid., 7–9.

7. Ibid., 8, 10, 12–13, 15, 17, 19–21, 32–33. The Rufus review panel had eliminated for consideration any million-ton blasts for sites in the coterminous United States. See Robert E. Miller to Rufus Group, Feb. 19, 1963, CIC 0133715.

8. Atomic Energy Commission, "Project Rufus Site Selection: Rejection and Preliminary Selection of Areas pt. 1," Feb. 1963, (Nevada Operations Office), 11–27; AEC, "Project Rufus," Feb. 1963, 33–34; Wouters, "Thoughts on Criteria"; James E. Reeves to A. W. Betts, Dec. 27, 1962, CIC 0133724; Robert E. Miller to Rufus Group, Apr. 3, 1963, CIC 0133706.

9. AEC, "Project Rufus," Feb. 1963, 34; Miller to Rufus Group, Apr. 3, 1963, CIC 0133706; L. F. Wouters, "Alaskan Site Selection Criteria for Possible High Yield Vulnerability Test, Sept. 26, 1962, ADEC, file 4, box 1; Allyn H. Seymour, "The Fisheries and the Wildlife Resources of the Aleutian Island Sites and Chirikof Island," Mar. 18, 1963, CIC 0133708; "Site Selection," Sept. 26, 1962, ADEC, file 4, box 1, 15.

10. "Consideration of Sites in Alaska," Mar. 21, 1963, CIC 0078235; Jack W. Reed to Otto H. Roehlk, Jan. 23, 1963, CIC 0133719; "Summary and Recommendations of the Sites Considered," n.d., CIC 0133704. Blast pressures from bursts in the Holitna area for one-, three-, and ten-million-ton shots were compiled for Nondalton, Koliganek, Dillingham, Nyac, Aniak, Russian Mission, Crooked Creek, Red Mountain, Sleetmute, Stony River, and Sparrevohn.

11. AEC Project "Rufus," Feb. 1963.

12. James E. Reeves to Harold C. Connelly, Mar. 4, 1963, CIC 0133713. Population figures are from U.S. Census, 1960, except for Point Lay, which is not listed. The estimate for it is taken from *Alaska Maritime National Wildlife Refuge Final Compre-*

hensive Conservation Plan (Anchorage: U.S. Fish and Wildlife Service, 1988), II-99. CIC 00078235; John H. Hancock to AP & TCC files, Dec. 17, 1962, and Otto H. Roehlk to Roland F. Beers, Dec. 21, 1962, ADEC, file 4, box 1.

13. CIC 0078235 and 0133719. Blast levels from bursts at Amchitka were expected to leave unscathed Atka's 199 people, about 300 miles to the east.

14. AMCHITKA, n.d., CIC 0133705; CIC 0078235.

15. AMCHITKA, Ibid.

16. Ibid.

17. "Consideration of Sites in Alaska," May 1963, CIC 0134723; CIC 0078235.

18. J. E. Reeves to Rufus II (Larkspur) List, Apr. 4, 1963, CIC 0133749 and CIC 0133751.

19. Spencer, Naske, and Carnahan, *Wildlife Refuges of Alaska,* 64; Kenyon, *Otter in the Eastern Pacific,* 2–3, 157.

6 / DURING A LONG SHOT

Epigraph from "Aleutian Islands National Wildlife Refuge and Izembek National Wildlife Range Narrative Report, Jan. 1, 1965–Dec. 31, 1965," Anchorage FWS.

1. Glenn T. Seaborg, *Kennedy, Krushchev, and the Test Ban,* with a foreward by W. Averell Harriman (Berkeley: University of California Press, 1981), 8–9; *U.S. Nuclear Tests,* 6.

2. Seaborg, *Test Ban,* 12; Atomic Energy Commission Minutes of Meeting 1353, Apr. 9, 1958, RG 326 AEC; Richard G. Hewlett and Jack M. Holl, *Atoms for Peace and War 1953–1961: Eisenhower and the Atomic Energy Commission,* with a foreword by Richard S. Kirkendall (Berkeley: University of California Press, 1989), 362.

3. Seaborg, *Test Ban,* 12–13; George B. Kistiakowsky, *A Scientist at the White House: The Private Diary of President Eisenhower's Special Assistant for Science and Technology,* with an introduction by C. S. Maier (Cambridge, Mass.: Harvard University Press, 1976), xliii–xlv.

4. Seaborg, *Test Ban,* 16–19, 20–21.

5. Congress, Joint Committee on Atomic Energy, *Developments in the Field of Detection and Identification of Nuclear Explosions (Project Vela) and Relationship to Test Ban Negotiations: Hearings before the Joint Committee on Atomic Energy,* 87th Cong., 1st sess., July 25, 26, and 27, 1961, 7, 37; Kistiakowsky, *Scientist at the White House,* 316.

6. Congress, *1961 Developments in Detection Hearings,* 58, 61–62; Lewis A. Dunn, ed., with Amy E. Gordon, *Arms Control Verification and the New Role of On-Site Inspection* (Lexington, Mass., and Toronto: Lexington Books, 1990), 58–65.

7. John [McCone] to George [B. Kistiakowsky], Apr. 28, 1960, and press release, *The White House,* May 7, 1960, National Archives, Record Group 359, Executive Office of the President, Office of Science and Technology, Subject Files, file Panel-Disarm-NT-Vela Seismic R+D, 1960, box 36 (hereafter cited as RG 359 Science); O'Neill, *Firecracker Boys,* 39–40, 51–54; U. S. President, *Public Papers,* Dwight D. Eisenhower, 1960–1961, 410; Kistiakowsky, *Scientist at the White House,* 346.

8. Barton C. Hacker, *Elements of Controversy: AEC and Radiation Safety in Nuclear Weapons Testing, 1946–1974,* 214–15, 244–45; Atomic Energy Commission, "Summary Notes of Meeting of the Commissioners with the Plowshare Advisory Committee," Feb. 10, 1961, DOE History, file 1/60–12/61, RG 326 AEC. In this meeting, Glenn T. Seaborg "noted that instrumentation [for military purposes in Vela] might be conjectured as an effort to circumvent the weapons test moratorium and overshadow the primary purpose of the seismic tests." References to test operations are based on data from *U.S. Nuclear Tests.*

9. Hacker, *Elements of Controversy,* 244–46.

10. Congress, *1961 Developments in Detection Hearings,* 83, n. 5, refers to chemical explosions in a Louisiana salt dome for decoupling data in Project Cowboy.

11. Congress, *1961 Developments in Detection Hearings,* 135, 189–91, 198; M. L. Merritt, "History, 1741–1967," in Merritt and Fuller, *Environment of Amchitka,* 132–33; Congress, Joint Committee on Atomic Energy, *Developments in Technical Capabilities for Detecting and Identifying Nuclear Weapons Tests: Hearings before the Joint Committee on Atomic Energy,* 88th Cong., 1st sess., March 5, 6, 7, 8, 11, and 12, 1963, 32, 115–16, 405.

12. U. S. Army Engineer District, Alaska, *Project Long Shot, Geologic and Hydrologic Investigations, Appendix C* (May 1965), 1–9.

13. Century Geophysical Corporation, *Final Report on Refraction Seismograph Survey,* "Project Toy Factory," *Amchitka, Aleutian Islands, Alaska* (July 1964), 1, k5–6; Vela Uniform also entailed the firing of sixty-one calibration explosions of one ton each underwater in a fifty-thousand square mile area from Amchitka to Atka during the 1964 summer. See *Vela Uniform Experiment in the Aleutian Islands,* U. S. Coast and Geodetic Survey, 1 April, 1964; H. Arnold Karo to Distribution List, 19 May and 10 June, 1964, FWS Adak, file Robert D. Jones.

14. U. S. Army Engineer District, Alaska, and U. S. Geological Survey, *Project Long Shot, Geologic and Hydrologic Investigations, Main Report* (May 1965), 1–3; Deputy Manager, *Long Shot,* 4, 57–59, 69.

15. Hacker, *Elements of Controversy,* 4–5, 7.

16. M. W. Knapp to J. E. Reeves, May 18, 1965, ADEC, file 3, box 5; Deputy Manager, *Long Shot,* 43; *Initial Feasibility Study, Project Long Shot,* August 15, 1965 (Seat-

tle: Laboratory of Radiation Biology, University of Washington), 1–2, 4–11, UA Fairbanks, Bartlett Papers, file AEC 1964, box 2.

17. Bethe, Hans A., *The Road from Los Alamos* (New York: American Institute of Physics, 1991), 39–40.

18. Delmar Crowson to H. C. Donnelly, Jan. 11, Dwight Ink to R. E. Hollingsowrth, Apr. 27, James E. Reeves to Delmar L. Crowson, May 12, 1965, ADEC, file 3, box 5; Merritt and Fuller, *Environment of Amchitka*, 133; Jones, "Narrative Report, Jan. 1–Dec. 31, 1965," 35, Anchorage FWS.

19. Richard D. Wolfe to D. A. Ink, "Notification of Alaskan Congressional Delegation and Governor on Project Long Shot Plans," Mar. 12, 1965, CIC 0137860. Also known as the Prince William Sound earthquake based on location of its epicenter, it generated destructive tsunamis. See U.S. Department of Commerce, National Oceanic and Atmospheric Administration, *United States Tsunamis, 1690–1988,* by James F. Lander and Patricia A. Lockridge (Boulder, Colo.: National Geophysical Data Center, 1989), 102.

20. Jones, "Narrative Report, Jan. 1–Dec. 31, 1965," 35.

21. Jones, "Narrative Report, Jan. 1–Dec. 31, 1965," 35–36; CIC 0137860 Attachment, proposed DOD public announcement, "DOD Seismic Experiment Will Assist Test Ban Negotiations."

22. CIC 0137860; "Alaska Atom Blast Scheduled," and "Egan is Certain Atomic Tests Are No Danger," *Anchorage Daily News,* March 19, 1965, 1–2; Howard C. Brown to Arthur Sylvester, May 7, 1965, and enclosure, "Public Information Plan, Project Long Shot," ADEC, file 3, box 5.

23. Governor Egan's speech was delivered at Elmendorf Air Force Base near Anchorage in March 1965, RG 01 Juneau, file 390.1, 1964–1968, box 4838. Test statistics are based on *U.S. Nuclear Tests,* 10–25.

24. Glasstone and Dolan, *Effects of Nuclear Weapons,* 61–62; Jones, "Narrative Report, Jan. 1–Dec. 31, 1965," 38.

25. "Amchitka Shaken, But Not Bad; Test Scored As Success," *Anchorage Daily News,* October 30, 1965, 1–2; "Amchitka Will Return Soon to Lonely Status," *Anchorage Daily Times,* October 30, 1965, 1; Deputy Manager, *Long Shot,* 46, 52, 82; Allyn H. Seymour and Roy E. Nakatani, *Long Shot Bioenvironmental Safety Program, Final Report* (Seattle: University of Washington Laboratory of Radiation Ecology, 1967), 45; Calvin J. Lensink to Wildlife Administrator, Kenai, Alaska, Nov. 23, 1956, FWS Adak, file Jones.

26. R. G. Fuller and J. B. Kirkwood, "Ecological Consequences of Nuclear Testing," in Merritt and Fuller, *Environment of Amchitka,* 632–33.

27. Charles I. Browne to James E. Reeves, n.d. [Mar. 1967?], David Shearer, Jr., to

Don Hendricks, Jul. 25, 1967, Charles Winter to Carleton Ray, Oct. 2, 1968, and Arthur J. Whitman to Donald H. Edwards, Apr. 18, 1969, ADEC, file 3, box 1; Deputy Manager, *Long Shot,* 54–56; D. C. Castagnola, *Tritium Anomalies on Amchitka Island, Alaska, Part III* (Palo Alto, Calif.: Teledyne Isotopes Company, 1969), iv, 1, 5, 9–11.

28. Castagnola, *Anomalies,* 15 and Part I, v; Allyn H. Seymour and Victor A. Nelson, "Radionuclides In Air, Water, and Biota," in Merritt and Fuller, *Environment of Amchitka,* 592–94.

29. Celia M. Hunter to Senator E. L. Bartlett, Mar. 18, 1965, and Hugh G. Gallagher to Hunter, Mar. 22, 1956, UA Fairbanks, Bartlett Papers, file Fallout 1965, box 3. Similarly, Gallagher, Bartlett's legislative assistant, wrote that the Department of Defense assures us "there will be no harm of any kind to the sea otters and the birds, the things that crawl or the creatures that swim." Gallagher to James E. Fisher, Mar. 3, 1965, file Amchitka Test Site 1964–65, box 7.

30. O'Neill, *Firecracker Boys,* 186–87; Ginny Hill Wood, "The Greening of Alaska: A Retrospect," *The Northern Line, Journal of the Northern Alaska Environmental Center,* 12 (April 1990): 4; for Hunter's reflections on the Alaska Conservation Society, see Maxine E. McCloskey, *Wilderness: The Edge of Knowledge* (San Francisco: Sierra Club, 1970), 186–88.

31. Alaska Conservation Society *News Bulletin* 6 (March 1965): 2–3.

32. Ibid., 3–4.

33. Ibid., 3. The nation's largest conservation society, the National Wildlife Federation, also supported the test. See its *Conservation News* 30 (October 1, 1965): 7.

34. *News Bulletin* 6 (October 1965): 9–1 1; Deputy Manager, *Long Shot,* 43.

35. Thomas P. O'Farrell to E. L. Bartlett, Aug. 9 and Sept. 30, 1956, UA Fairbanks, Bartlett Papers, file AEC 1965, box 2; "Uproar Over Otters," *Life,* October 15, 1956, 151–52.

36. Carl W. Buckheister, "Duplicity and Destruction at Amchitka," *Audubon,* Nov.–Dec. 1956, 381. (Original in bold print.)

37. Merritt and Fuller, *Environment of Amchitka,* 133–34; Steve McCutcheon, "Atomic Blast vs Otter," *Audubon,* Nov.–Dec. 1956, 377–79; W. W. Allaire to James E. Reeves, Nov. 8, ADEC, file 3, box 1.

38. Jones to C. M. Kirkpatrick, Mar. 23, 1962, Karl W. Kenyon to Jones, Mar. 30, 1964, Jones to Alfred G. Etter, June 10, 1965, Jim King to Wildlife Administrator, May 12, 1965, FWS Adak, file Robert D. Jones, Jr., "Narrative Report, Jan. 1–Dec. 31, 1965," 36–38; Senator Ernest Gruening, *Weekly Newsletter,* March 19 and April 2, 1965, in Alaska State Archives, Juneau, Record Group 03, Department of Law, Office of Attorney General, series 96, file Gruening, Ernest—Weekly Newsletter, box 5035; Lyman L. Woodman, *The Army Corps of Engineers in Alaska Starting in 1896 and His-*

tory of Its Alaska District During 1946–1974 (Elmendorf Air Force Base: U.S. Army Engineer District, Alaska, 1967), 78. Issues of *Amchitka News Shot* are in the Alaska Historical Library, Juneau. See copies of Aug. 17, 24, 31; Sept. 7, 14, 21, 28; Oct. 5, 1965.

39. Seaborg, *Test Ban*, 242; Senator E. L. Bartlett from Bill Boesch, May 16, 1967, Bartlett Papers, file Independent Agencies, Amchitka Test Site, box 7; to Ed Huizer from Ben Hilliker, RG 11 AK Fish and Game, Juneau, file AEC 1968, box 6863.

7 / THROUGH MILROW CALIBRATION

Epigraph from interview by author, Anchorage, Alaska, June 24, 1994. Farrell was 1969 chairman of Save Our State, a citizen committee opposed to nuclear tests on Amchitka.

1. *U.S. Nuclear Tests*, 36; *Ganja Planning Directive*, May 2, 1969, ADEC, file 1, box 10; Robert E. Miller to R. E. Batzel, et al., May 27, 1969, CIC 0156574; Karl B. Schneider to James Harper, Nov. 28, 1969, RG 11 AK Fish & Game, file AEC 1969, box 6863.

2. Neufeld, *Missiles in the Air Force*, 59–64; Fred Kaplan, *The Wizards of Armageddon* (New York: Simon and Schuster, 1983), 343; Atomic Energy Commission, *Weapons Part of Progress Report to the Joint Committee—December 1950 through May 1951*, CIC 0079406; Dwight D. Eisenhower, *Waging Peace, 1956–1961* (New York: Doubleday, 1965), 223.

3. Chuck Hansen, *U.S. Nuclear Weapons: The Secret History* (New York: Orion Books, 1988), 188. See also W. F. Biddle, *Weapons Technology and Arms Control* (New York: Praeger Publishers, 1972), 159–60; Edward Teller, *Better a Shield Than a Sword: Perspectives on Defense and Technology* (New York: The Free Press, 1987), 28–29.

4. Kaplan, *The Wizards*, 343–45; Hansen, *Nuclear Weapons*, 188–89. See also Atomic Energy Commission, Meeting 1308, Oct. 22, 1957, and meeting 1377, May 28, 1958, RG 326 AEC; *U.S. Nuclear Tests*, 7–8, 13, 15, 17; Herbert F. York, *Making Weapons, Talking Peace: A Physicist's Odyssey from Hiroshima to Geneva* (New York: Basic Books, Inc., Publishers, 1987), 148–49.

5. Kaplan, *The Wizards*, 345; Reeves, *President Kennedy*, 555. ABM is also referred to in the literature as ballistic missile defense (BMD) and the anti-intercontinental ballistic missile (AICBM).

6. Henry L. Trewhitt, *McNamara* (New York: Harper and Row, 1971), 124–25; Kaplan, *The Wizards*, 346; Lyndon Baines Johnson, *The Vantage Point: Perspectives of the Presidency, 1963–1969* (New York: Holt, Rinehart and Winston, 1971), 479–80.

7. Trewhitt, *McNamara*, 129–31; Kaplan, *The Wizards*, 347–48; Johnson, *Vantage Point*, 481, 483–85.

8. Merritt and Fuller, *Environment of Amchitka,* 134; Robert E. Miller to James E. Reeves, Jun. 10, and Delmar L. Crowson to J. E. Reeves, Aug. 12, 1966, ADEC, file 2, box 7; AEC Meeting 2230, Oct. 26, 1966, RG 326 AEC.

9. The Alaska Conservation Society Board resolved to ask for an AEC delay in considering this area for testing. See its press release, Feb. 27, 1967, Bartlett Papers, Independent Agencies, file Test Site, 1966, box 7.

10. Merritt and Fuller, *Environment of Amchitka,* 134; James E. Reeves to D. L. Crowson, Aug. 10, 1966, ADEC, file 2, box 7; *U.S. Nuclear Tests,* 31. The report of Faultless effects on the desert is found in Omar V. Garrison, *Howard Hughes In Las Vegas* (New York: Lyle Stuart, Inc., 1970), 211.

11. Merritt and Fuller, *Environment of Amchitka,* 651; Reeves to Crowson, Aug. 10, 1966, ADEC, file 2, box 7; Glenn Seaborg to Bartlett, Mar. 7, 1967, and William S. Boesch to Karl Armstrong, Mar. 31, 1969, Bartlett Papers, Independent Agencies, file Amchitka Test Site, 1966, box 7. Bartlett himself was interested in Alaska test sites, which would have more "economic impact" than one on Amchitka. So, too, was Karl Armstrong, editor of the *Kodiak Mirror* and executive director of the Native Association. He advised Kodiak, Afognak, Shugak, Sitkalidak Islands, and the Trinity Islands for supplemental test sites. Armstrong to Seaborg, Feb. 6, 1977, ADEC file 2, box 3.

12. Merritt and Fuller, *Environment of Amchitka,* 651; AEC Meeting 2230.

13. Donald L. Barlett and James B. Steele, *Empire: The Life, Legend, and Madness of Howard Hughes* (New York: W. W. Norton & Company, 1979), 318, 340–41, 342–47, 355–65; Robert Mahew and Richard Hack, *Next to Hughes* (New York: Harper Collins Publishers, 1992), 200–02, 204–08; Michael Drosnin, *Citizen Hughes* (New York: Holt, Rinehart and Winston, 1958), 183, 193, 196, 257–60, 276–80, 308–14, 346–56; Charles Higham, *Howard Hughes: The Secret Life* (New York: G. P. Putnam's Sons, 1993), 233–34, 242–46; Garrison, *Howard Hughes in Las Vegas,* 219–26. According to Drosnin, Gravel came to Las Vegas in April 1968 as a Senator, but at that time he was only a candidate. Based on an AEC report, Gravel and his staff were briefed in Las Vegas during April, 1969. See Congress, Senate, "Project Milrow—Public Affairs Report," 92nd Cong., 1st sess. *Congressional Record* (15 September, 1971), vol. 117, pt. 24, 31914; and E. B. Giller to Robert E. Miller, Apr. 15, 1969, ADEC, file 19, box 3. Drosnin also claims that President Nixon "ordered the biggest blasts moved to Alaska: because of worries about Hughes" (pp. 478, 490). This allegation was promoted by columnist Drew Pearson. See Garrison, 226. In light of Amchitka's long history with the bomb, the notion that Hughes caused the move to Alaska is questionable. AEC Chairman Seaborg thought the notion "exaggerated." Glenn T. Seaborg with Benjamin S. Loeb, *The Atomic Energy Commission under Nixon: Adjusting to Troubled Times* (New York: St. Martin's Press, 1993), 31.

14. Richard L. Garwin and Hans A. Bethe, "Anti-Ballistic-Missile Systems," *Scientific American* 218 (March 1968): 21–31.

15. *Congressional Quarterly Almanac* 24 (90th Congress, 2nd Session—1968): 80–81, 586, vote 247, p. 54; *Congressional Quarterly Weekly Report* 26 (Sept. 6, 1968): 2387 and (Oct. 4, 1968): 2616. Gruening had become a critic of Johnson's Vietnam policy and military spending.

16. Congress, House, Congressman Pollock, "No Logical Alternative to ABM Development," 91st Cong., 1st sess., *Congressional Record* (July 7, 1969), vol. 115 pt. 14, 18395–99; *Congressional Quarterly Almanac* 25 (91st Cong., 1st sess., 1969), 257–59, 267–72. For votes, see p. 13-S. The ABM's long history is discussed in Ernest J. Yanarella, *The Missile Defense Controversy: Strategy, Technology, and Politics, 1955–1972* (Lexington: University Press of Kentucky, 1977). Also see Terry Terriff, *The Nixon Administration and the Making of U.S. Nuclear Strategy* (Ithaca and London: Cornell University Press, 1995).

17. James E. Reeves to Walter J. Hickel, Feb. 3, Apr. 5, and Glenn T. Seaborg to Hickel, Oct. 13, 1967, RG 01 Juneau, file 390.5 Amchitka 1967–68, box 4838; statement from Bill Boesch, Oct. 12, 1967, UA Fairbanks, Bartlett Papers, Independent Agencies, file AEC General, 1968, box 4. Senator Bartlett was told that drilling near Point Lay would be held up until data from Amchitka were obtained, but reconnaissance of the area would go forward. See Delmar L. Crowson to Bartlett, Mar. 2, 1967, file Amchitka Test Site, box 7; W. D. Smith, Jr., to Alaska District Engineer, May 22, 1967, ADEC, file 2, box 7.

18. U.S. Atomic Energy Commission, "Project Milrow: Information Actions," Nevada Operations Office, n.d., 2; E. L. Bartlett to Robert D. O'Neill, Mar. 14, 1967, Bartlett Papers, Independent Agencies, file Amchitka Test Site, 1966, box 7; Robert G. Know, "Amchitka Blast To Make Long Shot Look Like Firecracker," *Alaska Construction and Oil Report* (May 1967): 16, 21–22.

19. Pamphlet, "The Story of Holmes & Narver, Inc.," University of Alaska Anchorage Library, Alaska Room, file AVFM—Amchitka Island, Alaska; Henry G. Vermillion to Alaska press media and Governor Hickel, Apr. 5, 1967, RG 01 Juneau, file 390.5, Amchitka 1967–68, box 4838.

20. Congress, Senate, Senator Gravel, "Joint Resolution to Provide for a Study and Evaluation Between Underground Nuclear Detonations and Seismic Disturbances," S. J. Res. 108, 91st Cong., 1st sess., *Congressional Record* (May 8, 1969), vol. 115 pt. 9, 11842–43.

21. Ibid., 11844–46. For science aspects of the debate, see Anne Hessing Cahn, *Eggheads and Warheads: Scientists and the ABM* (Cambridge: Massachusetts Institute of Technology, 1971).

22. Congress, House, introduction of H. J. Res. 899, 91st Cong., 1st Sess., *Congressional Record* (September 11, 1969), vol. 115, pt. 19, 25182; Congress, Senate introduction of S. J. Res. 155, 91st Cong., 1st sess., *Congressional Record* (September 24, 1969), vol. 115, pt. 20, 26815; *Congressional Quarterly Almanac* 25, 91st Cong., 1st sess., 1969, 734. For Fulbright's campaign against the ABM, see Randall Bennett Woods, *Fulbright: A Biography* (New York: Cambridge University Press, 1995), 519–25.

23. See endnote 22.

24. Congress, Senate, Committee on Foreign Relations, *Underground Weapons Testing:* Hearing before the Committee on Foreign Relations on S. J. Res. 155, 91st Cong., 1st sess., September 19, 1969, 4–5, 117–19.

25. Ibid., 54, 65–66.

26. J. W. Betit to "Tell It To Bud," July 22, 1968, RG 01 Juneau, file 390.1, 1964–1968, box 4838.

27. Amy Bollenbach to Gravel, Aug. 7, 1969, UA Fairbanks, Gravel Papers, file 1—Defense—ABM, box 71; Michaelene S. Pendleton to Pollock, Aug. 22; Huss and Sharon Malik to Pollock, Sept. 23, 1969, UA Fairbanks, Howard W. Pollock Papers, General File 1967–1970, file Amchitka Island Nuclear Test, box 1, and Legislative File, file Amchitka Island Nuclear Blast, box 1.

28. Alaska Conservation Society Press Release, Feb. 17, 1967, Bartlett Papers, Independent Agencies, file Amchitka Test Site, 1966, box 7; Ginny Wood, "A.E.C.—A Camel in the Tent," *Alaska Conservation Review* 8 (fall–winter 1967–1968): 1–2, and Henry G. Vermillion to Editor, 9 (spring 1968): 10; Ernest D. Campbell to Henry G. Vermillion, Apr. 3, 1968, ADEC, file 2, box 3.

29. Conservation Society Press Release, Feb. 17, 1967, Bartlett Papers, Independent Agencies, file Amchitka Test Site, 1966, box 7; Bartlett to Crowson, Mar. 23, 1967, and Crowson to Weeden, May 6, 1967, Bartlett Papers, Bartlett Papers, Independent Agencies, file Amchitka Test Site, 1966, box 7; Weeden to Crowson, May 17, 1969, and "Suggestions for an Approach to AEC on Amchitka," Sept. 17, 1969, UA Fairbanks, Alaska Conservation Society Papers, file 1, Nuclear Testing, box 11; Celia M. Hunter to President Richard M. Nixon, Sept. 28, 1969, Gravel Papers, file 3, box 599. For Society repugnance toward Milrow, see Ginny Wood, "AEC Having a Blast—In Wildlife Refuge," *Alaska Conservation Review* 10 (summer 1969): 10.

30. Miller to Boddy, June 2, 1969, Gravel Papers, file 3, AEC General Information: Amchitka Related, box 600. The AEC took this letter to be the first public opposition to Milrow. See *Congressional Record,* vol. 117, pt. 24, 31914.

31. Miller to Boddy, June 23, 1969, RG 01 Juneau, file Federal Government: AEC, box 4916.

32. *Congressional Record,* vol. 117, pt. 24, 31914–15; AEC News Release, Aug. 21,

1969, Gravel Papers, file 5, Arguments to Cancel, Postpone, box 598; Pendleton to Pollock, Aug. 22, 1969, Pollock Papers, General File 1967–70, file Amchitka Island Nuclear Test, box 1; Hollifield to Stevens, June 20, 1969, and attachment "Alaskans Contacted and/or Briefed by AEC," RG 01 Juneau, file Federal Government: AEC, box 4916.

33. Press Release from Democrat Headquarters, April 17, 1969, UA Fairbanks, Egan Papers, file 9, box 20; *Congressional Record*, vol. 117, pt. 24, 31915–16; *Alaska Legislative Council Transcript of Public Hearing on the Atomic Energy Commission Milrow Test at Amchitka*, Sept. 26, 1969, 1, 35, 51, 86, Rasmuson Library, University of Alaska Fairbanks.

34. Clifford E. Warren to Governor Miller, June 14, 1969, and "Resolution on Nuclear Testing at Amchitka Island, Alaska" and "Resolution on ABM," RG 01 Juneau, Boards and Commissions, file AEC, box 5057.

35. Mailing List, Democrats For Issues and Action, files of Martin A. Farrell, Jr., and interview by author, Anchorage, Alaska, June 15, 1994. Farrell remembered that other founders were Michael H. DeMan, Henry and Mary McKinnon, Herb and Kay Montoya, and Clifford and June Warren, in whose kitchen the group first met. Supporters included George A. Dickson, Gary H. Holthaus, Ed Isenson, John S. Parks, and John R. Roderick.

36. Interview, ibid. Money also came in later to pay expenses. Herbert Wilton Beaser to Farrell, Oct. 22 and Nov. 6, 1969; Stewart R. Mott to Farrell, Nov. 10, 1969, Farrell files. An example of SOS concern is found in its flier, "Amchitka—Our Fault," UA Ancorage, Woodman Collection, Amchitka AEC; *Anchorage Daily News*, September 10, 1969, sec. 1, 8, and October 2, 1969, sec. 1, 5; *Congressional Record*, vol. 117, pt. 24, 31915.

37. *Congressional Record*, vol. 117, pt. 24, 31913, 31917; AEC Memorandum, "Public Information Plan For Amchitka STS," April 12, 1967, FWS Adak, file HI, Amchitka—Info AEC Project; Augie Reetz to William D. Smith, June 10, 1969, RG 11 AK Fish and Game, file AEC 1969, box 6803; interview by author of Martin A. Farrell, Jr., June 24. Farrell introduced the first bill to create an Alaska Department of Environmental Conservation. Governor Egan, a friend of Farrell's, disagreed with the bill's language, and the Governor's bill finally passed. Farrell also was responsible for legislation creating Anchorage's Potter Marsh wetlands refuge, an addition to Kachemack Bay State Park, which expanded the Chilkat River reserve for protection of eagles. Letters in his files attest to this support.

38. Merritt and Fuller, *Environment of Amchitka*, 135; Clarence F. Pautzke to Charles Winter, June 23, 1967, Anchorage FWS; *Amchitka Island Status Report*, May 9, 1969; "Management and Research Needs," Apr. 10, 1967; "Memorandum of Under-

standing," no. AT(26-1)-320, May 17, 1967, and Supplemental Agreement, No. AT(26-1)-320, July 1, 1968, RG 22 FWS, Bureau of Sport Fisheries and Wildlife, General Correspondence, file 1-5-1-3a, box 5.

39. Merritt and Fuller, *Environment of Amchitka*, vi–vii, 134–35. Subcontractors are listed on the chapter heading pages in Merritt and Fuller. "Background Information Regarding AEC Activities on Amchitka Island, Alaska," Gravel Papers, file 2, Defense—Weapons, box 74.

40. Abram V. Tunison to Duane Bell, Aug. 25, 1967; Report on Conference on Sea Otters—November 7, 1967; Agreement no. AT(26-1)-380, May 10, 1968; Note YB to List, n.d., RG 22 FWS, files 1-5-1-3a and 1-5-1-3g, box 5; Walter J. Hickel to John N. Trent, May 9, 1967; Glenn Seaborg to Hickel, Oct. 13, 1967; *News from Alaska's Governor*, Oct. 20, 1967, RG 01 Juneau, file 390.5; Amchitka 1967–68, box 4838; Walter J. Hickel to Dr. Seaborg, n.d. [Jan. 1968?], ADEC, file 4, box 3. For transplant activities and estimated costs, see George Laycock, "Moving Day for Sea Otters," *Audubon* (January 1969): 58–78. Sea otter figures are reported in Wildlife Biologist to Supervisor, Aug. 16, 1968, FWS Adak, HI-Amchitka. See also U.S. Atomic Energy Commission, Nevada Operations office, *Amchitka Biological Information Summary*, R. Glenn Fuller (Las Vegas, Nev.: U.S. Atomic Energy Commission, 1969), 4.

41. *Amchitka Island Status Report*, May 9, 1969, and Averill S. Thayer to Assoc. Supervisor, Wildlife Refuges, May 15, 1967, RG 22 FWS, file 1-5-1-3a, box 5.

42. Palmer C. Sekora to Associate Refuge Supervisor, Aug. 1, 1967; Robert D. Jones, Jr., to R. Glen Fuller, Aug. 31, 1967; LeRoy W. Sowl to Assoc. Supervisor, Wildlife Refuges, Sept. 29, 1967, FWS Adak, files HI-Amchitka and Biologist—Amchitka Eagle Study; LeRoy W. Sowl to AEC Site Manager, Sept. 15, 1967, RG 22 FWS, file 1-5-1-3a, box 5.

43. George Laycock, "The Beautiful Sad Face of Amchitka," *Audubon* 70 (November/December 1968): 8–25; Michael Frome to Stewart L. Udall, Oct. 19, 1967, RG 22 FWS, file 1-5-1-3g, box 5; Udall to Frome, Dec. 16, 1967, FWS Adak, file HI-Amchitka.

44. John B. Hakala to Project Manager, AEC, Oct. 28, 1967; Vernon Ekedahl to David L. Spencer, Nov. 3, 1967; A. V. Tunison to List, Dec. 8, 1967; Ray E. Johnson to Director, Nov. 13, 1967, RG 22 FWS, file 1-5-1-3g, box 5.

45. Clarence J. Pautzke to E. L. Bartlett, Jan. 30, 1968, UAF Fairbanks, Bartlett Papers, Independent Agencies, file Amchitka 1968, box 4; LeRoy W. Sowl to Associate Refuge Supervisor, Feb. 7, 1968; John B. Hakala to Supervisor, Feb. 16 and Mar. 7, 1968; Sowl to Supervisor, Mar. 12, 1968, FWS Adak, file HI-Amchitka; Sowl to Assoc. Refuge Supervisor, June 14, 1968, RG 22 FWS, file 1-5-1-3g, box 5. The Alaska Department of Fish and Game also made an inspection of pollution from drilling mud and contacted the state attorney general's office with a view to legal action. Bob Wien-

hold to Ben Hilliker, Apr. 16, 1969, Gravel Papers, file 5—Amchitka Fish and Wildlife Statement, box 600.

46. Sowl to Supervisor, July 22, Sept. 18, and Nov. 5, 1968, FWS Adak, file HI-Amchitka; Abram V. Tunison to Regional Director, Aug. 16, 1968; Clay E. Cranford to Roland J. Marchand, Oct. 11, 1968, RG 22 FWS, file 1-5-1-3g, box 5. Pollution of streams by drilling mud from Long Shot was still visible. "Amchitka Damage Summary," July 9, 1969, Anchorage FWS.

47. Baine H. Cater to Assoc. Supervisor, Feb. 4, 1969; Clay E. Cranford to Roland J. Marachand, Apr. 25, 1969; Carl E. Abegglen to Yates Barber, May 1, 1969; Report on Joint Meeting FWS, AEC, and BMI, June 3, 1969, RG 22 FWS, file 1-5-1-3g, box 5; Sowl to Associate Supervisor, Apr. 23, 1969; David L. Spenser to Regional Director, Apr. 23, 1969, FWS Adak, file HI-Amchitka; Bob Jones to Alaska Conservation Society, July 3, 1969, UA Fairbanks, Alaska Conservation Society Papers, file 1, Nuclear Testing, box 11.

48. Larry R. Hafstad to Glenn T. Seaborg, Jul. 19, 1969, RG 325 AEC, General Advisory Committee, file 105th Meeting, box 11; Ronald C. Tracy to Under Secretary, Aug. 1, 1969, Gravel Papers, file 5—Amchitka Fish and Wildlife Statement, box 600; Walter J. Hickel to The President, Aug. 29, 1969, RG 22 FWS, file 1-5-1-3g, box 5.

49. Ronald F. Scott to Spurgeon M. Keeny, Jr., Nov. 8, 1968; Frank Press to Keeny, Nov. 15, 1968; David K. Todd to Keeny, Nov. 11, 1968, RG 359 Science, file Nuclear Underground Tests 1968, box 806.

50. Keeny to DuBridge, Mar. 27, 1969; DuBridge to Ken, Mar. 29, 1969; United States Atomic Energy Commission, Nevada Operations Office, *Safety of Underground Nuclear Testing* (April 1969), RG 359 Science, file Nuclear Underground Tests 1969, box 927.

51. Warren G. Magnuson to Glenn Seaborg, Sept. 2, 1969, CIC 0911434; Appendix A: Chronology, in Merritt and Fuller, *Environment of Amchitka,* 651; Henry A. Kissinger to Chairman, AEC, Sept. 25, 1969, CIC 0179133; Mike Gravel to the President, Sept. 27, 1969, Congress, Senate, 91st Cong., 1st sess., *Congressional Record* (October 1, 1969), vol. 115, pt. 21, 27884.

52. "6.6 Quake Jolts Amchitka," *Anchorage Daily News,* September 13, 1969, 4; "Attendees, Amchitka Trip," Sept. 13, 1969, ADEC, file 7, box 3; Bill Richmond, "Amchitka," *The Atom* 5 (September 1968): 19, 21; press release, Office of the Joint Committee on Atomic Energy, Sept. 27, 1969, UA Fairbanks, Gravel Papers, folder 6, box 600; AEC news release, Sept. 3, 1969, RG 11 AK Fish and Game, Office of the Commissioner, file AEC 1969, box 6863; AEC *Background Information—Amchitka* (July 30, 1969), 26.

53. See endnote 52.

54. U.S. Atomic Energy Commission, Nevada Operations Office, *Observed Seismic Data, Milrow Event,* by Environmental Research Corporation (Alexander, Vir.: March 1970), 1; Drill Hole Progress, Amchitka Island, Exhibit I, ADEC, file 2, box 12.

55. AEC Biweekly Status Report for October 7, 1969, RG 359, file Atomic Energy Commission, vol. II, 1969, box 862; U.S. Department of Commerce, Environmental Science Services Administration, *Aleutian Seismicity, Milrow Seismic Effects (May 1970)* by E. R. Engdahl and A. C. Tarr (Coast and Geodetic Survey, 1970), 21–29.

56. R. Glen Fuller and James B. Kirkwood, "Ecological Consequences of Nuclear Testing," Merritt and Fuller, *Environment of Amchitka,* 636; William R. Perret and Dale R. Breding, *Ground Motion In the Vicinity of Underground Nuclear Explosion in the Aleutian Islands: Milrow Event* (Albuquerque, New Mexico: Sandia Laboratories, 1972), 3.

57. Fuller and Kirkwood, "Ecological Consequences of Nuclear Testing," 636–37; James B. Kirkwood, *Bioenvironmental Safety Studies, Amchitka Island, Alaska, Milrow D+7 Days Report,* revised October 17, 1969 (Columbus, Ohio: Battelle Memorial Institute, 1969), 19.

58. Fuller and Kirkwood, "Ecological Consequences of Nuclear Testing."

59. Ibid., 633–36.

60. Ben Hilliker to Robert W. Ward, Sept. 23, 1969; telegram copy from undersigned citizens of Whitehorse to President Nixon, Sept. 26, 1969, RG 01 Juneau, files Reading 1971–72 and AEC, boxes 4892 and 5057; "Miller to See Nixon," *Alaska Daily News,* September 30, 1969, 6; "Amchitka Protest: The Way It Was in Canada," *Juneau Southeast Alaska Empire,* October 2, 1969, 10.

8 / FOR SAFEGUARD SECURITY

Epigraph from article quoting Moses, *Fairbanks Daily News-Miner,* April 6, 1970, 12.

1. Roger Auge, "Next Time?" *Alaska Conservation Society Review* 10 (fall 1969): 10.

2. Walter Sczudlo to Keith Miller, Oct. 7, 1969, and Leo A. Walsh to Miller, Oct. 8, 1969, RG 01 Juneau, reading file 1971–72, box 4892; *Ketchikan Daily News,* October 2, 1969, 2; John J. Shaffer and Mrs. John T. Chihuly to Miller, Oct. 3, 1969, RG 01 Juneau, reading file 1971–72, box 4892; Nissel A. Rose to Howard W. Pollock, Mar. 5, 1970, UA Fairbanks, Papers of Howard W. Pollock, Legislative files 1969–1970, file Amchitka Island Nuclear Test, box 1.

3. *Juneau Southeast Alaska Empire,* October 6, 1969, 7; *Ketchikan Daily News,* Oc-

tober 3, 1969, 8; Keith H. Miller to Eugene Guess, Jalmar Kertula, and Mike Bradner, Oct. 1, 1969, RG 01 Juneau, file 1971–72, box 4892.

4. News release, Oct. 13 and Dec. 2, 1969, RG 01 Juneau, reading file 1971–72, box 4892.

5. Robert E. Miller to Keith Miller, Nov. 5, 1969, RG 01 Juneau, reading file 1971–72, box 4892; Robert E. Miller to Melvin W. Carter, Nov. 24, 1969, CIC 0156512; news release, Dec. 2, 1969, CIC 0156512.

6. *Aleutian Islands National Wildlife Refuge and Izembek National Wildlife Range Narrative Report,* January 1, 1969–December 31, 1969, 5, and January 1, 1971–December 31, 1971, 26, Anchorage FWS.

7. See endnote 5.

8. Pamphlet and press release, National Committee Against Underground Nuclear Testing, Ernest Gruening Chairman, Jan. 8, 1970, Gravel Papers, file 4, box 596; Alaska, *House Journal,* Sixth Legislature—Second Session, Feb. 16, 1970, 331; copy of House Joint Resolution 98 in UA Fairbanks, Gravel Papers, file 5, box 597.

9. *Anchorage Daily News,* April 5, 1970, 1–2; *Fairbanks Daily News-Miner,* April 6, 1970, 12; Robert E. Miller to Geo. E. G. Giller, Apr. 9, 1970, ADEC, file 18, box 3.

10. *Anchorage Daily News,* April 5, 1970, 1–2; "Briefings" and copies of testimony, Gravel Papers, file 5, box 597 and file 4, box 108; *Juneau Alaska Empire,* April 6, 1970, 8.

11. *Juneau Southeast Alaska Empire,* April 2, 1970, 4; Martin A. Farrell, Jr., to Fellow Alaskans, Mar. 27, 1970, Gravel Papers, file Energy—Nuclear: Cannikin Juneau Hearings, box 597; "Briefings," Gravel Papers, file 5, box 597 and file 4, box 108; Miller to Giler, Gravel Papers, file 5, box 597 and file 4, box 108. For resolutions passed by the legislature, see *Alaska Statutes, Temporary and Special Acts and Resolutions, Alaska State Legislature, Sixth Legislature—Second Session,* 1970, 89–91. Joe P. Josephson to James H. Heller, Apr. 21, 1970, Gravel Papers, file 1, box 597.

12. Seaborg with Loeb, *AEC Under Nixon,* 38–39.

13. Ibid. For Seaborg's account of the environmentalist effect, see chapter 7, "The Environmental Onslaught," 113–22. One AEC official thought another shot in October rather than in the spring would better protect commercial fishing, bird hatchlings, and sea otters. He said it would also have "the desirable feature of abiding with the spirit and principles" of NEPA (see next paragraph). Elwood M. Douthett to Robert E. Miller, Jan. 30, 1970, ADEC, file 10, box 10.

14. *National Environmental Policy Act of 1969, Statutes at Large,* 83, sec. 2, 102 (1969). The statute creating NEPA is Public Law 91–190. Gravel's complaints about the AEC were a constant theme. See "International Commission on Radiological Protection," 91st Cong., 2nd sess., *Congressional Record,* Senate (May 13, 1970), vol.

116, pt. 11, 15429–30. After his election in 1968, Gravel depicted himself as a "nuclear opponent." See Seaborg and Loeb, *AEC Under Nixon,* 38 n.

15. "Memorandum on AEC's Proposed 'Cannikin' ABM Test at Amchitka," n.d., Gravel Papers, file 1, box 10; Mike Gravel to Glenn T. Seaborg, May 5, 1970, Gravel Papers, file 2, box 422; John A. Erlewine to Chairman Seaborg and Commissioners Raney, Johnson, Thompson, and Larson, June 9, 1970, CIC 0138468.

16. Egan O'Connor to Mike Gravel, June 24, 1970, Gravel Papers, file 2, box 598.

17. Ibid.

18. Gravel to Sen. Allen Ellender, July 2, 1970, and Gravel speech, Sept. 10, 1970, Gravel Papers, files 1 and 6, box 597; Edward B. Giller to R. E. Miller, Nov. 18, 1970, ADEC, file 6, box 1; Glenn Seaborg to Gravel, Dec. 5, 1970, Gravel Papers, file 6, box 597.

19. Seaborg to Gravel, enclosure, Dec. 5, 1970, Gravel Papers, file 1, box 597; *Congressional Quarterly Weekly Report* 28 (Aug. 14, 1970): 2035, 2079, and (Dec. 4, 1970): 2097, and (June 19, 1970): 1591–94. Alaska Representative Howard Pollock did not vote on the procurement bill, House Resolution 17123. See *Weekly Report* (May 15, 1970): 1320. He believed that opponents had not proven their case against the AEC, but favored establishing an independent commission for studying test effects. Pollack to Mr. & Mrs. Edward Duryea, Feb. 19, 1970, UA Fairbanks, Pollock Papers, Legislative file 8, box 1. The expanded ABM program also entailed preliminary site work in "the upper Northwest, central California, southern California, Texas, Florida-Georgia, southern New England, and Michigan-Ohio." Sites in Hawaii and Alaska were contemplated for future development. *Weekly Report* (Jan. 23, 1970): 208.

20. Seaborg to Gravel, Dec. 5, 1970, Gravel Papers, file 1, box 597; Seaborg and Loeb, *AEC under Nixon,* 39–40.

21. Seaborg and Loeb, *AEC under Nixon,* 40; Hacker, *Elements of Controversy,* 248; John G. Fuller, *The Day We Bombed Utah: America's most Lethal Secret* (New York: New American Library, 1984), 199.

22. Seaborg and Loeb, *AEC under Nixon,* 40; Hacker, *Elements of Controversy,* 248–49.

23. *Fairbanks Daily News-Miner,* October 3, 1969, 1, and October 7, 1969, 9; see also endnote 3.

9 / AMID MORE CANNIKIN CONTROVERSY

Epigraph from taped interview by author, Ester, Alaska, June 15, 1995, UA Fairbanks, Oral History Program. Feinberg is a freelance researcher and writer who is still interested in the morality of political action.

1. Hansen, *U.S. Nuclear Weapons,* 189; Miichael J. H. Taylor and John W. R. Taylor, *Missiles of the World* (New York: Charles Scribner's Sons, 1972), 139.

2. Shot Boxcar is listed as yielding 1.3 million tons, Cannikin less than 5 million. See *U.S. Nuclear Tests,* 32–42, for various high-yield test listings.

3. "Engineering & Construction Scope of Work, Cannikin Event, Amchitka," Apr. 27, 1970, 2, ADEC, file 13, box 4, and Phillip E. Coyle to Robert H. Thalgott, Sept. 8, 1971, file 2, box 7. Five deep exploratory holes were drilled in connection with Cannikin. The deepest reached 7,000 feet. R. O. Ross to Elroy Vento, Jul. 20, 1971, ADEC, file 1, box 6. The Plowshare program to recover natural gas detonated Shot Rulison at 8,430 feet deep in Colorado and Shot Miniata at 17,500 feet in Nevada. See Frank Kreith and Catherine B. Wrenn, *The Nuclear Impact: A Case Study of the Plowshare Program to Produce Gas by Underground Nuclear Stimulation in the Rocky Mountains* (Boulder, Colorado: Westview Press, 1976), 15–16. Also "Engineering & Construction," Apr. 27, 1970, 2–3, ADEC, file 13, box 4; Cannikin diagram, ADEC, file 5, box 4. Advertising for bids to mine this cavern began in 1968. It called for mining an area 30 feet in diameter, 61 feet deep. "It will be lined with a waterproof room liner consisting of steel outer shell lined with high strength plastic concrete." Telegram, Jun. 28, 1968, RG 01 Juneau, file Amchitka 1967–68, box 4838.

4. Amchitka Island, Exhibit I, ADEC, file 2, box 8; Samuel Glasstone and Philip J. Dolan, comp. and eds., *The Effects of Nuclear Weapons,* 3d ed. (Department of Defense and Department of Energy, 1977), 61–62.

5. *Anchorage Daily News,* May 25, 1971, 2; Henry G. Vermillion to Robert E. Miller, Apr. 20, 1971, ADEC, file 19, box 9.

6. Richard J. Denney, Jr., to the Files, Apr. 26, 1971, and John R. McBride to the Files, Apr. 29, 1971, CIC 0158614 and 0158613; Senators to William D. Ruckelshaus, Apr. 30, 1971, Gravel Papers, file 4, box 122; Text of Egan Press Release and Henry G. Vermillion to John A. Harris, May 11, 1971, ADEC, file 3, box 6; *Juneau Southeast Alaska Empire,* May 7, 1971, 1, 12. Egan was elected Alaska's first state governor, serving from 1959 to 1966 and then from 1970 to 1974. Minnesota Senator Hubert H. Humphrey had called for abandonment of Cannikin in April. See 92nd Cong., 1st sess., *Congressional Record,* Senate (April 14, 1971).

7. See endnote 6.

8. Edward B. Giller to R. E. Miller, Apr. 23, 1971, ADEC, file 3, box 6; William A. Egan to William D. Ruckelshaus, May 18, 1971, CIC 0158078; E. B. Giller to Robert E. Miller, May 10 and 21, 1971, ADEC, file 4, box 4, and file 8, box 6; *Juneau Southeast Alaska Empire,* May 24, 1971, 6. Department of Defense and AEC discussions about whether to reveal Cannikin data revolved around national security and public information questions. Some thought it would aid the enemy; others thought that it

was necessary to inform citizens in the face of growing opposition to the test. Edward B. Giller to Chairman Seaborg, Commissioners Ramey, Johnson, and Larson, Jan. 22, 1971, and Seaborg to Nelvin R. Laird, Mar. 2, 1971, CIC 0076111 and 0076109.

9. *Juneau Southeast Alaska Empire,* May 27, 1971, 1, 8; Carolyn Burg to Farrell, May 28, 1971, 6.

10. *Juneau Southeast Alaska Empire,* May 27, 1971, 1, 8; "Statement of Wallace H. Noerenberg . . . at the Amchitka-Cannikin Event Hearings—May 16, 1971, Juneau, Alaska, RG 11 AK Fish and Game, file AEC 1969, box 6863.

11. Stone's complete statement is in Gravel Papers, file 4, box 122; *Anchorage Daily Times,* May 28, 1971, 1, 2; *Anchorage Daily News,* May 29, 1971, 1, 2, and May 30, 1; *New York Times,* May 30, 1971, 40; "Presentation of Leo A. Walsh on Behalf of the Alaska Chapters of the Associated General Contractors of America," ADEC, file 2, box 8.

12. "A Brief Submitted to the United States Atomic Energy Commission Hearings on the Proposed Five-Megaton Underground Nuclear Test Scheduled for Amchitka Island in October, 1971," May 28, 1971, University of Alaska Anchorage, Alaska reading room, file AVF-Amchitka, Alaska. See also *Alaska Daily News,* May 30, 1971, 1, 2. "The Dominion of Canada and Project Cannikin: A Brief Presented to the Atomic Energy Commission by the Don't Make a Wave Committee," May 28, 1971, ADEC, file 1, box 8; *Anchorage Daily Times,* May 28, 1971, 1, and May 29, 2; *Anchorage Daily News,* May 29, 1971, 1, 2.

13. *Final Environmental Statement—Cannikin* (U.S. Atomic Energy Commission, June 1971), 1–4.

14. Gravel read into the record selections from the Alaska hearings. See 92nd Cong., 1st sess., *Congressional Record* (June 4, 1971): vol. 117, pt. 14, 18084–97. Also see (June 14, 1971): vol 117. pt. 15, 19629; *Congressional Record,* House (June 28, 1971): vol. 117 pt. 17, 22462–69; (July 14, 1971): vol. 117, pt. 19, 25209–10, 25228–44; *Congressional Record,* Senate (July 15, 1961): vol 117, pt. 19, 25304–05. See Daniel K. Inouye to Mike Gravel, Jul. 26, 1961, Gravel Papers, file 3, box 122. Besides his Amchitka opposition, Gravel picked another controversy. In June, he read the Pentagon Papers into the public record as a Senate subcommittee member. See Sanford J. Ungar, *The Papers and The Paper,* (New York: E. P. Dutton, 1972), 253–70, 290–92.

15. The focus of Gravel's position was anti-ABM. Egan [O'Connor] to Lenore, John, Bob, Jim Heller, Mar. 18, 1971, Gravel Papers, file 2, box 598. *Congressional Record,* Senate (July 19, 1971): vol. 117, pt. 20, 25820–24, 26045–60; *Congressional Record,* House (July 29, 1971): vol. 117, pt. 21, 28080–90. Gov. Egan had opposed the test program since 1969. See *New York Times,* August 1, 1971, 8. "Statement of William A. Egan . . . Regarding the Proposed Huge Amchitka Nuclear Explosions," June 25,

1969, ADEC, file 1, box 8. See also *New York Times*, July 21, 1971, 13; July 31, 1971, 26; and September 23, 1971, 37.

16. Seaborg and Loeb, *AEC under Nixon*, 41–45. Deputy Defense Secretary David Packard agreed on July 19 to announcing the test's purpose.

17. "Minutes," Milrow critique/Cannikin Planning Meeting, Feb. 20, 1970, ADEC, file 5, box 4; "Public Information Action Plan," Nov. 1, 1970, file 8, box 2; J. A. Harris to Robert E. Miller, Aug. 19, 1971, file 2, box 2. Gravel had complained to the Comptroller General that AEC public relations efforts were too costly and promoted the agency rather than informing the public. He asked for an investigation. Gravel to Elmer B. Staats, Jul. 30, 1971, Gravel Papers, file 2, box 598.

18. *Anchorage Daily News*, September 26, 1971, 28; September 27, 1971, 4; September 25, 1971, 1, 2, and advertisement, n.p.

19. *Anchorage Daily News*, September 17, 1971, 6; Statement of Lillie H. McGarvey, Oct. 18, 1971, Record Group 06, Records of the Alaska Department of Health, Alaska State Archives, Juneau (hereinafter cited as RG 06 Juneau), file Cannikin, Box 4704; *Alaska Mothers' Campaign against Cannikin*, (material prepared by Stephen Haycox), CIC 0160278; Dixon Steward to Robert E. Miller, Aug. 30, 1971, ADEC, file 9, box 9.

20. Other officers of Concerned Citizens Against Cannikin were vice-president Shirley Dean and treasurer Malcolm Doiron. *Ketchikan Daily News*, October 28, 1971, 1; October 30, 1971, 1; November 4, 1971, 1; James R. Musson to Mike Gravel, Oct. 30, 1971, and tearsheet of *Washington Post*, n.d., Gravel Papers, file Amchitka Memoranda, box 122.

21. See the student newspaper, *Polar Star*, October 1, 1971, 1; October 15, 1971, 3; October 22, 1971, 1; November 5, 1971, 1, UA Fairbanks. Anthropology Department Chairman John P. Cook, who conducted AEC-sponsored research on Amchitka, criticized the Commission for not considering possible blast damage to archaeological artifacts and for not giving researchers enough time to evaluate their finds. *Fairbanks Daily News-Miner*, October 26, 1971, 8.

22. Resolution By Alaska Nurses Association Regarding the Amchitka Blast, 92nd Cong., 1st sess., *Congressional Record*, House (July 13, 1971): vol. 117, pt. 19, 24829; *Anchorage Daily News*, October 23, 1971, 1. Figures of protest letters from computer-run printout of Amchitka citations, reference CIC 0160336 and 0160337. *Kodiak Island Times*, October 15, 1971, 2; *Fairbanks Daily News-Miner*, October 25, 1971, 2. Governor Egan asked the Defense Department to position rescue vessels along the Aleutian Chain, but the request was turned down. See *Anchorage Daily Times*, October 29, 1971, 1. One newspaper editorial argued that Senator Gravel's disclosure of the Aleutian nerve gas dumping had been a turning point. It converted conservative Alaska

dailies from spoofing his efforts to supporting them in a "swelling" of Cannikin opposition. *All Alaska Weekly,* June 4, 1971, 2.

23. Robert Keziere and Robert Hunter, *Greenpeace* (Toronto: McClelland and Stewart, Limited, 1972), n.p. For Hunter's story, see his *Warriors of the Rainbow: A Chronicle of the Greenpeace Movement* (New York: Holt, Rinehart and Winston, 1979), ch. I, "From Amchitka to Mururoa," 3–119.

24. Hunter, *Warriors of the Rainbow,* 9–17; Richard Fineberg, interview by author, Ester, Alaska, June 15, 1995; Richard A. Feinberg, "Amchitka Protest: Canadians to Anchor off Test Site," *Anchorage Daily News,* September 11, 1971, 15; Mike Gravel to Richard Feinberg, June 11, 1971, Gravel Papers, file 3, box 122.

25. Hunter, *Warriors of the Rainbow,* 7; Richard Feinberg, "The Voyage of the Greenpeace," *Anchorage Daily News,* October 29, 1971, 7.

26. *Anchorage Daily News,* September 15, 1971, 1–2; September 19, 1971, 2; October 14, 1971, 1; Hunter, *Warriors of the Rainbow,* 25–27, 32–33, 36–49, 52–63; Richard Fineberg, interview by author, Ester, Alaska, June 15, 1995; Telegram, CJTG 8.3 to RUWSSBA, ADEC file 1, box 2; Keziere and Hunter, *Greenpeace,* n.p. Feinberg mentioned "the magic and the strife" of his time on the ship. He was suspected as an undercover agent for the Central Intelligence Agency and resented for being an academician. In order to make the journey, he gave up a $9,600 National Endowment for the Humanities grant to do post-doctoral work. Feinberg to Hunter, Aug. 4, 1980, from the files of Richard A. Feinberg.

27. Hunter, *Warriors of the Rainbow,* 78–80, 86–87, 89–90, 96–112; *Kodiak Island Times,* October 22, 1971, 3; *Anchorage Daily News,* October 24, 1971, 1; Feinberg to Bob Sarti, Oct. 18, 1981, Feinberg files.

28. *Alaska Daily News,* May 27, 1971, 1; Robert E. Miller to W. E. Ogle, et al., Jun. 1, 1971, ADEC, file 4, box 8, and Dixon Stewart to H. G. Vermillion, May 17, 1971, file 19, box 9; "Hearings of the Atomic Energy Commission on Cannikin," May 18, 1971 [Begich statement], UA Fairbanks, Nicholas Begich Papers, file B, box Amchitka.

29. Hugh W. Fleischer, interview by author, Anchorage, Alaska, June 14, 1994; transcript, *The Aleut League, et al., v. The Atomic Energy Commission, et al.,* no. A-127-71 Civil, Judgment, vol II, Record Group 21-77B-0015, National Archives—Alaska Region, Anchorage; *Tundra Times,* September 29, 1971, 1, 6; transcript, *The Aleut League, et al., v. The Atomic Energy Commission, et al.,* no. A-127-71 Civil, Judgment, vol I, Record Group 21-77B-0015, National Archives—Alaska Region, Anchorage; Nelvin W. Carter to Robert Thalgott, Sept. 29, 1971, and E. B. Giller to Robert E. Miller, Oct. 1, 1971, ADEC, file 4, box 6; *Anchorage Daily News,* October 26, 1971, 4; *Tundra Times,* October 27, 1971, 1, 7.

30. *Anchorage Daily News,* October 14, 1971, 2; transcript, *The Aleut League, et al.,*

v. The Atomic Energy Commission, et al., no. A-127-71 Civil, Memorandum of Decision and Order, vol. II, Nov. 2, 1971, 34, 36, Record Group 21-77B-0015, National Archives—Alaska Region, Anchorage. See also *Aleut League v. Atomic Energy Commission,* 337 F. Supp. 534 (1971).

31. *The Committee for Nuclear Responsibility, et al., v. Glenn T. Seaborg, et al.,* Supreme Court, November Term 1971, No. A-482, Application for Injunction in Aid of Jurisdiction, 1–17, National Archives, Record Group 267, Records of the Supreme Court, entry 30, box 149; see also 463 F. 2d 782 (1971); 463 F. 2d 788 (1971); and 463 F. 2d 796 (1971).

32. Since Glenn Seaborg had resigned the AEC chairmanship, his successor, James R. Schlesinger, Jr., is named in the appeal. *The Committee for Nuclear Responsibility, Inc., et al, v. James R. Schlesinger, et al.,* Oral Arguments, National Archives, Record Group 267, Records of the Supreme Court, entry 30, box 149; Supreme Court *Bulletin,* 1971–1972 term, vol. I, no. A483, B165-177; *New York Times,* November 7, 1971, 1, 65.

33. *Anchorage Daily News,* November 5, 1971, 2, and November 7, 1971, 1; *Anchorage Daily Times,* November 6, 1971, 103; AEC News Release, Nov. 8, 1971, CIC 0147375; Henry G. Vermillion, "Cannikin and the Public," Jun. 21, 1972, ADEC, file 3, box 7.

34. "Substance of the Note Delivered to the United States Department of State by the Canadian Ambassador in Washington on February 22, 1971 . . . ," Gravel Papers, file 3, box 122; *External Affairs* 23 (November 1971): 421–27; *New York Times,* September 7, 1971, 2; October 28, 1971, 26; November 5, 1971, 20; C. Robert Pearson to Mike Gravel, Aug. 23, 1971, Gravel Papers, file 4, box 122; *Ketchikan Daily News,* October 7, 1971, 1; *New York Times,* November 3, 1971, 29.

35. See endnote 34.

10 / BEYOND THE LAST BOMB

Epigraph from Auke Tribe Council, Inc., to President Richard M. Nixon, Nov. 2, 1971, Gravel Papers, file 2, box 428.

1. M. O. Merritt to Charles Williams, Nov. 8, 1971, ADEC, file 5, box 6; James B. Kirkwood and R. Glen Fuller, *Bioenvironmental Effects Predictions for the Proposed Cannikin Underground Nuclear Detonation at Amchitka Island, Alaska* (Columbus, Ohio: Battelle, 1971), 1–2, 25–26; R. G. Fuller and J. B. Kirkwood, "Ecological Consequences of Nuclear Testing," Merritt and Fuller, *Environment of Amchitka,* 638, 641; Frank Jones to Wallace H. Noerenberg, Nov. 26, 1961, RG 11 AK Fish and Game, file Commissioner's Reading file, November 1971, box 6909, and Karl Schneider, "An

Evaluation of the Effects of Cannikin on Amchitka's Sea Otter Population," Dec. 2, 1971, file AEC 1971, box 6863. See also J. A. Estes and N. S. Smith, *Research on the Sea Otter, Amchitka Island, Alaska Final Report* (Tucson: University of Arizona, 1973). For other impressions of the test's effects, see George Laycock, "Amchitka Revisited," *Audubon* 74 (January 1972): 113–15.

2. Fuller and Kirkwood, "Ecological Consequences," 641–63; Robert L. Rausch, *Post Mortem Findings In Some Marine Mammals and Birds Following the Cannikin Test on Amchitka Island* (Fairbanks: Arctic Health Research Center, 1973).

3. Fuller and Kirkwood, "Ecological Consequences," 638–40, 643–44, 646–48; Baine H. Carter to Area Director, Bureau of Sport Fisheries and Wildlife, Nov. 16, 1961, FWS Adak, file Amchitka Information; Edward B. Giller to R. E. Miller, Nov. 17, 1971, ADEC, file 5, box 6. See also Melvin L. Merritt, *Physical and Biological Effects: Cannikin* (Las Vegas: AEC Nevada Operations Office, 1973), and Charles E. O'Clair, Jr., "The Effects of Uplift on Intertidal Communities at Amchitka Island, Alaska" (Ph.D. diss., University of Washington, 1977).

4. M. L. Merritt, *Cannikin: Effects on Archaeological Sites* (Albuquerque: Sandia Laboratories, 1972).

5. United States Atomic Energy Commission, *Project Cannikin D+30 Day Report: Preliminary Operational and Test Results Summary* (Las Vegas: Nevada Operations Office, 1972), ii; Eberline Instrument Corporation, *Project Cannikin On-Site Radiological Safety and Medical Services* (August 1973), 23; "Cannikin Post Re-Entry Water Sampling Program: UA-1 Post Shot Hole," Nov. 23, 1971; Robert E. Miller to Edward B. Giller, Feb. 23, 1972; V. E. Shockley and P. R. Prevo to P. E. Coyle, Mar. 6, 1972, ADEC, file 5, box 6.

6. Donald W. Hendricks to Elwood M. Douthett, Oct. 29, 1972, and Shockley and Prevo to Coyle, Mar. 6, 1972, ADEC, file 5, box 6; Merritt, *Physical and Biological Effects,* 49; Eberline, *Project Cannikin,* 29; L. J. O'Neill to G. A. Stafford, Mar. 16, 1972, ADEC, file 10, box 7.

7. E. B. Giller to Robert E. Miller, May 31, 1972; Elwood M. Douthett to William D. Smith, Jr., June 1, 1972; G. A. Stafford to William D. Smith, Jr., June 7, 1972, ADEC, file 5, box 6; Donald W. Hendricks to Perry N. Halstead, Feb. 14, 1973, ADEC, file 5, box 7; *Summary of On-Site Radiological Monitoring Operations For the Cannikin Event* (November 6, 1971), Amchitka, Alaska (Las Vegas: Department of Energy, Radiological Branch, 1978), 18.

8. Carolyn V. Brown, "Some Comments about Radiation Effects on Alaska Natives," September *1971* (unpublished), University of Alaska Anchorage Consortium Library; Melvin W. Carter to Brown, Dec. 10, 1971, CIC 0158421; Carter to John F. Lee, Mar. 2, 1972, ADEC, file 5, box 6; Carolyn V. Brown, "Cannikin Nuclear Explosion:

Human Surveillance" in Roy J. Shephard and S. Itoh, eds., *Circumpolar Health* (Toronto and Buffalo: University of Toronto Press, 1974), 647–50.

9. Carl M. Hild to Bev Aleck, Nov. 9, 1994, and Apr. 19, 1995, from the files of Carl Hild, Anchorage, Rural Alaska Community Action Program, Indigenous Peoples' Council For Marine Mammals; Bev Aleck, telephone conversation with author, December 29, 1996.

10. *Greenpeace Quarterly* 1 (fall 1996): 4; *San Francisco Examiner,* October 30, 1996, A10; *Village Voice,* November 5, 1996, 1; Pam Miller and Norman Buske, *Nuclear Flashback: The Return to Amchitka* (Washington, D.C.: Greenpeace, 1996), 4–5, 16, 20–21, 29.

11. *New York Times,* October 30, 1996, A15; *USA Today,* October 31, 1996, A3; *Village Voice,* November 5, 1996, 1; *Anchorage Daily News,* October 30, 1996, A1; October 31, B1; November 25, B6; and November 26, B4; Pam Miller to author, Nov. 7, 1996; Douglas H. Dasher, telephone conversation with author, April 10, 1997.

12. Clay E. Crawford to Roland J. Marchand, Apr. 28, 1970, report enclosure, and R. G. Fuller to E. D. Campbell, May 1, 1970, ADEC, file 8, box 8; Draft Roll-Up Items, Nov. 4, 1970, file 2, box 8; Henry G. Vermillion to Donald L. Bray, Jun. 8, 1971, and "Progress Report on Revegetation Trials of the Institute of Agricultural Sciences, University of Alaska," July 1971, file 1, box 6; David G. Jackson to Allan Frank, Apr. 6, 1972, file 5, box 6.

13. *Planning Directive: Demobilization, Restoration and Monitoring Amchitka Island Test Area* (Las Vegas: U.S. Atomic Energy Commission, 1972); Amchitka Sea Otter Studies Advisory Panel to Robert E. Miller, Jan. 24, 1972, and Miller to William A. Egan, Mar. 10, 1972, ADEC, file 4, box 3; E. B. Giller to Miller, Mar. 21, 1972, CIC 0158438; Giller to Miller, Apr. 13, 1972, ADEC, file 5, box 6.

14. Merritt and Fuller, *Environment of Amchitka,* 644–46, 652; E. B. Giller to Robert E. Miller, Jan. 26, 1962, and Mahlon E. Gates to Gordon Watson, Sept. 18, 1973, ADEC, file 4, box 6; information on photographs of brass plaque monuments, June 1996, courtesy of Pamela Miller; G. Vernon Byrd, wildlife biologist, interview by author, Adak Island, June 20, 1994.

15. Aleutian Islands National Wildlife Refuge and Izembek National Wildlife Range Narrative Report, Jan. 1, 1971–Dec. 31, 1971, 16, Anchorage FWS; *Washington Post,* September 18, 1974, clipping and list of biosphere reserves in FWS Adak, file LU-Biosphere Reserves 1974–1986.

16. Donna A. Dewhurst, "History of Amchitka Island, Alaska: Prehistory to 1988," Dec. 1988, 6–7, FWS Adak, file HI-Amchitka; Daniel L. Boone, Aleutian Islands Refuge Manager, interview by author, Adak Island, June 20, 1994.

17. Jeffrey B. Staser, "Defense Environmental Restoration Program," July 11, 1985;

U.S. Army Engineer District, Alaska, "Environmental Assessment: Defense Environmental Restoration Program," July, 1985; Alaska Construction Management to Coffman Engineers Inc., July 22, 1985, FWS Adak, file LU-Restoration Program, and L. R. Marsh to John Martin, June 11, 1991, file HI-Amchitka; R. L. Frazier to John Martin and Dan Boone, July 1, 1992, file Agreement Navy.

18. D. Colt Denfeld, *The Cold War in Alaska: A Management Plan for Cultural Resources, 1994–1999* (Alaska District: U.S. Army Corps of Engineers, 1994), 213–14; Donna Dewhurst, "History of Amchitka," Dec. 1988, 6–7, FWS Adak, file HI-Amchitka, 7–8.

19. Denfeld, *The Cold War in Alaska*, 14; Robert Bowker to Wilbur T. Gregory, Jr., Mar. 8, 1988; Tom Crane to Files, Dec. 5, 1988; Walter O. Stieglitz to Tom Crane, Dec. 6, 1988; Donna A. Dewhurst to Shaun Sexton, Jan. 24, 1989; J. F. Lebiedz to U.S. Environmental Protection Agency, Jan. 26, 1989, FWS Adak, file Agreement Navy; *Second Relocatable-Over-the-Horizon Radar (ROTHR) System Amchitka Island, Alaska: Draft Environmental Impact Statement* (Department of the Navy, 1991); Daniel Boone, interview by author, Adak Island, June 22, 1994; *Amchorage Daily News,* October 31, 1996, B5.

20. For details of Refuge work on Amchitka, see Narrative Reports by year, Anchorage FWS; John Martin, "Amchitka," Apr. 4, 1980, FWS Adak, file HI-Aleutians, and Byrd to RM, Aug. 12, 1988, file Biologist Amchitka; G. Vernon Byrd, interview by author, June 20, 1994, and Kevin Bell, interview by author, June 21, 1995, Adak Island.

21. Richard Milhouse Nixon, *RN: The Memoirs of Richard Nixon* (New York: Grosset & Dunlap, 1978), 415–16; Allan M. Winkler, *Life under a Cloud: American Anxiety About the Atom* (New York and Oxford: Oxford University Press, 1993), 183–84. Literature on the SALT talks is extensive. A helpful, early study, for instance, is John Newhouse, *Cold Dawn: The Story of SALT* (New York: Holt, Rinehart and Winston, 1973). The best by a participant is Gerard Smith, *Doubletalk: The Story of the First Strategic Arms Limitation Talks* (Garden City, NY: Doubleday & Company, Inc., 1980).

22. Seaborg with Loeb, *AEC under Nixon,* 30n, 34, 47; Hanson, *U.S. Nuclear Weapons,* 189. One estimate for the cost of developing nuclear weapons alone was $45.5 billion. See "Cost of Developing and Producing Atomic Weapons from Fiscal Year 1940 through Fiscal Year 1975," Gravel Papers, file Nuclear Weapons B, box 963. Clean-up costs at five production sites, however, are estimated at $230 billion over a seventy-five year period. See U.S. Department of Energy, *Estimating the Cold War Mortgage: The 1995 Baseline Environmental Management Report Executive Summary March 1995* (U.S. Department of Energy, 1995), i.

INDEX

Abegglen, Carl E., 84

Acheson, Dean, 35

Adak Island, 15, 25, 116

Advanced Research Projects Agency, 56

Agattu Island, 7, 30

Agnew, Spiro, 74

Airfields, 19–20

Akutan Island, 12, 106

Alaska: AEC relations with, 79, 100;
economic benefits of testing, 74–75;
geography of, 3, 5; islands, 5–6; oil
pipeline, 100; World War II's effect
on, 14

Alaska Army Scouts, 17–18

Alaska Coalition Against Cannikin, 104

Alaska Conservation Society, 63, 77, 105,
140n9

Alaska Department of Environmental
Conservation, 143n37

Alaska Legal Services Corporation, 106

Alaska Medical Association, 105

Alaska Mothers' Campaign Against
Cannikin, 104

Alaska Nurses Association, 105

Alaska Railroad, 74

Alaska Sportsmen's Council, 78

Aleck, Beverly, 112

Aleck, Nick, 112

Aleutian Islands: construction's effect
on, 15–16; geography of, 6, 119n11;
hunting of furbearers on, 8–9; as
imbued with spirit, 109; indigenous
people of, 5; map of, 4; names for,
118n2; resources of, 6–7; soldier's
impressions of, 24–25; under
Russian rule, 7–9

Aleutian Islands National Wildlife
Reservation, 11, 45, 121n19

Alexander Archipelago, 3, 5

Algae, 88

Amaknak Island, 12, 13

Amchitka: archeological sites, 23;
biological surveys, 46; as biosphere
reserve, 115; cleanup of, 114; cycles of
habitation of, 9; exploratory air raid
on, 18; geography of, 7–8; invasion
of 1943, 18–19; long-term radiation
on, 113; map of, 10; and military, 17-
18, 19–22; Milrow's environmental
damage, 82–84, 87–88; naming of,
7–8; as nuclear graveyard, 117;
restoration of, 31–32, 117; value as
nuclear test site, 52–54; withdrawal
for military use of, 30, 110

"Amchitka Express" (Japanese air raids), 19

Amchitka Two, 107

Americium *241*, 113

Anchorage Daily News, 104

Anchorage Daily Times, 36, 40, 76, 80

Anti-ballistic missiles (ABMs), 68–71, 73–74, 95, 98, 116, 148*n19*

Arctic Health Research Laboratory (Public Health Service), 45

Armed Forces Special Weapons Project, 32–33

Armstrong, Karl, 140*n11*

Army Corps of Engineers, 15, 21, 75

Army Ordnance Corps, U.S., 69

Arthur Middleton (transport ship), 18

Asahi Shimbun (newspaper), 96

Asplund, John, 90

Association on American Indian Affairs, 107

Atka Island, 24, 112

Atomic bombs. *See* Nuclear weapons

Atomic Energy Commission (AEC): and Alamogordo, 27; Cannikin role of, 99–104, 108, 149*n8;* cleanup of Amchitka, 114; decoupled detonations, 57; expenditures of, 42; Long Shot role of, 59, 61, 64; Military Application Division, 69, 100; Military Liaison Committee, 33; Milrow role of, 79–87, 90; Native Alaskans and, 107; nuclear safety, 75, 85–86; Operation Windstorm role of, 35–37; Project Larkspur role of, 54; Public Information Department, 61; public relations campaigns of, 61, 80–81, 90–92, 99–104, 110, 151*n17;* secrecy by, 91–93, 103–104; security

issues as emphasis of, 89; supervision of construction work by, 82–84

Attu Island, 13–19

Atwood, Robert B., 90

Audubon, 65, 83

Bacher, Robert F., 56

Bartlett, Bob, 41, 45, 60, 62–63, 77, 83–84, 140*n11*, 141*n17*

Bashmakov, Petr, 8

Battelle Columbus Laboratories, 81–82

Beals, Frank, 29

Bell Laboratories, 69

Bentonite, 111

Berger, Warren, 107

Bering, Vitus, 7

Bethe, Hans B., 73–74

Bikini atoll, 27

Biological Survey, U.S. Bureau of, 12

Birds: fatalities from Cannikin, 110; garbage dumps as havens for, 88; geese, 30–31, 66; loss of habitat for, 87, 115; in post-bomb test era, 116; restoration programs, 66; Soviet test's effect on, 43; surveys on Amchitka of, 8, 46; after the Trinity test, 28

Black flies, 84

Blackmun, Harry A., 107

Bockstoce, John, 7

Boddy, A. W. ("Bud"), 78, 90

Bomb shelters, 41

Bombs, atomic. *See* Nuclear weapons

Bradbury, Norris E., 37

Bragin, Dimitri, 8

Brakel, Bernard, 101

Breakwaters, 21–23

Brennan, William J., Jr., 107
Brezhnev, Leonid I., 116
Brooks Range, 50–52, 71, 74, 77
Brown, Carolyn V., 112
Buckheister, Carl W., 65–66
Buckner, Maj. Gen. Simon B., 16, 18, 25
Bureau of Fisheries, 12
Burg, Carolyn, 101

Canada, 33, 76, 94, 96, 108
Canadian Coalition to Stop the
    Amchitka Nuclear Blast, 108
Cannikin (test): AEC role in, 99–104,
    108, 149n8; bird losses from, 110;
    detonation of, 98, 108;
    environmental damage from,
    110–111; Greenpeace protest over,
    105–106; international reaction to,
    96; litigation over, 106–108; post-
    shot drilling, 111; Senate opposition
    to, 95; site preparation for, 99, 149n3;
    size of, 98
Carbon 14, 112
Castner, Col. Lawrence V., 17
Cats, feral, 45–46
Century Geophysical Corporation, 58
Chadwick, Jerah, 13
China, 32, 71, 74
Chirikof Island, 51
Chuginadak Island, 5
Clams, 29
Committee for Nuclear Responsibility,
    107
Commoner, Barry, 73
Concerned Citizens Against Cannikin,
    104–105
Confidence (cutter), 106
Congressional Record, 45

Conqueror (movie), 73
Constantine Harbor, 18, 20–21
Construction: of airfields, 19–20; effect
    amenities for workers in, 86; effect
    on Aleutians of, 15–16; of harbor
    facilities, 20–22; for Long Shot,
    58–59; for Milrow, 82–84; of roads,
    21
Council on Environmental Quality, 100
Cranston, Alan, 75
Creation tales, 5
Crowson, Brig. Gen. Delmar L., 72, 77
Cuban Missile Crisis, 54, 55
Curtis, Hugh, 96
Czechoslovakia, 74

Dasher, Douglas H., 113
Dean, Frederick C., 63–64
Dean, Gordon, 35–36
Defense, U.S. Department of, 61, 63–64,
    89, 115, 133n22, 149n8
DeMan, Michael H., 143n35
Democrats for Action and Issues (DIA),
    79–80, 143n35
Dickson, George A., 143n35
Diomede Islands, 5, 40, 130n2
Dogs, feral, 45–46
Dolly Varden trout, 88, 110
Don't Make a Wave, 105
Doty, Dale E., 38
Douglas, William O., 107
Duck Cove, 87–88
Dufresne, Frank, 25
Dunning, Gordon, 57
Dutch Harbor, 13

Eareckson, Col. William O., 18
Early warning systems, 42

Earthquakes: fears of, 85, 94, 103; Great
    Alaska Earthquake, *1964*, 60, 137*n19*;
    from Milrow test, 87; oil spills and,
    75–76; in the Soviet Union, 59
Edwards, G. Kent, 107
Egan, William A., 60–62, 78, 100–101,
    130*n5*, 132*n14*, 143*n37*, 149*n6*
Eisenhower, Dwight D., 56–57, 70
Ellender, Allen J., 95
Elliott, Henry W., 6
Energy, U.S. Department of, 113
Enewetak Atoll, 28
Environmental Impact Statements
    (EISS), 93–94, 101–102, 107
Environmental and External
    Operational Safety Group, 53–54
Environmental damage: from
    Cannikin, 110–111, 113; from hunting
    and fishing by workers, 16–17, 88;
    from Long Shot, 61–62; from
    Milrow, 82–84, 87–88; post-bomb
    test survey of, 113–114; from ROTHR,
    115–116; at Trinity Site, 27–28; from
    World War II bombing, 16, 18–19
Environmental Protection Agency
    (EPA), 100, 113
Erosion, 16
Executive Order *1773*, 11

Fallout, nuclear: Alaskan public
    opinion on, 45; from the Baneberry
    shot, 96; from Bikini, 26; danger of,
    80, 132*n14*; government unconcern
    over, 44; in high-latitude areas, 44,
    51–52; leakage from Long Shot, 62;
    on the "Lucky Dragon", 43; from
    Nevada, 39; from Soviet tests, 44. *See
    also* Radiation, nuclear

Farrell, Martin A., Jr., 68, 80–81,
    143*n37*
"Fat Man" (atomic bomb), 26
Federal Water Pollution Control
    Administration, 84
Feinberg, Richard A., 98, 106, 152*n26*
Feral animals, 45–46
The Firecracker Boys (O'Neill), 43
Fish and Game Department, Alaskan,
    45, 144*n45*
Fish and Wildlife Service, U.S., 25, 30,
    38, 81–82, 84–85, 115
Fishing, 78
Fleischer, Hugh W., 106–107
Fletcher, Rear Adm. Frank J., 16
Fong, Hiram L., 76
Fortas, Abe, 16
Fostor, John S., 96
Foxes, 25, 29, 31, 46
Friends of the Earth, 107
Friends Service Committee, 105
Fuchs, Klaus, 32
Fujii, Maj. Kazumi, 17
Fulbright, J. William, 70, 76

Gabrielson, Ira N., 17, 29
Gallagher, Hugh G., 63, 138*n29*
Game Commission, Alaska, 12, 16, 25
Garbage dumps, 88
Garfield, Brian, 15, 18, 23
Garwin, Robert L., 73–74
Geese: Aleutian, 66; Emperor, 30–31
Geological Survey, U.S., 12, 35
Geophone detectors, 58
Giller, Gen. Edward, 100–101
Glassboro Summit, 70–71
Good Friday earthquake, 60, 137*n19*
Gough Island, 69

Gravel, Mike, 73, 75, 77, 86, 90, 93–95, 102, 147*n14*, 150*n14*
Gray, H. Douglas, 29–31
Great Alaska Earthquake, *1964*, 60, 137*n19*
Greenpeace, 105–106, 112–113
"Greenpeace" (boat), 106, 152*n26*
Groves, Gen. Leslie R., 33
Gruening, Ernest, 41, 60, 80, 132*n14*, 141*n15*
Grumbly, Thomas P., 113
Guess, Eugene, 90
Guggenheim, Capt. Paul, 23–24

Haakanson, Swen, 105
Hacker, Barton, 27
Hakala, John B., 83–84
Hart, George L., Jr., 107
Helicopters, 82
Herter, Christian A., Jr., 114
Hickel, Walter J., 74–75, 78, 81, 85, 105
Hild, Carl M., 112
Hilliker, Ben, 88
Hillstrand, Earl D., 92
Hirohito, Emperor of Japan, 104
Holifield, Chet, 79, 87
Holmes and Narver, 54, 75, 82
Holthaus, Gary H., 143*n35*
Hrdlička, Aleš, 23
Hughes, Howard, 73, 75, 140*n13*
Humphrey, Hubert H., 73, 104, 149*n6*
Hunter, Celia M., 62–63
Hunting, 8–9, 11, 16–17, 25
Hutchinson, Capt. Howard B., 29
Hutchinson, Isabel, 12
Hydrogen bombs, 42

Ickes, Harold L., 16
Indian Affairs, Bureau of (BIA), 45

Inouye, Daniel K., 76, 103
Institute of Agricultural Sciences, 114
Intercontinental Ballistic Missiles (ICBMs), 48–49, 98
Interior, U.S. Department of, 114
Irwin, John, 96
Isenson, Ed, 143*n35*
Islands, Alaskan, 5–6
Isotopes, radioactive, 44, 62, 111
Izembek National Wildlife Refuge, 45
Izvestia (newspaper), 96

Jackson, Henry M., 36
Japan: AEC contacts with, 94; Cannikin, reaction to, 96; nuclear bombing of, 26; testing complaints, 76; World War II activities of, 16, 19
Johnson, Lewis A., 69
Johnson, Lyndon B., 70–71, 73, 116, 141*n15*
Joint Chiefs of Staff, 33, 35, 38, 49, 70
Joint Task Force *131*, 34, 36, 38
Jones, Brig. Gen. Lloyd E., 18
Jones, Robert D., 31–32, 38, 45–47, 55, 59–60, 66, 82

Katerina Archipelago, 118*n2*
"Kee bird" (mascot), 24
Kennedy, Edward, 73
Kennedy, John F., 70
Kennedy, Robert F., 73
Kenyon, Karl W., 46, 66
Kertulla, Jalmar, 79
Khrushchev, Nikita, 56
Kinkaid, Rear Adm. Thomas C., 17
Kiska Island, 13–19, 25
Kistiakowsky, George, 57
Kodiak Island, 112

Korean War, 32
Kosygin, Aleksei, 70–71
Krypton, 62, 111

Lake Cannikin, 110
Lawrence Radiation Laboratory, 62
Laxalt, Paul, 73
Laycock, George, 83
Lazarev, Maksim, 9
Lewisite, 102
Libby, Willard F., 44
Life magazine, 25, 65
Lisenkov, Prokopii, 8
"Little Boy" (atomic bomb), 26
Logistical Survey Group, 54
Long Shot (test): A E C role, 59, 61, 64;
    announcement of, 60–61; conflict
    over, 65–67; environmental effects
    of, 61–62, 145*n46;* government
    spin on, 63–64; for nuclear test
    detection, 56, 66; secrecy around,
    59–60; site preparation for, 58–59;
    wildlife damage studies, 59
Los Alamos Scientific Laboratory,
    69
Lucky Dragon (ship), 43
Lynch Brothers, 35

Magnuson, Warren G., 36, 86
Mao Tse-tung, 32
Mardsen Mats, 20
Marshall, George C., 37–38
Marshall, Thurgood, 107
Massacre Harbor, 15
Matthews, Courtland W., 24
McCarthyism, 90
McGarvey, Lillie H., 104
McKinnon, Henry and Mary, 143*n35*

McMahon, Brian, 27, 37
McNamara, Robert S., 70–71, 133*n22*
Merritt, Melvin L., 24, 50, 79, 102
Miller, Keith H., 78, 87, 90–91
Miller, Les, 106
Miller, Robert E., 92
Milrow (test): A E C role in, 79–87, 90;
    detonation of, 87; environmental
    damage from, 82–84, 87–88;
    government spin on, 77–79;
    international reaction to, 96–97; site
    selection for, 63
Mink, Patsy T., 76, 103
Minuteman missiles, 49, 54, 74
Montoya, Herb and Kay, 143*n35*
Moses, Carl E., 89, 91
Mount Redoubt, 77
Muir, John, 6
Murie, Margaret E., 83
Murie, Olaus J., 7, 17
Muskie, Edward, 75
Musson, James R., 105
Mustard gas, 102, 151*n22*

National Environmental Policy Act
    (N E P A), 93, 100, 147*n14*
National Geographic, 25
National Parks and Conservation
    Association, 107
Native Alaskans: the A E C and, 107; in
    the Aleutians, 7; Aukes, 109;
    bombing of Aleut church, 18;
    creation tales of, 5; decline in *19th*
    century of, 9; destruction of
    archeological sites of, 111, 151*n21;*
    fallout's effect on, 44, 112; Inupiats,
    40; lawsuits over testing by, 106–107;
    in nuclear test workforce, 79;

spiritual beliefs, 109; theft from ancient sites of, 23, 84

Navy Mobile Construction Battalion Three, 35

Nelson, Gaylord, 76

Nichols, Gen. Kenneth D., 32–33, 35

Nike-Zeus missiles, 69–70

Nixon, Richard M., 73–74, 76, 85–86, 105, 116

Noerenberg, Wallace H., 101

North Pacific Sealing Convention (1911), 11, 17

Nuclear power, 130n5

Nuclear Test Ban Treaty, 1963, 48, 54, 68–69, 72, 131n7

Nuclear test shots: Aardvark (Nevada), 58; Baneberry (Nevada), 96, 101; Boxcar (Nevada), 73, 99, 149n2; Bravo (Bikini), 43; Faultless (Nevada), 72; Ganja (Amchitka), 68; Handley (Nevada), 93; Haymaker (Nevada), 58; Joe-4 (Soviet), 43; Joe One (Soviet), 32; Mike (Enewetak), 43; Miniata (Nevada), 149n3; Orange (Johnson Island), 69; Rulison (Colorado), 149n3; Sugar (Nevada), 39; Teak (Johnson Island), 69; Trinity (Alamogordo), 32; Uncle (Nevada), 39. See also Cannikin (test); Long Shot (test); Milrow (test)

Nuclear test sites: Australia (proposed), 33, 48; Bikini, 27; Brooks Range (proposed), 50–52, 71, 74, 77; Camp Irwin (proposed), 37; Chirikof Island (proposed), 51; criteria for selection of, 33; Enewetak, 28; Fallon, Nevada, 57; Gough Island, 69; Hot Creek Valley, Nevada, 72; Johnson Island, 69; Little Diomede (proposed), 40; Nevada Test Site, 37; Outer Banks (proposed), 28; Pagan Island (proposed), 50; Pahute Mesa, Nevada, 72; search for, 48–50, 140n11, 141n16; Tatum Salt Dome, Mississippi, 57; Trinity, 32. See also Amchitka

Nuclear testing: calibration shots, 72, 136n13; decoupled detonations, 57–59; detection of, 55–56, 66; as diplomacy, 41; safety issues, 75, 85–86; by the Soviet Union, 32, 43–44, 66–67; underground, 56

Nuclear weapons: cost of development of, 156n22; creation of H-bomb, 42; peaceful uses of, 42–43, 149n3; use on Japan of, 26, 126n2

O'Connor, Egan, 94–95

Oil pipeline, 100

Oil spills, 75–76

O'Neill, Dan, 43

Operations: Castle, 43; Cottage, 13; Crossroads, 27; Crosstie, 72; Dropshot, 41; Grommet, 99; Hardtack II, 56; Ivy, 43; Jangle, 39; Landcrab, 13; Longview, 18; Mandrel, 68; Safeguard, 76, 95; Windstorm, 34–37, 39, 115. See also Projects

Packard, David, 93

Parker Drilling Company, 74

Parks, John S., 143n35

Parsons, Rear Adm. William S., 28

Pastore, John O., 103

Paul I, Czar, 9

Pautzke, Clarence J., 84

Penney Trailer Sales, 75

Pentagon Papers, 150*n14*

Philemonof, Iliodor, 106–107

Phillips, Brad, 79

Phyllis Cormack (ship), 106

Pitzer, Kenneth S., 75, 85–86

Plummer, Raymond E., 107

Plutonium, 111, 113

Polaris missiles, 54

Pollock, Howard W., 77, 87, 90, 148*n19*

Potter Marsh refuge, 143*n37*

President's Council on Environmental
    Quality, 93

Press, Frank, 85

Press leaks, 36

Pribilof Islands, 50

Prince William Sound earthquake, 60,
    137*n19*

Princeton, U.S.S., 87

Projects: Chariot, 43, 51, 131*n7;* Cowboy,
    136*n10;* Hardtack I, 69; Larkspur,
    53–54; Plowshare, 43, 149*n3;* Rufus,
    49–53; Scroll, 58; Toy Factory, 136*n13;*
    Vela, 56–57, 136*n8;* Windstorm,
    34–37, 39, 115. *See also* Operations

Pruitt, William O., Jr., 63

Public Acceptance Group, 54

Public Health Service, U.S., 45

Public opinion, 89

Public relations, 61, 80–81, 90–92,
    99–104, 110, 151*n17*

Qagus (Rat Islanders), 8

Radar, 14, 42, 52, 115

Radiation, nuclear: from the Bikini
    tests, 27; from post-shot drilling,

111–112; radioactive isotopes, 44, 62,
    111; sickness, 43, 73; from surface
    detonations, 39; threat to fishing, 78;
    from underground testing (actual),
    94, 96, 112–113; from underground
    testing (potential), 59, 62, 85, 102. *See
    also* Fallout, nuclear

Radionuclides, 62

Rat Islands, 7–8, 60

Rats, 7, 30, 46

Rausch, Robert L., 45

Raytheon Corporation, 115

Reagan, Ronald W., 73

Reclamation, Bureau of, 58

Relocatable-Over-the-Horizon Radar
    (ROTHR), 115

Resor, Stanley R., 102

Reynolds, Harry L., 92

Reynolds Electrical and Engineering,
    54

Rivers, Ralph J., 60

Rodenticides, 46

Roderick, John R., 143*n35*

Rogers, William P., 108

Roosevelt, Theodore, 41

Ruckelshaus, William D., 100

Rufus Maximum Allowable Yield
    Group, 50

Russell, Capt. James S., 28

Russian American Company, 9

Salinger, Pierre, 133*n22*

SALT I. See Strategic Arms Limitation
    Treaty

Sandia Laboratory, 53

Sane, Inc., 107

Sassara, Charles, 79

Save Our State Committee (SOS), 80

Scheffer, Victor B., 7

Schlesinger, James R., 108, 153*n*32

Scientific American, 73

Scott, Ronald F., 85

Sea lions, 16

Sea Otter Studies Advisory Panel, 114

Sea otters: Amchitka as refuge for, 31; capture for testing of, 82; deaths from testing, actual, 110; deaths from testing, projected, 53; harvesting of, 54; recovery of, 12; studies on, 29, 31, 81; transfer from Amchitka of, 38, 46–47, 82; urchins in diet of, 46

Seaborg, Glenn: A B Ms, 117; A E C-Alaska relations, 79, 100; Bikini test, 27; blast damage, 85; Congressional relations, 86, 93, 95, 103; government differences over testing, 96; Project Vela, 136*n*8; resignation of, 153*n*32; sea otter threat from blast, 81–82; Soviet clandestine tests, 66–67

Seal hunting, 8–9, 11

Seals, 50, 102, 110

Secrecy, 91–93, 103–104

Sekora, Palmer C., 82

Sentinel missiles, 71, 74

Settle, Rear Adm. Thomas G. W., 34, 36, 38

Seymour, Allyn H., 50

Sharp, Mitchell W., 108

Sierra Club, 105, 107

Smith, William D., Jr., 92

Smithsonian Institution, 12, 81

Smyth, Henry D., 37

Soviet Union: A B M development, 70; Amchitka testing's impact on, 35, 40; bomb testing by, 32, 43–44; clandestine tests, possibility of, 66–67; earthquakes in, 59; easing of Cold War tensions, 55; invasion of Czechoslovakia, 74; on-site nuclear inspections, 56

Sowl, LeRoy W., 82, 85

Spartan missiles, 98–99, 117

Spencer, David L., 60, 84

Spirit, 109

Sports Fisheries and Wildlife, Bureau of, 83

St. Lawrence Island, 5

Stahr, Elvis J., 76

Stalin, Josef, 130*n*2

Stevens, Ted, 79

Stewart, Dixon, 91

Stewart, Potter, 107

Stone, Jeremy L., 101–102

Strategic Arms Limitation Treaty (S A L T I), 116

Strauss, Lewis F., 28

Sturges, Lt. Col. W. R., Jr., 37

Submarines, 17

Supreme Court, U.S., 107–108

Taft, William H., 11

Tanaga Island, 16, 17, 30

Technical Criteria Group, 53

Teledyne Isotopes Corporation, 94

Teller, Edward, 42, 44, 70

Tigalda Island, 5

Todd, David K., 85

Train, Russell, 95–96

Trans-Alaska oil pipeline, 100

Tritium, 62, 85, 94, 101

Truman, Harry S, 33–35, 126*n*3

Tsunamis, 85, 94, 103, 136*n*19

UCLA Medical School, 27
Udall, Stewart, 63, 83
Umnak Island, 5, 24, 42
Unalaska Island, 30
Undersecretaries Committee, 95
Unga Island, 106
United Nations Educational, Scientific, and Cultural Organization (UNESCO), 115
Urchins, sea, 46

Vela Hotel, 56
Vela Sierra, 56
Vela Uniform, 56–58, 136n13
Vermillion, Henry G., 108
Vidal, Gore, 24
Viereck, Leslie, 63
Vorb'ev, Aleksei, 8

W-71 warhead, 98, 117
Walsh and Company, 75
Ward, Robert, 90
Warren, Clifford, 143n35
Warren, June, 143n35
Warren, Shields, 37
Water pollution, 62, 84, 88, 94, 110–111, 145n46
Weeden, Judy, 63

Weeden, Robert B., 63, 77–78
West Construction Company, 21, 23
Western Electric, 69
Whaling stations, 12
Wheeler, Gen. Earle G., 93
White, Byron R., 107
White Alice Creek, 113
Whitebrook, Robert B., 24
Wilderness Society, 107
Wildlife: damage from testing to (actual), 88, 101, 110–111; damage from testing to (potential), 59, 85; early abundance of, 8; in the post-testing era, 116; reservations, 121n19; unprotected, 12
Wood, Ginny Hill, 63, 77
Worden (destroyer), 18
World War II: Aleutian Campaign's value, 13–14; bombing during, 16, 18–19, 26, 126n2; cleanup of debris from, 114–115; construction during, 15, 19–22; Japanese activities during, 16, 19; population increase in Aleutians during, 22; refuse of, 23; social problems during, 125n34

Yomuri Shimbun (newspaper), 96